Jörg Rogge (ed.)
Killing and Being Killed: Bodies in Battle

Mainz Historical Cultural Sciences | Volume 38

Editorial

The **Mainzer Historische Kulturwissenschaften** [Mainz Historical Cultural Sciences] series publishes the results of research that develops methods and theories of cultural sciences in connection with empirical research. The central approach is a historical perspective on cultural sciences, whereby both epochs and regions can differ widely and be treated in an all-embracing manner from time to time. Amongst other, the series brings together research approaches in archaeology, art history, visual studies, literary studies, philosophy, and history, and is open for contributions on the history of knowledge, political culture, the history of perceptions, experiences and life-worlds, as well as other fields of research with a historical cultural scientific orientation.

The objective of the **Mainzer Historische Kulturwissenschaften** series is to become a platform for pioneering works and current discussions in the field of historical cultural sciences.

The series is edited by the Co-ordinating Committee of the Research Unit Historical Cultural Sciences (HKW) at the Johannes Gutenberg University Mainz.

Jörg Rogge (ed.)
Killing and Being Killed: Bodies in Battle
Perspectives on Fighters in the Middle Ages

[transcript]

The print was sponsored by the Research Unit Historical Cultural Sciences (HKW).

Bibliographic information published by the Deutsche Nationalbibliothek
The Deutsche Nationalbibliothek lists this publication in the Deutsche Nationalbibliografie; detailed bibliographic data are available in the Internet at http://dnb.d-nb.de

© 2017 transcript Verlag, Bielefeld
transcript Verlag | Hermannstraße 26 | D-33602 Bielefeld | live@transcript-verlag.de

All rights reserved. No part of this book may be reprinted or reproduced or utilized in any form or by any electronic, mechanical, or other means, now known or hereafter invented, including photocopying and recording, or in any information storage or retrieval system, without permission in writing from the publisher.

Cover design: Kordula Röckenhaus, Bielefeld
Proof-reading & typesetting: Judith Mengler
Printed in Germany
Print-ISBN 978-3-8376-3783-0
PDF-ISBN 978-3-8394-3783-4

Content

Preface 7

Killed and Being Killed.
Perspectives on Bodies in Battle
in the Middle Ages – an Introduction....................... 9
Jörg Rogge

"The Goths Drew their Swords Together".
Individual and Collective Acts of Violence
by Gothic Warlords and their War Bands................. 15
Guido M. Berndt

The Torture of Bodies in Byzantium
After the Riots (Sec. IV-VIII) 43
Bogdan-Petru Maleon

"One man slashes, one slays, one warns,
one wounds". Injury and Death in
Anglo-Scottish Combat, c.1296-c.1403 61
Iain MacInnes

Willing Body, Willing Mind: Non-Combatant
Culpability According to
English Combatant Writers 1327-77 79
Trevor Russell Smith

Body Techniques of Combat: The Depiction of
a Personal Fighting System in the Fight Books
of Hans Talhofer (1443-1467 CE) 109
ERIC BURKART

Six Weeks to Prepare for Combat: Instruction and
Practices from the Fight Books at the End
of the Middle Ages, a Note on Ritualised
Single Combats 131
DANIEL JAQUET

The Body of the *Condottiero.* A Link Between
Physical Pain and Military Virtue as it was
Interpreted in Renaissance Italy 165
GUILIA MOROSINI

Two Kinds of War? Brutality and Atrocity in
Later Medieval Scotland.. 199
ALASTAIR J. MACDONALD

Logistics and Food Supply in the *Crònica* of
Ramon Muntaner 231
JUDITH MENGLER

Summary and Conclusions:
Silent Men and the Art of Fighting........................... 251
DOMINIK SCHUH

Contributors 267

Preface

JÖRG ROGGE

The collection of articles based on papers provided and discussed at a conference with a focus on the experiences fighters make through their lifetime and especially in violent conflicts. Central questions have been how they have communicated their fighting experience and what they regarded as necessary to prepare their bodies for fighting.

The conference took place at the Johannes Gutenberg University in Mainz, April 16th – 18th 2015, and was founded by the research unit Historical Cultural Sciences. I like to thank the contributors for their articles, Christine Reinle (Gießen), Martin Kaufhold (Augsburg) and Thomas Scharf (Braunschweig) for their input during the conference, and especially Judith Mengler for her excellent support during the publication process.

Mainz, July 2016   Jörg Rogge

Introduction

JÖRG ROGGE

Research on medieval bodies prospers. We have learned a lot about body concepts in medicine, theology and philosophy. A lot of work has been done to help us understand how body has been used as a metaphor in prose, poetry, etc.[1] The medieval religious concept of the body was not in favour of the physical body. It was regarded as a tool or means to carry the immortal soul. The faithful believers had to worry about their soul, not about their body. Physical discomfort was regarded a consequence of the fall of mankind. The body could be neglected and famous preachers and ascetics, such as Franz von Assisi, have claimed that the body has been their greatest enemy.[2]

However, this was only one body concept in the middle ages. There was also a more optimistic view on the bodies to find; a view that regarded the human body in God's own likeness. Therefore, one should maintain the body or even exercise to keep the body in good shape. This was very important for the epic heroes in court literature for example. They had been very important for the development of chivalric culture in late medieval Europe for they could be used as some kind of role model for the real fighters. Such a warrior had to exercise his bodily abilities and fighting skills as well. To be in good shape was, together with boldness and skill, a requirement to become a good and

---

1 See for example KALOF, 2010; KALOF/BYNUM, 2010.
2 FRANZISKUS-QUELLEN, 2009, p. 86.

successful fighter. To be a fighter implies to take good care of your body because it was your most important tool.[3]

To be a fighter implies also that you are prepared to expose yourself to the dangers of battles and other forms of military activities. In all cases, the men had to deal with two very important aspects – two sides of one coin. On one side, the fighters had to anticipate in killing other men, in most cases fellow Christians. On the other side, there was the possibility that their body was injured by swords, arrows, pikes etc. or even by horses. In the context of the famous and fierce battles in France, England, Scotland and Spain a fighter was lucky if he was not slain on the spot but able to survive – sometimes without bodily wounds, sometimes injured. In case where a fighter survived his injuries, he may have had the chance to show the scars as a sign or signature of his boldness. However, if he had lost a leg or an arm, it was likely that he had to live as a beggar the rest of his life – given that he was not a member of a noble family.

The conference was an attempt to obtain an impression of the way in which the fighters handled the experience of the clash on the battlefields, of killing other men or being wounded by other men. We want to know more about the practices they have used to communicate their bodily experiences to others. Therefore, the focus of the articles in this volume is on shaping bodies for battle, using bodies in battle, bodily injuries by means of battle and on dead bodies of fighters.

As far as I can discern, we cannot find the immediate experiences of the fighters in our sources. They have always undergone a process of reflexion and they are imbedded in the practice of narrating such experiences in a social group or society. I believe we can distinguish between two principle forms of that type of narratives. There are the stories of famous battles told by the well-known chroniclers such as Jean Froissart and Jean Le Bel for the Hundred Years War, or Walter Bower, writing about war and fighting in his *Scotichronicon*. These men were not fighters themselves, and have written their accounts based on second hand knowledge, which they collected from fighters through interviews or other means. These texts are of great value, of

---

3   This point has been stressed by the authors of mirrors of chivalry like Geoffrey de Charny or Ramon Llull. See CHARNY, 1996; LLULL, 2013.

course, because they deliver important information about the practice of "talking" about war with specific text patterns.[4]

Then we have the so-called self-assessments of fighters who wrote down or dictated their experiences on the battlefields at some point in their lives. Like Thomas Gray did in his *Scalacronica* or several German and Swiss fighters such as Georg von Ehingen or Ludwig von Diesbach. Even when we read their accounts, we must bear in mind that the writer is not identical with the protagonist in the narrated past. However, the bodies in these texts can function as a link because they are object and symbol at the same time. We can assume that the writer had used the bodies in the texts to communicate his experiences.[5]

Thomas Gray, for example, constitutes the bodies of fighters by using specific narrative patterns, which are the performance of Deeds of Arms, physical toughness or resilience, the ability to recuperate after injuries and the description of horse and fighter as a common fighting body.[6] These stylistic devices are also present in Froissart's Chronical. When he describes the heroic death of James Douglas on the battlefield by Otterburn in August 1388, he uses comparisons with ancient heroes: Douglas was fighting like a hardy Hector. It takes three spears to stop this human fighting machine – one struck him in the belly, the second in the shoulder the third in the thigh. "Sore hurt" in that way Douglas died on the battlefield.[7] Ralph Percy was another fighter who was sore hurt during the battle of Otterburn. When he was taken prisoner by a Scottish knight because he was too exhausted to fight any longer, he said, "My chausses and my greave are full of blood already".[8] These examples show that the real valiant fighters had been those who fought until exhortation – ignoring the injuries they received in the press. It is likely that the contemporary readers or listeners to such narrative understood the argument well.

One focus of the articles is on the preparation of bodies for fighting;[9] another on the description or narration of physical pain caused by weapons, and how it felt to give and receive blows or even

---

4 CLAUSS, 2016.
5 See ROGGE, 2016.
6 GRAY, 2005; ROGGE, 2011, p. 270.
7 FROISSART, 1978, pp. 342f.
8 IBID., p. 343.
9 See the contributions by MENGLER; BURKHART; JAQUET in this volume.

being killed on the battlefield.[10] They contribute to the ongoing debate on the practice of writing or telling pain and other emotions in the Middle Ages.[11] This, for example, concerns the problem that physical pain is felt by all humanity, but could not be shared directly. This is why the writers have used similes, metaphors or specific narrative patterns to describe or convey their experiences.[12] By asking how pain is denoted in our sources, we can obtain further information about the practice that has been used to express pain in different historical contexts. Furthermore, we can learn how the written expression of physical pain was culturally conditioned – in our cases the culture of war and fighters of course.[13]

Bibliography

Sources

CHARNY, GEOFFRY DE, The Book of Chivalry, Text, Context and Translation, ed. by RICHARD KAEUPER/ELSBETH KENNEDY, Philadelphia 1996.
FRANZISKUS-QUELLEN. Die Schriften des heiligen Franziskus, Lebensbeschreibungen, Chroniken und Zeugnisse über ihn und seinen Orden, ed. by DIETER BERG/LEONHARD LEHMANN, Kevelaer 2009.
FROISSART, JEAN, Chronicles, selected, translated and edited by GEOFFREY BRERETON, London 1978.
GRAY, THOMAS, Scalacronica, 1272-1363 (Surtees Society 209), ed. by ANDY KING, Woodbridge 2005.
LLULL, RAMON, The Book of the Order of Chivalry, trans. by NOEL FALLOWS, Woodbridge 2013.

---

10 See the contributions by BERNDT; RUSSELL SMITH; MOROSINI; MACINNES in this volume.
11 See COHEN, 2000.
12 See the contribution by SCHUH in this volume.
13 See the examples from the Byzantine Empire given by MALEON in this volume.

Literature

CLAUSS, MARTIN, Krieg der Ritter. Erzählmuster des Heroischen in den Chroniken zum Hundertjährigen Krieg, in: Kriegserfahrungen erzählen (Mainzer Historische Kulturwissenschaften), ed. by JÖRG ROGGE, Bielefeld 2016, pp. 31-45.

COHEN, ESTHER, The animated Pain of the Body, in: American Historical Review 105 (2000), pp. 36-68.

KALOF, LINDA (ed.), Cultural History of the Human Body. In the Middle Ages, Oxford/New York 2010.

KALOF, LINDA/BYNUM, WILLIAM (eds.), Cultural History of the Human Body. In the Renaissance, Oxford/New York 2010.

ROGGE, JÖRG, Kämpfer als Schreiber. Bemerkungen zur Erzählung von Kampferfahrung und Verwundung in deutschen Selbstzeugnissen des späten Mittelalters, in: Kriegserfahrungen erzählen (Mainzer Historische Kulturwissenschaften), ed. by ID., Bielefeld 2016, pp. 73-106.

ROGGE, JÖRG, Tote Ritter – tote Pferde. Bemerkungen zu Körpern im Kampf während des 14. Jahrhunderts, in: Körperbilder. Kulturalität und Wertetransfer, ed. by ANDREAS CESANA et al., Frankfurt a. M. 2011, pp. 261-272.

The used contributions to the volume at hand are not listed separately here.

"The Goths Drew their Swords Together"
Individual and Collective Acts of Violence by Gothic Warlords and their War Bands*

GUIDO M. BERNDT

Introduction

In Germany and other German-speaking countries, there is a long tradition of dealing with the history of the Goths. Since the end of the 19th century, there has been intense academic research, and some of these early scholarly publications are still worth reading.[1] One can find an

---

* This article has been written in the course of a project on "Gothic Warriors in the Later Roman Empire" (Gotische Kriegergruppen im spätrömischen Reich), which has been conducted from 2009 to 2015 at the Friedrich-Alexander-University Erlangen-Nuremberg. The project was funded by the German Research Foundation (Deutsche Forschungsgemeinschaft) in the framework of research group 1101 on "Communities of Violence" (Gewaltgemeinschaften). I would like to thank the organizers of the conference at Mainz for their kind invitation and all participants for the discussions and suggestions. My thanks also go to Sabine Held (Erlangen) and Ellora Bennett (Berlin) for help with the English.
1 In the first half of the 20th century, one of the most important works (in German) concerning Gothic history was *Geschichte der deutschen Stämme bis zum Ausgange der Völkerwanderung* by Ludwig Schmidt, that had been published between 1934 and 1941. The history of the Ostrogoths is

unpretentious explanation for the admiration of the Goths: Up to the middle of the 20th century, they have been considered a "Germanic tribe" and have been declared ancestors of the Germanic people.[2] Gothic history was German history. The traditional *Meistererzählung* ("master-narrative") told it roughly like this: Once upon a time, the Gothic people emerged somewhere in the far North (Scandza[3]/Scandinavia). From there, the Goths repeatedly launched vast migrations. After centuries of living on the frontiers and the hinterland of the Roman Empire, a powerful group of Gothic warriors reached Italy at the end of the fifth century. Here, a war-hero named Theoderic – the famous Dietrich of Bern of legendary epics[4] – founded a splendid kingdom on former Roman soil.

In the 19th century, there was a common belief that each *Volk* (people) has its own characteristic *Volksgeist* (literally meaning "spirit of the people" or "national character"), and there was a need for a unique identity based on national and cultural idiosyncrasies. The Goths were considered an especially unique, heroic and most noble nation. Many Germans were proud when considering the deeds of the Goths.[5] These notions finally led to an idea of an incessant continuation of history from the early Germans up to the German Reich.[6] Because the migrations of the Goths had once led them to the Crimean peninsula,[7] the Goths were used to legitimise the war of conquest ordered by Adolf Hitler during the Third Reich.[8] In the course of the planned re-Germanisation of Eastern

---

    described in the first part, second book. Still, in 1970 this work has been reprinted.
2 For the modern history of reception: HELBLING, 1954, pp. 53-95; PIZZI, 1994/95.
3 The name appears in the *Getica* of Jordanes.
4 ZIMMERMANN, 1972.
5 The historical novel *Ein Kampf um Rom* ("A Struggle for Rome") of Felix Dahn (1834-1912), first published in 1876, was very popular and surely contributed to the widespread veneration of the Goths as ancestors of the modern German people. There are a couple of modern studies on the influence of Dahn's work, e.g. FRECH 1996; KIPPER 2002. Besides his many historical novels Dahn has also written a comprehensive history of the early medieval kingdoms in 12 volumes (*Die Könige der Germanen*, published 1861-1911).
6 BLECKMANN, 2009, pp. 38f.; VON SEE, 1972; VON SEE 1994.
7 VASILIEV, 1936; for a modern view see WOLFRAM, 2009, pp. 52-62.
8 KLETZIN, 2002.

Europe, Gdynia (Germ. Gdingen) – a seaport in Poland – was given the name Gotenhafen in 1939. Following the conquest of the Crimea by the Wehrmacht, the city Simferopol was renamed Gotenburg and Sewastopol Theoderichshafen.[9] This blatant misuse[10] of history resulted in the decline of research on Germanic peoples in Germany and Austria after World War II. Consequently, Herwig Wolfram appropriately described Gothic history as a "topic [with a] burden".[11]

Today, historians look at the history of the Goths from another perspective, in particular due to the internationalisation of scientific research.[12] Many older views and ideas that were based on exaggerated national or even nationalistic convictions have now been largely deconstructed: Germanic loyalty, Germanic sacral kingship and the *Gefolgschaftswesen* (the mode of organising the following).[13] Furthermore, the idea that the *gentes* of the migration period were homogeneous and cohesive groups, but rather heterogeneous with ephemeral characteristics, has generally gained acceptance.[14] These groups did not share a single biological origin. Rather, it is a belief in common history that gave these groups a collective identity. Such

---

9   GRUCHMANN, 1962.
10 For different forms of misuses of medieval history see BAK et al., 2009; GOFFART, 1995 focuses on Germanic history.
11 WOLFRAM, 1997, p. 194. "The topic and its burden" is a subtitle of the chapter concerning Theoderic the Amal.
12 E.g. WOLFRAM, 2009; HEATHER, 1996; GIESE, 2004.
13 Walter Schlesinger once defined "Gefolgschaft" as follows (SCHLESINGER, 1953, S. 235): "Unter Gefolgschaft wird [...] ein Verhältnis zwischen Herrn und Mann verstanden, das freiwillig eingegangen wird, auf Treue gegründet ist und den Mann zu Rat und (kriegerischer) Hilfe, den Herrn zu Schutz und 'Milde' verpflichtet." For Schlesinger these forms of loyalty already existed very early in Germanic history making references to the *Germania* of Tacitus (cap. 14). This conception was criticised by GRAUS, 1959, especially the idea of a specific Germanic element in the oath of allegiance and its sacral implications. Reinhard Wenskus has pointed out that "Gefolgschaft" is an overloaded term that does not occur in our sources and should only be used by historians when considering all the implications and traditions it transports. WENSKUS, 1992; Stefanie Dick has thoroughly analysed the whole controversy and pointed out that there never has been something specific Germanic in the mentioned fields, DICK, 2008, pp. 201-203.
14 E.g. POHL, 1998.

histories could be designed according to the current leader's will.[15] From time to time, these leaders ordered the creation of genealogical traditions for their communities.[16] Overall, the specific ethnic identities of these groups have proved to be almost entirely social constructs.[17] In Late Antiquity and the Early Middle Ages, ethnic identities often appear to be linked to warrior groups. So, if historians no longer consider Goths, Vandals or Lombards as Germanic tribes, what else may they have been?

Late Antique and Early Medieval War Bands as Communities of Violence

In Late Antiquity and the Early Middle Ages, there were social groups that mainly consisted of men who lived their lives as warriors. Their specific *Lebensform* (way of life) was violent and warlike.[18] The Goths had to have exceptional skills in this regard; otherwise, it would be difficult to explain how they managed to compete against numerous opponents throughout their history and even got Roman emperors into trouble. A research group, founded in 2009 at the University of Gießen, coined the term *Gewaltgemeinschaften* (communities of violence) for such units. These communities of violence include groups that formed, developed and became stabilised due to the use of violence within their socio-political environment. For them, physical violence determined a major, even fundamental, factor of their existence.[19] Thus, violence

---

15 WENSKUS, 1961. Wenskus ideas were accepted quite soon in German research and consequently built the starting point for the so-called Viennese School (lead by Herwig Wolfram and Walter Pohl), but it took a while since they were perceived in English speaking countries. Only in 2002 there has been published a volume that strongly criticised the book of Wenskus. GILLETT, 2002.
16 TÖNNIES, 1989; HEATHER, 1989; HEATHER, 1991, pp. 34-67; CHRISTENSEN, 2002, pp. 124-157.
17 GEARY, 1983.
18 There is an excellent study for Frankish warriors and warriorship: BODMER, 1957. No comparable work has been published for Gothic warriors so far.
19 The current bibliography on violence is vast. Important studies aiming at understanding the significance of violence include: POPITZ, 1986, pp. 43-66; VON TROTHA, 1997; VON TROTHA/RÖSEL, 2011. There are some recent general studies worth mentioning that deal with the role of violence in

existed in individual and collective forms, aided the construction of identity and was even integral to the group's self-perception. Particularly, these war bands could find extraordinary success in regions where there were power-vacuums and therefore no longer a monopoly on violence (*Gewaltmonopol des Staates* in the sense of Max Weber) by the 'state'.[20]

Currently, the term and its exact connotations have not been given precise definition in sociology, political science or historiography. In this regard, some remarks are necessary:

Violence is a resource at the hand of every single person, because human beings are fundamentally capable of violence due to their physicality. Humans are able to cause other humans or living beings pain with their bare hands: They are capable of breaking bones, strangling, drowning or beating to death. If several people come together to commit violence, the potential for injury and death increases. The use of weapons, again, increases the potential of violence. Social groups such as those described in this chapter generally make use of weapons to threaten or actually commit violence.[21]

The use of violence may form a sense of community, it may polarise and exclude, but it also determines their collective behaviour in all aspects of their lives. The success of a community of violence, as well as an individual's chances of survival, depends on one's ability to handle weapons. It is not the quality of the weapon itself, but rather the skill of the person who handles it that determines the efficacy of the weapon.

For this chapter, violence may be defined as intentional action, which aims to violate the physical integrity of at least one person. This narrow definition does not take into consideration forms of structural or cultural violence.

In Late Antiquity and the Early Middle Ages, there were a great many groups that could be classified as "communities of violence" according to the given criteria.[22] However, few of these groups aside from the Goths

---

different pre-modern epochs: DRAKE, 2006; HALSALL, 1998; BARAZ, 2003; BROWN, 2011.
20 SPEITKAMP, 2013. For the case of the Ostrogoths: WIEMER, 2013.
21 For the role of weapons and weaponry for Gothic warrior groups: WIEMER/BERNDT, 2016 (forthcoming).
22 WIEMER, 2013; BERNDT, 2013.

benefit from a sufficient written record. It is therefore possible to identify the activities of Gothic war bands from the third to seventh century.[23] These groups had been repeatedly taking advantage of the political and military weakness of the Imperium Romanum, then in the throes of crisis, to establish their own power by fighting and exercising violence. Their primary aim was to secure a sustainable livelihood, but they also aimed at institutionalising their gained position to enjoy economic advantages as well as gaining prestige and honour. Their actions had usually been violent conflicts with either competitive groups of warriors or, if still existing, with the imperial armed forces. Eventually, a great number of these groups were beaten, eliminated or integrated into new political systems that had been established by other, more successful groups.

The new kingdoms (*regna*), which arose on soil formerly belonging to the Western Roman Empire, were by no means the outcome of a peaceful process.[24] When written sources report on Gothic war bands, the violence collectively committed by these warriors very often takes centre stage. On the other hand, there are depictions of violence involving only a single person. These persons were frequently the leaders of a group or (at least) someone who aspired to a leading position.

Warlords

The leaders of war bands may be described as warlords.[25] Sources persistently emphasise their common individual willingness to use violence and their ability to kill foes even with their bare hands.[26] They proved themselves on the battlefield, took booty for themselves and their followers and thereby strengthened their outstanding social position within the group. Aside from their physical strength and military skills, they needed to possess some qualities of leadership. A warlord had a better chance of increasing his following as his success grew; the promise of gold and glory under his leadership could attract more warriors to his

---

23 BERNDT, 2013.
24 Overview: WOLFRAM, 1997, some case studies have been published in: GOETZ et al., 2003. More detailed on violence in the barbarian kingdoms: LIEBESCHUETZ, 2006.
25 WHITTACKER, 1993; MACGEORGE, 2002; LIEBESCHUETZ, 2007.
26 BERNDT, 2014.

band. Thus, the greater the number of warriors, the greater the group's collective potential for further success through violence. Solidarity within the group was based on mutual obligations. Individual warriors probably had to pledge allegiance to their leader, however, only few documents provide detailed information in this context. In this case, it may be useful to compare the ritual of how Roman commanders dealt with their soldiers in Late Antiquity.[27] In social groups, which do not have written rules or similar other stabilising institutions, trust-building measures are of great significance to strengthen personal relationships between the members of the group. To join a war band, men needed to possess exemplary physical skills and an unshakable willingness to affiliate themselves to the leader's plans. Indeed, Gothic warlords were more than leaders of brutal gangs of marauders. Even though clear political intentions are not discernible in every case, their actions were not conducted without awareness of their resulting political impact. They were neither paramilitaries nor rebels, because they usually showed willingness to cooperate with the institutions of the 'state' as long as it seemed useful to them.[28] Warlords had a much greater individual power of disposition over their hard-won loot than a Roman general, whose loot was normally considered to belong to the state. Ideally, a Roman soldier had a salary and therefore had no need to find remuneration in goods won in battle. Leaders used specific ways to distribute booty to create and perpetuate the aspired hierarchy within in the group.[29] From time to time, the "official leader" recognised a warlord's position, either on his own initiative or due to pressure, without fundamentally changing the warlord's position. This acceptance could be expressed by awarding an official military position, or by acknowledging a hard-earned lordship. A number of warlords managed to formalise their violently obtained

---

27 Roman soldiers had to swear an oath (*sacramentum militare*) when joining the army. Following Vegetius (*Epitoma rei militaris* 2,5) the wording was: *Iurant autem milites omnia se strenue facturos quae praeceperit imperator, numquam desertuos militiam nec mortem recusaturos pro Romana republica* ("The soldiers swear that they will strenuously do all that the Emperor may command, will never desert the service, nor refuse to die for the Roman state"). See BECHER, 2009, p. 169.
28 This is not the place to discuss the concept of "state" in the Early Middle Ages. A good starting point are the two volumes AIRLIE et al., 2006 and POHL/WIESNER, 2009.
29 BERNDT, 2011.

positions and to transform it into a kingdom, or at least into a position of similar status. A warlord had to be concerned about the group's social cohesion and his place at the head of the hierarchy in order to limit contests for leadership and ensure permanent stability. Only measures such as those could uphold the functionality of the community, which had to protect the position of the group and the individual against external threats. Gothic warlords constantly tried to expand their spheres of activity according to their prevailing economic and political interests. Particularly, expanded areas of operation based on high mobility[30] of the warrior communities made them dangerous players in the world of Late Antiquity and the Early Middle Ages. Warlords had to launch raids or wage war to become the head of their war bands – and such wars had to be conducted regularly. Not only to provide new goods to secure the provision of the group, but also to prove the legitimacy of their own preeminence – normally, this also included an open expression of the individual willingness to use violence. One well-studied example is the Amal Theoderic, who operated as a warlord in the east of the Roman Empire for several decades before he managed to become king of Italy in the 490s. Another warlord worthy of consideration is Fritigern who was the leader of a Gothic war band at the end of the fourth century.

Fritigern

Fritigern was a Gothic warlord, whose leading position within the Gothic-Tervingian society was most likely based on both his military competences and his family background. However, he was the leader of only one Gothic group and not king of the Goths overall. There are a number of different terms for his position: chief, chieftain or king.[31] He is one of the earliest Gothic warlords for whom there is reliable written source material; thus, it is possible to reconstruct at least some parts of his actions. He appears in at least six different late antique historical sources, largely due to the victory of his warrior group at the Battle of Adrianopel (Edirne) in 378. It is said that about 20,000 Roman soldiers

---

30 BERNDT, 2013.
31 PLRE I, p. 374.

and the Roman emperor Valens were killed in this battle.[32] Nothing can be said about Fritigern's date of birth his childhood or youth. His name seems to be a compound of the two words *fridu* and *gernus*, possibly from Gothic **Frithugairns* ("desiring peace").[33] When he appears in written sources for the first time – in the 31st book of Ammianus Marcellinus,[34] whom we have to thank for the majority of our information – he is already depicted as the established leader of his warrior community. However, he was in fact hierarchically below a man called Athanaric, referred to as *iudex* (judge) of the Goths.[35] On several occasions, this man was accepted by the Roman Emperor or by one of his delegates as partner in negotiations. Whatever the exact status of Athanaric, he did not manage to keep the Gothic-Tervingian association together.

Fritigern appears in the context of a quarrel among Tervingi and Romans, which started in 365. At that point in time, the Goths had given military support to a usurper called Procopius – which was ultimately unsuccessful – who rose in revolt against the Roman Emperor Valens. Therefore, in the Roman's view, the Goths had been in league with the enemy. Finally, Athanaric signed a peace treaty with the Romans in 369, in which the Gothic side was obviously disadvantaged, even though their military strength had not been entirely defeated.[36] They had to provide hostages and did not receive annuities, although the war band sorely needed them. This must have worsened an already difficult supply situation.

Additionally, conflicts within the Gothic community arose during the early 370s. One group, led by Fritigern together with another leader called Alaviv, consequently left the Gothic association.[37] Besides this instance, there are several historical examples of this dyarchic separation of rule within groups of warriors in Late Antiquity.[38] The two leaders,

---

32   Amm. 31,13,12.
33   His Gothic name is not sufficiently proven. In historical research he sometimes is equated with *Friþareiks,* named in a calendar fragment (in the *Codex Ambrosianus A*) in the early sixth century. SCHÄFERDIECK, 1998.
34   KULIKOWSKI, 2012 with some controversial ideas concerning the 31st book of Ammianus' Roman History.
35   PLRE I, pp. 120f.
36   The patterns of events are described in detail in WANKE, 1990.
37   WOLFRAM, 2009, p. 81.
38   Some examples are studied in CASTRITIUS, 2008.

acting independently of one another, together with their union of warriors soon aspired to an agreement with the Roman Emperor. This agreement should have guaranteed them their own area of settlement in *Thracia*, located on Roman soil. In return, they promised the Roman Emperor to behave peacefully in the future, to help the Romans with troops if required and, above all, to convert to Arian (better Homoean) Christianity, which was predominant in the eastern empire at this time.[39]

After long and difficult negotiations, the Goths of Fritigern and Alaviv were finally allowed to cross the Danube in summer of 376, which consequently made entering the Roman Empire possible.[40] However, the Goths soon fell victim to the common Roman anti-Barbarian policies and particularly to those of certain Roman officials described by Ammianus as being incompetent and corrupt. Those politicians took advantage of the Goth's existential hardship. They allowed the Goths to cross the border river (nearby Durostorum = Silistra, Bulgaria) as *dediticii* (the subjugated); however, due to heavy rainfall, the Danube had been in full spate resulting in many Goths drowning while trying to reach the opposite bank of the river.

In 377, the Gothic warrior group moved up to the city Marcianopolis, which was the capital of the province *Moesia inferior*. However, the Roman commander Lupicinus did not want the Goths to enter the city under any circumstances. He evidently feared the Goths would attack the city's population as they had already run out of food. Nevertheless, Lupicinus invited both Gothic leaders to a feast, most likely discuss the delicate situation. In the meantime, outside the city gates, considerable unrest was brewing amongst the people, leading to Roman soldiers capturing a number of Goths. When Lupicinus got word of this, he ordered the Gothic delegation to be killed, which broke with every prevailing law. Several men fell victim to this attack, probably including Alaviv, whereas Fritigern managed to escape.[41] He consequently became sole leader of the group and started to plunder the area around Marcianopolis together with his warriors. Lupicinus wanted to stop the Goths' actions as quickly as possible and sent out his soldiers. In the end, he lost the battle, apparently because his attack had been unsystematic

---

39   BRENNECKE, 2014.
40   HEATHER, 1986.
41   Amm. 31,5,4.

and overly hasty. Numerous Roman soldiers died and – which was especially shameful – the *signa* (banners of arms) fell into the hands of the enemy. As the Goths' problem of supply had not yet been solved, further raids and plundering followed.[42] This time, Fritigern chose the Thracian province as their next target, exactly the region that the emperor had supposedly previously granted to the Goths. There they freed many Goths, which had been forced into Roman slavery. In addition, a considerable number of Romans joined Fritigern's group of warriors. Henceforth, Ammianus no longer referred to these groups as *Tervingi*, but only as the Goths. By examining the emperor's reaction, the perceived threat of these actions becomes clear: On the one hand, he sent troops normally stationed in Armenia (due to the ongoing conflict with the Persians) to Thracia. On the other hand, he called his co-emperor in the West for help. Because of this massive deployment of troops – Gratian had sent several units to the crisis zone – Fritigern's Goths were forced on the defensive. Nevertheless, the battle, in which both sides suffered heavy losses, did not lead to a final decision in late summer of 377 (*Ad Salices*).[43] It must have been evident to Fritigern that he would not be able to keep up his war band without food and an influx of additional warriors. Consequently, he sought and gained the support of Alanic and Hunnic warriors who were attracted by his promise to reward them richly. This meant that Fritigern's retinue once again underwent fundamental changes concerning its compositions and military force. Fritigern immediately took the offensive and managed to escape the Roman stranglehold. The Goths once again invaded Thracia and took the necessary supplies by force. In response, and in an attempt to put an end to this "Gothic" problem, the Romans raised all available troops. The decisive battle, which could not be avoided despite the efforts of mediating legates, took place in August 378.[44] It ended in the destruction of huge swathes of Roman legions, possibly one third of the total armed forces Valens had been able to mobilise.

The *History* of Ammianus not only reflects his great dismay over the massacre on the battlefield and the battle's catastrophic ending, but also his indignation at the incompetence of the emperor and his strategists.

---

42 BERNDT, 2011.
43 Amm. 31,7.
44 BRODKA, 2009.

The historian acknowledges that Fritigern's warriors had a numerical advantage, but – contrary to other battle-descriptions – Ammianus does not praise the warlord's skills in tactics and strategy. However, although Fritigern was then at the height of his career, he was not able to establish a stable and permanent livelihood for his warrior group. They were neither able to capture the city of Adrianopel, where they suspected the emperor's treasure and war chest to be, nor take steps against Constantinople itself. Still far from the city gates, they had to evade some Saracene warrior groups, which were in the service of the Romans.[45] Up to the year 380, the sources describe Fritigern's Goths raiding and plundering at *Thessaly, Epirus* and *Achaia*. However, Fritigern probably did not live to see the *foedus* of the year 382. Their warlord managed to neither transform his military success into a stable or institutionalised position, nor win territories for a permanent settlement of his followers. At the end of the fourth century, Roman power was still strong enough to limit the influence of a Gothic warlord.

Theoderic the Amal

During the second half of the fifth century, the conflicts between the Western and Eastern part of the Roman Empire had taken a turn for the worse, making military cooperation difficult. At increasing intervals, ambitious military men were able to take advantage of the weakness of the Empire in regions where a 'state' monopoly on violence was no longer maintained. The second example for this chapter is the Amal-Gothic leader Theoderic.[46] His Gothic name is a compound of the Germanic words *þiudô* (people) and *rîkja* (mighty, rich), which could be understood as "ruler of the people".[47]

After the fall of Attila and the breakup of the Hunnic realm at the middle of the fifth century, fundamental changes took place at the north-eastern frontiers of the Roman world.[48] The Ostrogoths, who had been

---

45   Amm. 31,16,3.
46   For biographical approaches, see ENSSLIN, 1959; MOORHEAD, 1992; HEATHER, 1995.
47   On the name, see SCHÖNFELD, 1911, pp. 232-234.
48   HEATHER, 1996, pp. 151-154.

under the dominion of the Huns for several decades, seized this opportunity to reorganise themselves as an independent group of warriors. At the age of eight (or a little older) Theoderic was given by his father, the Gothic leader Thiudimir, as a hostage in the context of a peace treaty to Constantinople.[49] It is possible that he grew up in the imperial palace, or at least in close proximity.[50] Around the age of 18, he was released from custody and able to return to his people, who dwelt in *Pannonia* at that time.

Shortly after his return, most likely in the year 471, Theoderic organised a raid against a group of Sarmatians led by a certain Babai, who – it is said – was killed by Theoderic himself.[51] This raid, involving no less than 6,000 Gothic warriors, is best interpreted as a serious attempt by Theoderic to be accepted by the Gothic war band. In particular, the fact that Theoderic had killed their enemy's leader himself might have demonstrated Theoderic's undeniable right to the leadership. The chronicler Jordanes strongly emphasised that Theoderic remained in control over the occupied territory around Singidunum (Belgrade), which was a border town of the eastern Roman Empire located on the Danube.[52] Thiudimir led the Goths out of the frontier area and further into the Empire, firstly to Greece, where they plundered in Macedonia. During these campaigns, his son Theoderic again distinguished himself as a brave and competent leader, although it must be noted that he had been supported by the leaders Astat and Invilia during the attack on the city of Stobi, capital of the province of *Macedonia Salutaris*. The Goths captured Ulpiana, Heraclea Lyncestis, Larissa and other cities that were plundered afterwards.[53]

Following a number of additional raids, the Goths settled in and around Kyrrhos, where the Amal died in 474. Now Theoderic was seemingly able to claim the leadership position within the group without causing internal conflict. There is nothing to indicate a competition for the leadership, even though it is evident that Theoderic had a brother

---

49 Jordanes, *Getica* 269; Theophanes, *Chron.* 5977.
50 Ennodius, *Panegyricus* 11; John Malalas, *Chron.* 383; SHEPARD, 2006. Theoderic obviously was able to communicate in Greek and Latin, besides his mother tongue Gothic.
51 Jordanes, *Getica* 281-282.
52 IBID., 282.
53 IBID., 285-286.

called Theodimund[54], who had also been entitled to claim this position. Theoderic was evidently unwilling to share his leading position, as had been common practice in his father's time. He needed this unchallenged position within the Gothic warrior community in order to counter his strongest competitor, a man also named Theoderic who went by the cognomen Strabon.[55] At the peak of his power, Strabon was the leader of the so-called Thracian Goths and commander of 30,000 men. The Roman emperor Leo I accepted Strabon as Gothic supreme authority and granted him 2,000 pounds of gold a year. This was a considerable amount compared to the 300 pounds previously received by the Amals.

Emperor Zenon, who ascended the throne in Constantinople in 474, devoted himself to dealing with the Goths in a different manner. He tried to take advantage of the Goth's difficulties in securing a stable livelihood and tried to play them off against each other. In the beginning, the Amals had enjoyed his favour. He made Theoderic "Waffensohn" and appointed him *magister militum*. The *adoptio per arma* was an act that established artificial kinship through the donation of weapons.[56] Connected to this honour was the granting of new subsidies to the Goths. Consequently, Strabon lost considerable prestige in the capital as well as within his own retinue. This was further compounded by Zenon declaring him enemy of the state (*hostis publicus*) and ordering his allies out of the city. However, through military strength and his negotiating skills, Strabon soon revived his influence at the imperial court. As early as in the autumn of 478, he had won back his position as *magister militum*, received salaries for his 13,000 warriors, was in supreme command of two units of the palace and eventually was able to collect the subsidies and supplies, which had been due since 476.[57] Those who suffered from these intrigues were the civilian population as well as the Amal Goths, who now no longer received supplies from the Romans. To help his warriors and their families through the cold season, Theoderic again started to plunder. Malchus states that farmers in Thracia were particularly affected. The Goths, under attack by imperial troops, moved to Stobi and devastated the city – all soldiers stationed there were apparently killed during this

---

54 PLRE II, p. 1084.
55 IBID., pp. 1073-1076.
56 WOLFRAM, 2006 with further examples and KISS, 2015.
57 Malchus, *fr.* 14 (BLOCKLEY).

attack. Subsequently, Theoderic led his warriors to Thessaloniki, where the urban population remembered the Goths all too well and went into a panic. Unrest spread, statues of the Emperors were torn down and the official seat of the prefect was stormed by the crowd. In the end, the conflict was settled by diplomatic negotiations. Theoderic had again managed to force the Emperor into reacting by exercising his military power. During new negotiations with a Roman envoy, Theoderic announced that he planned to take action against the Thracian Goths with a troop of only 6,000 men. Evidently, the size of his war band had decreased considerably. Many had fallen into Roman captivity after general Sabinianus attacked the Gothic warriors in the Epirotic Mountains and Theudimund, Theoderic's brother, had abandoned his people. Thus, Theoderic's position was by no means permanently secured. This tenuous position is made clear by the consequences of a direct confrontation with Theoderic Strabon at the foot of the mountain Sondis (its precise location cannot be identified) in the border region between *Moesia* and *Thracia* in 478. Here, Theoderic's warriors, who had intended to fight Strabon alongside Roman troops, came across the enemy unexpectedly. The Roman soldiers were yet to arrive and Theoderic felt betrayed by the Emperor.[58] Perhaps due to the persistent supply difficulties and preceding defeats, many of Theoderic's warriors were discouraged and very likely considered deserting to the enemy.[59] This constituted an immediate and serious threat to Theoderic's position as a warlord.

The rivalry between the two warlords only ended with the accidental death of Strabon in 481.[60] His group of warriors soon disbanded after his son, Recitach, was unable to win the loyalty of his father's men. Many of them then joined the Amal warlord. Now substantially strengthened, Theoderic restarted his policy of manipulating the Roman Emperor by threatening the use of violence. He let his men devastate Greece, which again resulted in raids on the population.

Violence only ended when the Emperor had given the promise to promote Theoderic to the office of *magister militum*, appointed him *patricius* and promised him the consulship for the year 484. Theodoric

---

58   IBID., *fr.* 16 (BLOCKLEY).
59   IBID., *fr.* 18 (BLOCKLEY).
60   Marcellinus Comes, *Chron.* a. 481.

received this extraordinary honour and it was openly displayed through the erecting of a statue at Constantinople. Only two years later, the Emperor and Theoderic were again engaged in open conflict. The Goths, as usual, reacted to this dispute with the exertion of excessive violence. In the meantime, the Goths had set up their base of operations in Novae. From there, Theoderic let his warriors plunder and prepared to launch an offensive against the capital itself. After the Goths occupied several suburbs and cut off one of the city's aqueducts, the Emperor realised the seriousness of the situation and was only able to induce the Goths to leave by endowing them richly.[61] The threats of Theoderic had once again been successful. The withdrawal of his warriors to Italy in 488 must have been a relief for Eastern Rome.

Together with a group of warriors, which was considered very large for the 5th century – estimates give a number of 20,000 battle-hardened men (plus dependents) – Theoderic moved to Italy to overturn the rule of Flavius Odoacer on behalf of the Emperor Zenon in 489.[62] At that time, Theoderic's positions as leader of his warriors was indisputable. Nevertheless, during the previous 15 years he repeatedly experienced how brittle the group's social cohesion could be if he was not able to satisfy the needs of his followers. Particularly, during periods when he was not able to achieve military success, the danger of internal disintegration increased. To prevent such situations in the future, he searched for and found an alternative concept of power in Italy. However, he first needed to get rid of Odoacer and his warriors, who had already been in power in Italy for more than a decade.[63]

The course of the four years of war cannot be reconstructed in detail, as coherent reports did not survive. The sources contain indications of two larger battles, namely the Battle of Verona in September 489 and the

---

61 John of Antioch, *fr.* 214,8-9; Marcellinus Comes, *Chron.* a. 487; *Anonymus Valesianus* 11,49: *cui Theodericus pactuatus es tut, si victus fuisset Odoacar, pro merito laborum suorum loco eius, dum adveniret, tantum praeregnaret.* Much ink has been spent on the meaning of these words. See the recent argument ARNOLD, 2014, pp. 66-68.

62 Jordanes, *Getica* 289-290; Jordanes, *Romana* 348; *Anonymus Valesianus* 11,49; Procopios, *BG* 1,1,9; Theophanes Confessor, *Chron.* A.M. 5977; Evagrius Scholasticus, *HE* 3,27.

63 In the year 476 Odoacer had dethroned the Roman Emperor Romulus (Augustulus) and set himself up as ruler of Italy.

Battle of the Adda (Addua) near Milan in August 490.[64] Although the Goths emerged as the victor in both battles, Odoacer's resistance had not yet been broken. Theoderic had to besiege the capital Ravenna, where his opponent had entrenched himself.[65] It was only in March 493 that the Gothic warriors were able to enter the city. Odoacer withdrew and peace negotiations commenced. After four years of violence, an agreement was concluded. Then, Odoacer fell victim to an assassination attempt at a banquet, which ostensibly had been organised to support the peacekeeping.[66] The early Byzantine historian John of Antioch, who wrote his work at the beginning of the 7th century, describes this in terms of blood feud:

> "Theoderic and Odoacar agreed in a treaty with each other that both should rule the Roman Empire, and thereafter they talked together and frequently went to see each other. But ten days had not passed when Odoacar was at Theoderic's headquarters and two of the latter's henchmen came forward as though suppliants and grasped Odoacar's hands. Therewith those hidden in ambush in the rooms on either side rushed out with their swords. They were panic-stricken at the sight of their victim, and when they did not attack Odoacar, Theoderic himself rushed forward and struck him with a sword on the collarbone. When he asked 'Where is God?' Theoderic answered, 'This is what you did to my friends.' The fatal blow pierced Odoacaer's body as far as the hip, and they say Theoderic explained, 'There certainly wasn't a bone in this wretched fellow.'"[67]

There is no additional evidence to verify the event taking place as Johannes von Antioch describes it; he wrote a century later and, besides, he used sources, which are no longer identifiable. It is also not clear which family members Theoderic meant here and how they had lost their lives, but another source[68] suggests that Odoacer is said to have killed relatives of the Amal. Theoderic also had Odoacer's family members

---

64 *Anonymus Valesianus* 11,53. Cassiodor, *Chron.* a. 490.
65 Jordanes, *Getica* 293; Procopius, *BG* 1,1,14-15; Marcellinus Comes, *Chron.* 489.
66 *Anonymus Valesianus* 11,55. The killing is mentioned in a couple of sources.
67 John of Antioch, *fr.* 307.
68 Ennodius, *Panegyricus* 25.

killed, including his wife Sunigild, his son Thela and some of his close followers. Whatever the precise details, it is evident that Theoderic carried out a bloody purge that destroyed both the family and the political support of Odoacer. Consequently, even Hunulf (Onoulphus[69]), Odoacer's brother, was killed by an arrow as he ran for shelter in a church in Ravenna.[70] Interestingly, the *Anonymus Valesianus*, two (now) fragmentary Latin chronicles compiled in the middle of the sixth century, tells us that Odoacer himself planned to eliminate Theoderic. The Amal, as on many previous occasions, committed a murder from which his men – if we believe the sources – had shied away at the last moment. By the means of a single sword stroke, Theoderic proved his personal ability to perform violence and (judging from a modern perspective) his cold-bloodedness. It is not clear if Theoderic also bore a sword in times of peace; however, the fact that he was repeatedly able to kill enemies with a surprise blow suggests that this was the case, at least at the beginning of his kingship in Italy.[71]

Individual violence of "ordinary" Gothic warriors rarely appears in the sources. Numerous examples illustrate that Gothic warriors did not hesitate to use their swords off the battlefield. One such incident took place in the city Arcadiopolis in Thracia in the course of the year 474. This episode is found in the historical work of Malchus of Philadelphia, written at the end of the 5th century, and of which only fragments are preserved. Malchus described in detail the competitive situation among the different Gothic war-bands in the Balkans and around Constantinople. The historian wrote that the Byzantine general and *magister militum per Thracias* Heraclius[72] had been ransomed from captivity of the Goth Theoderic Strabon. However, the Roman was not to enjoy his newly won freedom for long:

"When he was making a public appearance at Arcadiopolis, some Goths rushed up to him, and one of them struck him hard on the shoulder as he was walking along. One of Heraclius' escorts rebuked the Goth, saying,

---

69 PLRE II, p. 806.
70 John of Antioch, *fr.* 214; *Chronica Gallica 511*, 670.
71 He had – for example – killed the son of Theoderic Strabon, Recitach, on the open road in a suburb of Constantinople (Bonophatianae) in 484. John of Antioch, *fr.* 214,3.
72 PRLE II, pp. 541f. (Heraclius 4).

'Don't you know who you are, man? Don't you know whom you struck?' The other replied that he knew very well and was going to bring him to a nasty end. The Goths drew their swords together and one cut of Heraclius' head, another his hands. They say that Heraclius was killed in revenge."[73]

This instance of violence was the outcome of a prolonged conflict and took the form of a brutal act of revenge. Revenge appears as a recurring motive for action in our sources, not only for the Goths but also for other groups of warriors in early medieval times. Retribution without boundaries and rules could set into motion a cycle of vengeance that threatened the survival of the entire group.

To return to Theoderic: One might say that the killing of Odoacer marks the end of Theoderic's warlord-career. He became king over the Goths and Romans in Italy, thus marking a fundamental change to his exercise of power.[74] Very little is known about the internal arrangement of Gothic war-bands. Until the conquest of Italy, the warlord Theoderic always acted as supreme commander who stood in the thick of the fight and did not operate as a strategist in the background, as recommended by eastern Roman military theorists. As far as is known, Theoderic no longer personally participated in military campaigns as a king, but charged experienced military men of the Gothic nobility with this task, making them *ad hoc* leaders of his troops. His successors, Athalaric and Theodahad, also retired from personal combat. Theoderic had transformed the war band, which had been a mobile association for decades, into a standing army and settled or trained these soldiers in garrisons. He had an impregnable capital at his disposal and lived more or less peacefully with the Italian population for most of the time.

Meanwhile, Anastasius I had ascended the throne in Constantinople. During the following years, Theoderic worked to gain his recognition by repeatedly sending ambassadors. Eventually, in an agreement in 497,[75] the Emperor acknowledged Theoderic's position in Italy. This

---

73 Malchus, *fr.* 6,2 (BLOCKLEY).
74 WIEMER, 2013 with a detailed description of the transformation of the Gothic war-band into a regular standing army and WIEMER, 2014 with a profound comparison of the different concepts of power of Odoacer and Theoderic in Italy.
75 *Anonymus Valesianus* 12,64; Procopius, *BG* 1,1,26.

arrangement was clearly illustrated by the transfer of the *ornamenta palatii* to Theoderic. These symbols of power had been sent by Odoacer to Constantinople after the displacement of Emperor Romulus about 20 years earlier. By this act, Theoderic's rise from Gothic warlord to established king was formally concluded. He and his followers succeeded where Fritigern and his men had failed a century earlier.

Bibliography

Sources

Anonymus Valesianus, ed. by THEODOR MOMMSEN (MGH AA 9), Berlin 1892 (repr. Munich 1981), pp. 306-328.

Ammianus Marcellinus, ed. by WOLFGANG SEYFARTH, *Rerum gestarum libri qui supersunt*, Leipzig 1978; trans. by JOHN C. ROLFE (LCL), Cambridge 1935-1940.

Cassiodor, *Chronica*, ed. by THEODOR MOMMSEN (MGH AA 11), Berlin 1894 (repr. 1961), pp. 109-161.

Chronica Gallica, ed./trans. by RICHARD BURGESS, in: Society and Culture in Late Antique Gaul. Revisiting the Sources. ed. by RALPH W. MATHISEN/DANUTA SHANTZER, Aldershot 2001, pp. 85-100.

Ennodius, *Panegyricus*, ed./trans. by CHRISTIAN ROHR, Der Theoderich-Panegyricus des Ennodius (MGH Studien und Texte 12), Hannover 1995.

Evagrius Scholasticus, *The Ecclesiastical History*, trans. by MICHAEL WHITBY (Translated Texts for Historians 33), Liverpool 2000.

John of Antioch, *fr.*, ed. by UMBERTO ROBERTO, *Ioannis Antiocheni Fragmenta ex Historia chronica*, Berlin/New York 2005; trans. by COLIN D. GORDON, The Age of Attila. Fifth-Century Byzantium and the Barbarians, Michigan 1960.

Jordanes, *Getica*, ed. by THEODOR MOMMSEN, De origine actibusque Getarum (MGH AA 5/1), Berlin 1882 (repr. Munich 1982), pp. 53-183; trans. by CHARLES C. MIEROW, Princeton 1915.

Johannes Malalas, *Chronographia*, ed. by JOHANNES THURN (Corpus Fontium Historiae Byzantinae 35), Berlin/New York 2000; trans. by

ELIZABETH JEFFREYS et al. (Byzantina Australiensia 4), Melbourne 1986.

Malchus, *fr.*, Malchus of Philadelphia, Fragments, ed./trans. by ROGER C. BLOCKLEY, The Fragmentary Classicising Historians of the Later Roman Empire. Eunapius, Olympiodorus, Priscus and Malchus (ARCA Classical and Medieval Texts, Papers and Monographs 10) Liverpool 1983, pp. 401-462.

Marcellinus Comes, *Chronicon*, ed. by THEODOR MOMMSEN (MHG AA 11), Berlin 1894 (repr.1961), pp. 37-108, trans. by BRIAN CROKE, The Chronicle of Marcellinus (Byzantina Australiensia 7), Sydney 1995.

Procopius, *BG*, ed. by JAKOB HAURY, Procopius Caesariensis, Opera omnia, Vol. II: De Bellis libris V-III, Leipzig 1905 (repr. 1963); trans. by ANTŌNIOS KALDELLĒS, The Wars of Justinian, translated by Henry B. Dewing, revised and modernized, with an introduction and notes, maps and genealogies by Ian Mladjov, Indianapolis 2014.

Theophanes, Confessor, *Chronicle*, trans. by CYRIL MANGO/ROGER SCOTT, The Chronicle of Theophanes Confessor. Byzantine and Near Eastern History AD 284-813, Oxford 1997.

Vegetius, *Epitoma rei militaris*, trans. by NICHOLAS P. MILNER (Translated Texts for Historians 16), Liverpool 1993 (second revised edition 2011).

Literature

AIRLIE, STEWARD et al. (eds.), Staat im frühen Mittelalter (Forschungen zur Geschichte des Mittelalters 11), Vienna 2006.

ARNOLD, JONATHAN, Theoderic and the Roman Imperial Restoration, Cambridge 2014.

BAK, JÁNOS M. et al. (eds.), Gebrauch und Missbrauch des Mittelalters, 19.-21. Jahrhundert (MittelalterStudien 17), Munich 2009.

BARAZ, DANIEL, Medieval Cruelty. Changing Perceptions, Late Antiquity to the Early Modern Period, Ithaca/London 2003.

BECHER, MATTHIAS, 'Herrschaft' im Übergang von der Spätantike zum Frühmittelalter. Von Rom zu den Franken, in: Von der Spätantike zum Frühmittelalter. Konzeptionen und Befunde (Vorträge und Forschungen 70), ed. by THEO KÖLZER/RUDOLF SCHIEFFER, Ostfildern 2009, pp. 163-188.

BERNDT, GUIDO M., Murder in the Palace. Some Consideration on Assassinations in Late Antiquity and the Early Middle Ages, in: Rules and Violence – Regeln und Gewalt. On the Cultural History of Collective Violence from Late Antiquity to the Confessional Age – Zur Kulturgeschichte der kollektiven Gewalt von der Spätantike bis zum konfessionellen Zeitalter, ed. by CORA DIETL/TITUS KNÄPPER, Berlin/Boston 2014, pp. 31-47.

ID., Aktionsradien gotischer Kriegergruppen, in: Frühmittelalterliche Studien 47 (2013), pp. 7-52.

ID., Beute, Schutzgeld und Subsidien. Formen der Aneignung materieller Güter in gotischen Kriegergruppen, in: Lohn der Gewalt. Beutepraktiken von der Antike bis zur Neuzeit (Krieg in der Geschichte 72), ed. by HORST CARL/HANS-JÜRGEN BÖMELBURG, Paderborn et al. 2011, pp. 121-147.

BLECKMANN, BRUNO, Die Germanen. Von Ariovist bis zu den Wikingern, Munich 2009.

BODMER, JEAN-PIERRE, Der Krieger der Merowingerzeit und seine Welt. Eine Studie über Kriegertum als Form menschlicher Existenz im Frühmittelalter, Zürich 1957.

BRENNECKE, HANNS CHRISTOF, Introduction. Framing the Historical and Theological Problems, in: Arianism. Roman Heresy and Barbarian Creed, ed. by GUIDO M. BERNDT/ROLAND STEINACHER, Farnham 2014, pp. 1-19.

BRODKA, DARIUSZ, Einige Bemerkungen zum Verlauf der Schlacht bei Adrianopel (9. August 378), in: Millennium 6 (2009), pp. 265-279.

BROWN, WARREN C., Violence in Medieval Europe, London 2011.

CASTRITIUS, HELMUT, Das vandalische Doppelkönigtum und seine ideell-religiösen Grundlagen, in: Das Reich der Vandalen und seine (Vor-)geschichten (Forschungen zur Geschichte des Mittelalters 13), ed. by GUIDO M. BERNDT/ROLAND STEINACHER, Vienna 2008, pp. 79-86.

CHRISTENSEN, ARNE SØBY, Cassiodorus, Jordanes and the History of the Goths. Studies in a Migration Myth, Kopenhagen 2002.

DAHN, FELIX, Die Könige der Germanen. Das Wesen des ältesten Königtums der germanischen Stämme (Teil 2: Die kleineren gotischen Völker – Die Ostgothen, München 1861; Teil 3: Verfassung des ostgotischen Reiches in Italien, Würzburg 1866, Teil 4: Anhänge zur dritten Abtheilung, Würzburg 1866).

DICK, STEFANIE, Der Mythos vom "germanischen" Königtum. Studien zur Herrschaftsorganisation bei den germanischsprachigen Barbaren bis zum Beginn der Völkerwanderungszeit (RGA Ergänzungsbände 60) Berlin/New York 2008.

DRAKE, HAROLD A. (ed.), Violence in Late Antiquity. Perceptions and Practices, Aldershot 2006.

ENSSLIN, WILHELM, Theoderich der Große, Munich, 1947, 2nd ed.,1959.

FRECH, KURT, Felix Dahn. Die Verbreitung völkischen Gedankenguts durch den historischen Roman, in: Handbuch zur "Völkischen Bewegung" 1871–1918, ed. by UWE PUSCHNER et al., Munich et al. 1996, pp. 685-698.

GEARY, PATRICK J., Ethnic Identity as a Situational Construct in the Early Middle Ages, in: Mitteilungen der Anthropologischen Gesellschaft in Wien 113 (1983), pp. 15-26.

GIESE, WOLFGANG, Die Goten (Urban-Taschenbücher 597), Stuttgart 2004.

GILLETT, ANDREW (ed.), On Barbarian Identity: Critical Approaches to Ethnicity in the Early Middle Ages (Studies in the Early Middle Ages 4), Turnhout 2002.

GOETZ, HANS-WERNER et al. (eds.), Regna and Gentes. The Relationship between Late Antique and Early Medieval Peoples and Kingdoms in the Transformation of the Roman World (The Transformation of the Roman World 13), Leiden/Boston 2003.

GOFFART, WALTER, Two Notes on Germanic Antiquity Today, in: Traditio 50 (1995), pp. 9-30.

GRAUS, FRANTIŠEK, Über die sog. Germanische Treue, Historica I., Prag 1959.

GRUCHMANN, LOTHAR, Nationalsozialistische Großraumordnung (Schriftenreihe der Vierteljahreshefte für Zeitgeschichte 4), Munich 1962.

HALSALL, GUY (ed.), Violence and Society in the Early Medieval West, Woodbridge 1998.

HEATHER, PETER, The Goths (The Peoples of Europe), Malden/MA 1996.

ID., Theoderic, King of the Goths, in: Early Medieval Europe 4 (1995), pp. 145-173.

ID., Goths and Romans 332-489, Oxford 1991.

ID., Cassiodorus and the Rise of the Amals. Genealogy and the Goths under Hun Domination, in: Journal of Roman Studies 79 (1989), pp. 103-128.

ID., The Crossing of the Danube and the Gothic Conversion, in: Greek, Roman and Byzantine Studies 27/3 (1986), pp. 289-318.

HELBLING, HANNO, Goten und Vandalen. Wandlung der historischen Realität, Zürich 1954.

KIPPER, RAINER, Der völkische Mythos. "Ein Kampf um Rom" von Felix Dahn, in: Der Germanenmythos im deutschen Kaiserreich. Formen und Funktionen historischer Selbsthematisierung, ed. by ID., Göttingen 2002, pp. 118-150.

KISS, ATTILA, Per arma adoptio. Eine gotische in den frühmittelalterlichen schriftlichen Quellen, in: Romania Gothica II. The Frontier World: Romans, Barbarians and Military Culture (Proceedings of the International Conference held at the Eötvös Loránd University, Budapest, 1-2 October 2010), ed. by TIVADAR VIDA, Budapest 2015, pp. 95-108.

KLETZIN, BIRGIT, Europa aus Rasse und Raum. Die nationalsozialistische Idee der Neuen Ordnung (Region – Nation – Europa 2), Münster et al., 2nd ed., 2002.

LIEBESCHUETZ, JOHN H. W. G., Warlords and Landlords, in: A Companion to the Roman Army, ed. by PAUL ERDKAMP, Malden/MA 2007, pp. 479-494.

ID., Violence in the Barbarian Successor Kingdoms, in: Violence in Late Antiquity. Perceptions and Practices, ed. by HAROLD A. DRAKE, Aldershot 2006, pp. 37-46.

MACGEORGE, PENNY, Late Roman Warlords, Oxford 2002.

MOORHEAD, JOHN, Theoderic in Italy, Oxford 1992.

NEUHAUS, STEFAN, 'Das Höchste ist das Volk, das Vaterland!'. Felix Dahns "Ein Kampf um Rom" (1876), in: ID., Literatur und nationale Einheit in Deutschland, Tübingen 2002, pp. 230-243.

PIZZI, ANTONIO, Teoderico nella grande storiografia europea, in: Romanobarbarica 13, (1994/95), pp. 259-282.

PLRE = MARTINDALE, JOHN R., The Prosopography of the Later Roman Empire. Vol. I: A.D. 260-395, Cambridge 1971; Vol. II: 395-527, Cambridge 1980.

POHL, WALTER, Conceptions of Ethnicity in Early Medieval Studies, in: Debating the Middle Ages. Issues and Readings, ed. by LESTER K. LITTLE/BARBARA H. ROSENWEIN, Malden/MA. 1998, pp. 13-24.

POHL, WALTER/WIESNER, VERONIKA (Eds.), Der Frühmittelalterliche Staat – Europäische Perspektiven (Forschungen zur Geschichte des Mittelalters 16), Vienna 2009.

POPITZ, HEINRICH, Phänomene der Macht, Tübingen, 2nd ed.,1986.

SCHÄFERDIEK, KNUT, Das gotische liturgische Kalenderfragment – Bruchstück eines Konstantinopeler Martyrologs, in: Zeitschrift für Neutestamentliche Wissenschaft 79 (1988), pp. 116-137.

SCHLESINGER, WALTER, Herrschaft und Gefolgschaft in der germanisch-deutschen Verfassungsgeschichte, in: Historische Zeitschrift 176 (1953), pp. 225-275.

SCHMIDT, LUDWIG, Geschichte der deutschen Stämme bis zum Ausgang der Völkerwanderung, Berlin 1904-1918. Bd. 1: Die Ostgermanen, Munich, 2nd ed.,1941 (repr. 1970).

SCHÖNFELD, MORITZ, Wörterbuch der altgermanischen Personen- und Völkernamen nach der Überlieferung des klassischen Altertums, Heidelberg 1911.

VON SEE, KLAUS, Deutsche Germanen-Ideologie, Frankfurt a. M. 1972.

SHEPARD, JONATHAN, Manners maketh Romans? Young Barbarians at the Emperor's Court, in: Byzantine Style, Religion and Civilization, ed. by ELIZABETH M. JEFFREYS, Cambridge 2006, pp. 135-158.

SPEITKAMP, WINFRIED, Gewaltgemeinschaften, in: Gewalt. Ein interdisziplinäres Handbuch, ed. by CHRISTIAN GUDEHUS/MICHAELA CHRIST, Stuttgart 2013, pp. 184-190.

ID., Barbar, Germane, Arier. Die Suche nach der Identität der Deutschen, Heidelberg 1994.

TÖNNIES, BERNHARD, Die Amalertradition in den Quellen zur Geschichte der Ostgoten. Untersuchungen zu Cassiodor, Jordanes, Ennodius und den Excerpta Valesiana (Beiträge zur Altertumswissenschaft 8), Hildesheim et al. 1989.

VON TROTHA, TRUTZ, Zur Soziologie der Gewalt, in: Soziologie der Gewalt (Kölner Zeitschrift für Soziologie. Sonderheft 37), ed. by ID., Opladen/Wiesbaden, 1997, pp. 9-56.

VON TROTHA, TRUTZ/RÖSEL, JAKOB (eds.), On Cruelty. Sur la cruauté. Über Grausamkeit, Cologne 2011.

VASILIEV, ALEXANDER, The Goths in the Crimea, Cambridge/MA 1936.

WANKE, ULRICH, Die Gotenkriege des Valens. Studien zu Topographie und Chronologie im unteren Donauraum von 366 bis 378 n. Chr. (Europäische Hochschulschriften, Reihe 3, Geschichte und ihre Hilfswissenschaften 142), Frankfurt a. M. et al. 1990.

WENSKUS, REINHARD, Die neuere Diskussion um Gefolgschaft und Herrschaft in Tacitus' Germania, in: Beiträge zum Verständnis der Germania des Tacitus, Teil II. (Abhandlungen der Akademie der Wissenschaften in Göttingen. Phil.-hist. Klasse, 3. Folge 195), ed. by GÜNTER NEUMANN/HENNING SEEMANN, Göttingen 1992, p. 311-331.

ID., Stammesbildung und Verfassung. Das Werden der frühmittelalterlichen gentes, Köln/Graz 1961.

WHITTACKER, DICK, Landlords and Warlords in the Later Roman Empire, in: War and Society in the Roman World, ed. by JOHN RICH/GRAHAM SHIPLEY, London/New York 1993, pp. 277-302.

WIEMER, HANS-ULRICH, Odovakar und Theoderich. Herrschaftskonzepte nach dem Ende des Kaisertums im Westen, in: Chlodwigs Welt. Organisation von Herrschaft um 500 (Roma Aeterna. Beiträge zu Spätantike und Frühmittelalter 3), ed. by MISCHA MEIER/STEFFEN PATZOLD, Stuttgart 2014, pp. 293-338.

ID., Die Goten in Italien. Wandlungen und Zerfall einer Gewaltgemeinschaft, in: Historische Zeitschrift 296 (2013), pp. 593-628.

WIEMER, HANS-ULRICH/BERNDT, GUIDO M., Instrumente der Gewalt. Bewaffnung und Kampfesweise gotischer Kriegergruppen, in: Millennium 13 (2016) [forthcoming].

WOLFRAM, HERWIG, Die Goten. Von den Anfängen bis zur Mitte des sechsten Jahrhunderts. Entwurf einer historischen Ethnographie, Munich 1979 (5th ed. 2009).

ID., Waffensohn, in: Reallexikon der Germanischen Altertumskunde 33 (2006), pp. 49-51.

ID., The Roman Empire and its Germanic Peoples, transl. by Thomas Dunlap, Berkeley et al. 1997.

ZIMMERMANN, HEINRICH JOACHIM, Theoderich der Große – Dietrich von Bern. Die geschichtlichen und sagenhaften Quellen des Mittelalters (Diss.), Bonn 1972.

The Torture of Bodies in Byzantium After the Riots (Sec. IV-VIII)*

BOGDAN-PETRU MALEON

The Byzantine state was a world power that inherited the ethnolinguistic diversity of the Roman period. The consistency of the empire was ensured by the subjects' loyalty to the central government and, since the 4th century, by belonging to the Christian religion. In terms of political ideology, the territory was inalienable, which implied the preservation of the right over all provinces that had been under the rule of Rome over time. Although Constantinople no longer effectively controlled many of them, their temporary masters were subjects of the empire, whose title could be revoked at any time. From this point of view, any form of insubordination of those who governed various territories was considered a crime of lese majesty. Typically, this accusation was brought to those who wanted to usurp the throne, asserting these claims by assuming the symbols of imperial power, among which the purpura had the strongest meanings. In the struggle for power, the success marked the difference between a contender and the legitimate emperor chosen by God through the senate, army, and people.[1] After gaining the throne, sovereigns always strived to make violent changes in order to ensure succession among their own families, but failed to do so before the 8th century.[2] Starting from the 10th century, when the principle of birth in the purple was imposed, only the

---

* This work was supported by CNCSIS-UEFISCSU, NO. 215 /5.10.2011, PN-II-ID-PCE-2011-3-0730.
1 ANASTOS, 1979, pp. 183f.
2 SCHREINER, 1991, p. 184.

fact of being a member of the leading family justified imperial aspirations.³

The conflicts between pretenders and the imperial power are designated in historiography by the generic term of "insurrection", "revolt", or "riot".⁴ Such a choice in terms of terminology is justified by the difficulty to distinguish between "civil" and "military" spheres, as both components participated in actions against the imperial power.⁵ The explanation lies in the fact that Constantinople was very difficult to conquer by external pretenders without relevant support from the inhabitants. The inhabitants of the capital often sanctioned government abuse and sometimes their opposition resulted in emperor's overthrow.⁶ The causes of these urban riots are complex, ranging from military threats hanging over the Empire to social and economic reasons.⁷ Urban violence was also present in urban centers in Italy, its intensity reflecting the solidity or the weakness of imperial power in the peninsula.⁸

The annihilation of riots resulted in a large number of victims, and their leaders were considered enemies of imperial power, which determined exceptional punitive measures taken against them. Thus, it was preferred that the enemies were captured alive, only to be subjected to public torture with their bodies or parts thereof to be exposed in public space. The display of prisoners in humiliating poses and their corpses' exposure were widely practiced in ancient times. In Ancient Rome, such treatment was applied to those sentenced for serious crimes, especially if they were guilty of rebellion against the central power. This was because Roman emperors⁹, who had a monopoly over body violence through the justice that they managed, performed the execution of sentences in public.¹⁰ However, during the Roman Republican period, freemen could not be legally torture, but in the imperial era, this interdiction applied also to men of the lower classes as

---

3 IBID., pp. 186f.
4 KAEGI JR., 1981, p. 4.
5 IBID., p. 11.
6 GREGORY, 1979, pp. 220-223.
7 NICHANIAN, 2010, pp. 28f.
8 BROWN, 2002, pp. 76-86.
9 BELL, 1997, p. 129.
10 GIL, 1998, pp. 265-267.

well as slaves.[11] Our goal here is to reconstruct how these practices applied to the bodies of the defeated in the struggle for power evolved since the Christianization of the Roman Empire. We also aim to highlight new meanings of these practices over the 4th-8th centuries.

The subject we propose has been mentioned in historiography among the researches on triumphal ceremonies. Specialized studies have shown that there was certain continuity between pagan Rome and Christian Constantinople of the 4th-5th centuries in terms of how victories were celebrated and the treatment applied to the bodies of the defeated.[12] However, the ceremonies in late antiquity accentuated the imperial majesty, as they became ritualized and staged.[13] The crowd continued to participate in the parade, gathered on both sides of the road, and launched various insults.[14] Once the Roman capital was moved to Constantinople, the celebration of military victories was organized in an almost liturgical manner, and the most important moments consisted in the exposure of prisoners and spoils and the cheers of the crowd in honor of emperors. On these occasions, sovereigns entered the capital on the road that began at Hebdomon[15], the Byzantine equivalent of the Field of Mars in Rome.[16] The 5.5 km long road started from the Golden Gate, passed through the Augustaion Forum, and ended at the Hippodrome, where prisoners and trophies were exposed. The triumphal path was created in about 100 years and remained unchanged after 435.[17] Triumphal ceremonies were auxiliary elements indispensable for the power, as military victories were the main factors that legitimated emperors since the 7th century.[18] The Hippodrome became the place where all celebrations of imperial victory took place.[19] The architectural configuration favored "crowd control" and the repression of popular riots, as it was the case in the Nika riot.[20] Many practices applied to prisoners were abandoned, such

---

11 BURY, 1958, II, p. 414.
12 MCCORMICK, 1986, p. 89.
13 IBID., p. 90.
14 RIVIÈRE, 2004, pp. 86-88.
15 MANGO, 2000, pp. 173f.
16 DAGRON, 1974, p. 98; pp. 108-110.
17 MANGO, 2000, p. 180.
18 NICHANIAN, 2010, p. 33.
19 MCCORMICK, 1986, p. 92.
20 BROWNING, 1971, pp. 111f.

as the show with wild beasts set on barbarian prisoners and the gladiatorial fights, which were replaced by horse races.[21]

Captive enemies were brought before the emperor who stood in the imperial box (*kathisma*) in the Hippodrome, and prostrated (*proskynesis*) in front of him thus recognizing his supremacy.[22] This practice was inherited from the Roman past, when the defeated leaders were brought in front of the victorious emperor, who stood on a throne in the presence of the troops. Those guilty of attempts of usurpation were ritually stripped of their insignia before being forced to prostrate before the legitimate emperor. In 534, to celebrate the victory of General Belisarius against Vandals[23], King Gelimer was brought to Constantinople with his family, 15,000 prisoners, and the treasure.[24] The ceremony consisted of two parts, the first being the parade along the most important street of the capital, and the second, the display of spoils and prisoners in the Hippodrome. King Gelimer was brought before the imperial box and bowed in front of Justinian I (527-565), a gesture that turned him into a "defeated usurper, a rebel against the Roman order".[25] The emperor humbled the defeated by *calcatio colli*, the ancient gesture in which the latter was trampled, as an expression of the former's total victory.[26] After the defeat of the Isaurian revolt in 498, its leaders were driven through Constantinople in chains, then taken to the Hippodrome and placed under the feet of Emperor Anastasius I, who watched the race from the imperial box.[27]

Continuity in early medieval victory celebration does not imply identity with pagan Antiquity, as emperors took care to thank the deity for the help in achieving the victory. Since the time of Theodosius I, the rituals of power underwent a significant Christianization process. The main aspect was the celebrated liturgical processions of supplication with priests and people, in order to obtain divine guidance for victory.[28] For example, when he received the news of Vitalian's defeat, Emperor

---

21 MCCORMICK, 1986, pp. 78f.
22 GUILLAND, 1969, pp. 462-490.
23 EVANS, 1996, pp. 132f.
24 DOWNEY, 1960, p. 41.
25 MCCORMICK, 1986, pp. 128f.
26 IBID., pp. 56-58.
27 EVAGRIUS, 2000, p. 180.
28 MCCORMICK, 1986, p. 107.

Anastasius (581-518) organized a procession of thanks giving and victory spectacles.[29] Very importantly, the rites of Christian victory developed independently of other secular festivities, like the triumphal parades and circus show.[30]

After Christianity became official, the celebration of victories continued to include the parade of heads on poles. According to Roman tradition, beheading was not applied to all those sentenced to death, but only to citizens[31], and was traditionally executed with the ax.[32] After the removal of the heads, they were displayed in the city, while the bodies were thrown into the Tiber, and into the sea, after the capital was moved to Constantinople.[33] The parade of usurpers' heads exerted a profound and sinister impact on the collective mind, while their exposure was destined to prove the victory and to attract the subjects' loyalty, by showing who the winner was.[34] From this perspective, it was not by chance that John Malalas, author in the 6th century, mentioned in his chronicle the entry of David in Jerusalem, with Goliath's huge head on a pole, as a sign of victory.[35] Emperor Constantine the Great had Maxentius' head thrust onto a spear and carried through the city of Rome so everyone could see it.[36] In 411, the usurper Constantine's head was presumably sent to Ravenna, from which it was dispatched to provinces.[37] During the next year, the usurpers Jovian and Sebastian's heads were carried in triumph through the streets of Ravenna.[38] After the defeat of Isaurians Illus and Leontius, and their beheading in 488[39], emperor Zeno revived the ancient ritual of the parade of heads in Constantinople.[40] The ritual ended at the Hippodrome; the heads were

---

29 MALALAS, 1986, p. 227.
30 MCCORMICK, 1986, p. 111.
31 RIVIÈRE, 2004, pp. 141f.
32 CANTARELLA, 1991, pp. 154-156.
33 RIVIÈRE, 2004, pp. 86-88.
34 MCCORMICK, 1986, p. 85.
35 MALALAS, 1986, p. 251.
36 LENSKI, 2006, p. 70.
37 MCCORMICK, 1986, p. 56.
38 Theophanes Confesor believed that the head was sent to rome (THEOPHANES, 1997, p. 126), but Michael McCormick thought that the destination was ravenna (MCCORMICK, 1986, p. 56, n. 72).
39 BURY, 1958, I, p. 398.
40 MCCORMICK, 1986, p. 60.

subsequently taken to St. Canons in Syncae, where the show continued to attract the crowd.[41] Anastasius I also faced an Isaurian revolt, which he defeated in 498 and the heads of the dead rebel leaders were sent to the capital.[42]

The repressions of riots of the population of Constantinople were treated as real armed confrontations, and the riot leaders were punished, like usurpers, in an exemplary manner, even though triumphal ceremonies were not organized on these occasions. Emblematic in this regard is the Nika revolt that took place between 11 and 18 January 532, an occasion where the irrational force of the crowd manifested, epitomized by circus parties[43] developed in the Hippodrome.[44] The population of the capital proclaimed Hypatius as emperor[45], a nephew of the former emperor Anastasius I[46], and acclaimed him in the arena.[47] Encouraged by Theodora[48], Justinian I (527-565) turned to the army[49], and the repression occurred also at the Hippodrome.[50] The intervention of Generals Belisarius and Mundus[51] caused major damage in Constantinople[52], as the tradition claimed the huge number of 30,000 deaths.[53] Hypatios and his brother Pompeius were arrested[54] and beheaded, and their bodies were thrown into the sea.[55] Since the usurper's body was washed ashore, the emperor exposed him in public with an inscription naming him the false emperor; subsequently, he was

---

41 MALALAS, 1986, p. 218.
42 EVAGRIUS, 2000, p. 180.
43 DVORNIK, 1974, p. 127; CAMERON, 1976, pp. 105f.; p. 123.
44 EVANS, 1996, p. 119.
45 EVAGRIUS, 2000, p. 213; EVANS, 1996, pp. 121f.
46 JANIN, 1964, pp. 62-64; DOWNEY, 1960, p. 42.
47 CHRONICON PASCALE, 1989, p. 122.
48 EVANS, 1984, pp. 380-382.
49 GREGORY, 1979, p. 30.
50 BURY, 1958, II, pp. 46f.; BROWNING, 1971, pp. 111f. The Hippodrome became the place were political punishments (capital, or mutilations) were performed (JANIN, 1964, pp. 183-194).
51 GUILLAND, 1964, pp. 510-514. On Belisarius' role in the supression of this riot in the Hippodrome see CHASSIN, 1957, pp. 56f.
52 EVANS, 1996, pp. 124f.
53 CAMERON, 1976, pp. 278-280.
54 CHRONICON PASCALE, 1989, p. 125.
55 EVAGRIUS, 2000, p. 213.

given to his relatives after a few days.[56] The repression of the Nika revolt was seen as a military victory, since Emperor Justinian made public its defeat in a newsletter sent to "all the cities".[57]

The overthrow of Emperor Mauricius (582-602) was a turning point in terms of political violence[58], which brutally reactivated the massive involvement of the army in changes of power on the imperial throne.[59] The events of 602, which were the culmination of ten years of military unrest in the Balkans[60], began when the army refused to obey the imperial command and hailed Phocas as emperor.[61] After this moment, the soldiers left for Constantinople[62], where they arrived on November 21st-22nd.[63] The military revolt coincided with the failure in the relationship between the emperor and the population of the capital, the dissatisfaction of the latter being caused by the fact that the very harsh winter of 601-602 delayed the delivery of grains from Egypt.[64] After an incident caused by famine, the emperor was stoned and insulted on his way to church.[65] Maurice was forced to rely on the demes to defend the long walls of the city, but these had few fighters[66], who soon deserted anyway[67], so the situation more and more resembled the Nika riot.[68] Therefore, the cause of Mauricius' overthrow was not that he "had been betrayed by the demes", according to the traditional interpretations suggested by Theophylact Simocatta, but "the result of negligent and unpopular rule".[69] The patriarch crowned the usurper Phocas on November 23 in the church of St. John of Hebdomon[70], and on Sunday,

---

56 CHRONICON PASCALE, 1989, p. 126.
57 MALALAS, 1986, pp. 280f.
58 Broadly on the genesis and progress of this military riot and mauricius' execution on november 27, 602, see KAEGI JR., 1981, pp. 101-114.
59 TREADGOLD, 1995, p. 206.
60 KAEGI JR., 1981, p. 101.
61 JONES, 1986, I, p. 413.
62 SHLOSSER, 1994, p. 73.
63 STRATOS, 1968, I, p. 45.
64 IBID., p. 41. After an incident caused by famine, the emperor was stoned and insulted on his way to church (SHLOSSER, 1994, p. 74).
65 SHLOSSER, 1994, p. 74.
66 CAMERON, 1976, pp. 280f.
67 DVORNIK, 1974, p. 128.
68 CAMERON, 1976, p. 122.
69 OLSTER, 1993, p. 49.
70 STRATOS, 1968, I, pp. 49f.

November 25, he entered the city and crossed it in a triumphal procession, which ended in the Hippodrome.[71] Theophylact described the execution of Maurice and his family according to whom the former emperor's sons were murdered before their father's eyes, followed by his own beheading.[72] Their bodies were thrown into the sea, and the heads were brought to Phocas, who had them exposed for several days on a stand in Hebdomon.[73]

Between 602 and 717, the empire's political life was marked by the end of peaceful ascension to the throne. The struggle for power became endemic and involved both military forces and civilian population. The absence of emperors from the army camp and military campaigns during the 5th-6th centuries was one of the factors that facilitated the military unrest. Political ambitions of several generals, the delay of military pays and the soldiers' difficult living conditions were additional factors. Most riots in Constantinople were generated by economic causes, such as excessive taxation and gaps in food supply. Others referred to various abuses of the imperial power and the persecution of certain categories of citizens. Moreover, riots multiplied during the 7th century due to increasing external military pressures.[74] The success of several pretenders was determined by the concentration of soldiers for campaigns under the command of some ambitious generals.[75]

At the end of the 7th century and the beginning of the following, violence was exacerbated, so the defeated suffered extreme tortures. Such punitive excesses were meant to strengthen the power of some emperors who ascended the throne by force and to discourage potential candidates. At this time, the burning of bodies, which was a punishment from archaic Roman past, was reactivated. In fact, this practice continued, as evidenced by the fact that in 332, the usurper Kalokairos of the island of Cyprus was defeated, and along with those responsible, he was executed at Tarsus in Cilicia by being burned alive.[76] Moreover, such penalties were applied for sexual vices of the monks and for

---

71　THEOPHYLACT, 1986, p. 225.
72　IBID., p. 227.
73　IBID., pp. 228f.
74　KAEGI JR., 1981, p. 139.
75　IBID., pp. 201f.
76　THEOPHANES, 1997, p. 49.

witchcraft[77], but Byzantine sources mentioned them also in some cases of heretics' punishment.[78]

The reign of Phocas (602-610) was a military and economic disaster[79]; the emperor was known for the ferocious suppression of his opponents, which made him the image of a tyrant par excellence.[80] From the beginning of his reign, he faced the uprising of Narses in Mesopotamia, whom he burned alive in the Hippodrome, in front of the people, as an example to all other generals with ambitions of plotting against the emperor.[81] More and more rebels challenged the legitimacy of the emperor, due to his seizing power violently, which was seen as an act of desecration of power, and his arbitrary government marked by cruelty.[82] In 610, the exarch of Africa[83] decided to send his son Heraclios the Younger to Constantinople to capture Phocas[84], after the city defenders had betrayed the latter.[85] According to the information provided by Patriarch Nikephoros and by Chronicon Pascale, Phocas' genitals and right arm were amputated, and the corpse was carried through the city.[86] His head was exposed in public[87], and the body was taken to the Forum Bovis and thrown into the fire, along with those of some collaborators.[88] This incident triggered an annihilation process, which aimed both the destruction of images[89], and the damnation of the tyrant's memory.[90] Thus, his body was dismantled in order to show the

---

77 BURY, 1958, II, pp. 412f.
78 THEOPHANES, 1997, p. 260.
79 HALDON, 1990, pp. 36f.
80 JENKINS, 1966, p. 19.
81 STRATOS, 1968, II, p. 60.
82 On the perception about Phocas' reign and the legend around it, see OLSTER, 1993, pp. 1-21.
83 KAEGI, 2003, p. 80.
84 OLSTER, 1993, pp. 17-19.
85 KAEGI, 2003, pp. 38-45.
86 JANIN, 1964, pp. 59-62.
87 KAEGI, 2003, pp. 38-45.
88 NIKEPHOROS, 1990, p. 37. See KAEGI, 1973, p. 310. On Forum Bovis, where Phocas' body was burnt, see JANIN, 1964, pp. 69-71.
89 STRATOS, 1968, I, p. 91.
90 On Heraclios' return to Constantinople, after the victory against the persians in 628, the triumphal procession arrived to Forum Bovis, where 18 years before the bodies of Phocas and his lieutenants had been burnt, for celebrating the day when tyrany was crashed (IBID., pp. 240-245).

fraudulent character of the power he had exercised. The act symbolized the downgrading to the lowest stage of social organization, as the body was subjected to humiliating punishment, which was usually applied to ordinary criminals or slaves, according to legal codes.

The early years of Constans II's reign (641-668) were emblematic for the political, economic, and military crisis the empire was facing. A series of centrifugal tendencies occurred at this time[91] in Africa[92] and Italy.[93] The following emperor, Constantine IV (668-685) captured and suppressed his fathers' killers, Patrician Justinian being among those executed. The latter's son, Germanos, the future ecumenical patriarch, protested violently, but was punished by castration, although he had already become a member of the monastic race.[94] However, emasculation was applied in exceptional cases, here to punish a potential usurper; the act preceded its preventive application, for the sons of some pretenders or deposed emperors. Nasal mutilation remained dominant, also in the struggle for power within the imperial family.

During the second half of the 7th century, the influence of the military power increased, as proven by the frequent rebellions in this period and particularly during the twenty years of anarchy between 685 and 717, which was probably the most obscure period of Byzantine history.[95] In this context, mutilation was used to eliminate both potential claimants within the imperial family and deposed emperors charged of tyranny. The most common mutilation was the cutting of nose, used also in 695 when Justinian II was overthrown.[96] In this latter case, people also played a key role, as shown by Theophanes Confesor.[97] The supporters of the pretender Leontios surrounded the imperial palace and captured Justinian II, who was taken to the Hippodrome.[98] The citizens of the capital wanted an execution, but Leontios spared the life of the deposed emperor and had his nose and

---

91 HALDON, 1990, pp. 60-63.
92 STRATOS, 1975, III, pp. 62-67.
93 IBID., pp. 106-111.
94 IBID., 1978, IV, pp. 8-14.
95 KAEGI, 1981, pp. 157-185; pp. 186-208; TREADGOLD, 1990, p. 203.
96 See the progress of events in STRATOS, 1980, V, pp. 69-74.
97 THEOPHANES, 1997, p. 515.
98 HEAD, 1972, p. 93; TREADGOLD, 1990, pp. 94f.

tongue cut off, after which he exiled him to Cherson.[99] The crowd took revenge also on the main collaborators of the deposed emperor, namely the monk Theodotos, who was logothete of the genikon, and the sakellarios Stephen the Persian, and dragged them through the main street to the Forum Bovis, where they burnt them.[100]

Following a series of adventures that took him to the courts of Khazar and Bulgarian khans, whose support he managed to obtain, Justinian II took back the throne in the spring of 705 and captured the two emperors who reigned after his overthrow.[101] On February 15, 706, he celebrated his restoration by parading his rivals, decked in chains, through the streets of the capital. They were taken to the Hippodrome, and the emperor placed his feet on their necks for the period of the first race, after which they were sent to the Kynegion for execution, like criminals.[102] During his next reign, Justinian II proved to be a bloody tyrant, so that he was suppressed during a riot, which had started in Crimea[103] under the leadership of Philippicos Bardanes.[104] The execution was not followed by a Christian burial, but his beheaded body was thrown into the sea, and his head sent to be exposed in Rome and Ravenna.[105] To follow the same line, according to Patriarch Nikephoros, after Justinian's overthrow, his son Tiberius was killed "like a senseless animal".[106] These violent practices alternated with decisions taken in the spirit of Christianity, so that the Life of St. Stephan the Younger mentioned that on March 25, 717, Emperor Theodosius III agreed to abdicate, as he did not want Christian blood to flow. There were other cases when exemplary punishment was applied to those defeated in the struggle for power. Thus, the former Emperor

---

99 NIKEPHOROS, 1990, p. 97.
100 THEOPHANES, 1997, p. 515.
101 HEAD, 1972, pp. 114f.; TREADGOLD, 1990, pp. 212f. Justinian II returned to the throne on August 21st, but acted against the two barely on February 15th 706, as the last of them was captured in December (TREADGOLD, 1990, p. 212).
102 HEAD, 1972, pp. 102-111; pp. 116f. On the celebration of triumph, see also MCCORMICK, 1986, p. 73.
103 TREADGOLD, 1990, p. 217.
104 The latter was exiled by Tiberius III Apsimarus because he was telling of a dream in which he became emperor (SUMMER, 1976, pp. 287-289).
105 HEAD, 1972, p. 148.
106 NIKEPHOROS, 1990, p. 113.

Anastasius II did not resign himself to losing the throne and, with the support of the Bulgarians, started a revolt against Leo III (717-740). The rebel was betrayed and handed over to the sovereign, who beheaded him on June 1, 719, along with the archpriest of Thessalonica. Patriarch Nikephoros also showed that "an equestrian race was performed and their heads, affixed to poles, were paraded through the Hippodrome"[107] after the execution. Moreover, common punishments at the time were applied to other conspirators, such as cutting noses off, confiscation of assets and exile.

The issue of succession continued to generate violence throughout the 8th century, as was the case when, after Leo III's death on June 18, 741, his son Constantine succeeded on the throne.[108] Shortly after, he had to face a two-year insurrection instigated by his brother-in-law Artavasdos, an important military commander in Anatolia.[109] Taking advantage of the emperor's departure on an expedition against the Arabs, the claimant was able to obtain support from Patriarch Anastasios, who accused Constantine V of having embraced Arianism. The crowd gathered in front of the Cathedral of Hagia Sophia proclaimed Artavasdos, who was thus able to enter the city, was crowned, and reined with full rights for a year.[110] This period ended after Constantine V's victory in August 742, which made him gain control over Anatolia and allowed him to land in Europe. As famine was raging in Constantinople, Artavasdos allowed non-fighters to leave the city, which turned into a general exodus, and on November 2, he attempted to follow, but was soon captured.[111] Constantine V killed many important people in Artavasdos' entourage, and blinded others or even cut off their limbs.[112] To show the people that the usurpation was over, the head of the chief of the party, who supported the rebels in the capital, was hung from the Arch of the Milion for three days.[113] The

---

107 IBID., pp. 127-129.
108 Constantine V was born in 718 and was baptised on October 25th, the same year (LOMBARD, 1902, p. 22).
109 IBID., pp. 22f. artavasdos gave the action a significant religious content, asociating it with the iconiphile resistance (GERO, 1977, pp. 14-20).
110 LOMBARD, 1902, pp. 24-26.
111 IBID., pp. 27f.
112 THEOPHANES, 1997, p. 581.
113 MCCORMICK, 1986, p. 134.

usurper and his two sons were blinded and, together with other supporters, were paraded in chains in the Hippodrome during the games organized to celebrate the triumph.[114] Patriarch Anastasius, who had collaborated with the usurper, was also brought into the arena, beaten, and forced to ride backwards.[115]

After confrontations with enemies outside the empire, Constantine V also organized triumphal entries, such as those celebrating the victories against the Bulgarians.[116] Therefore, according to Theophanes Confessor, after the defeat of Khan Telez at Anchialos, on June 30, 763, the emperor entered the capital fully armed, accompanied by the soldiers and the Bulgarian prisoners yoked to wooden shackles, after which the members of *demes* beheaded them outside the Golden Gate.[117] This gesture can be considered as rather an exception, which must be understood in terms of the emperor's extreme hostile attitude toward the Bulgarians and an expression of imperial propaganda.[118] According to the cited source, a strange episode occurred shortly thereafter; Constantine V captured a "renegade from the Christian faith" in the Balkans, who was fighting against the empire. The emperor ordered, "they amputate his arms and legs […] in the presence of physicians, dissect him alive from the genitals to the chest so as to comprehend the construction of the human body". After this operation, which reminded of experiments that took place ancient medical science, his body was burned.[119]

Although many practices during the 8th century were still maintained from the pagan Roman period with respect to how the bodies of prisoners of war were treated, the trend of keeping them alive and mutilating them was increasingly evident. In 793, Constantine VI quashed a revolt in the Armeniakon theme and, after the execution of the leaders, he organized a triumphal entry into the capital through Blachernai gate on June 24. On this occasion, one thousand rebels paraded with "their faces tattooed in ink with the words 'Armeniac

---

114 IBID.
115 LOMBARD, 1902, p. 29.
116 MCCORMICK, 1986, p. 135.
117 CAMERON, 1976, pp. 302-304.
118 HALDON, 2003, p. 245.
119 THEOPHANES, 1997, p. 603.

plotter'", after which they were exiled to Sicily and other islands.[120] According to classical antiquity thinking, the destruction of the face was equivalent to the cancelation of personal identity, which automatically implied marginalization. Political offenses were sanctioned by mutilation with strong symbolic significance, most of them directed towards the face, which is explained by that the face was the main channel of social communication. Moreover, disfigurement was practiced extensively since the 8th century when – amid the iconoclastic doctrine – it was associated with the fight against the fascination for human face from the early Byzantine period.[121]

Once Christianity was adopted, emperors were seen as guarantors of the unity of faith and integrity of the state. Any claim against these envoys of God signified the challenging of the order established by the Divinity. Despite these ideological transformations, the general frame of the celebration of military triumphs of the pagan past was maintained during the analyzed period. However, since the late 4th century, there was a more pronounced Christian influence, like liturgical procession of thanksgiving and church service. They developed parallel with the classic scenario of imperial victory celebration. Large-scale human sacrifices, held in the arena by facing the beasts, and gladiators fighting were abandoned. However, the defeated bodies took the central place in these events, as the celebration of victory implied their and their accomplices' public humiliation. However, the practice of beheading the corpses of defeated enemies and the exposure of skulls in the city was maintained. This way of action was based on the ancient tradition of the supernatural power of the head, to which Christian thinking added the belief that the head was the seat of the soul.

Since the 7th century, a number of changes occurred in terms of the treatment applied to the defeated bodies. They more rarely resorted to a series of pagan practices, such as throwing them into the sea or burning the body. Nevertheless, the burning of bodies continued to have profound meanings from a Christian perspective, equivalent to eternal damnation. Although in 775, Emperor Constantine V, the main promoter of iconoclasm, was buried in Justinian's mausoleum, Michael III ejected his remains and burnt them after the restoration of the icons'

---

120 IBID., p. 644.
121 MCCORMICK, 1986, p. 142.

veneration. From this moment the mutilation of those attempting to usurp the supreme power was preferred, and the change of emphasis was related to the Christian view of corporal punishment, which allowed the individual to regret his deeds. The bodies of the convicts had to carry the traces of the guilt, as any crime against the power was treated as a sin. Therefore, the mutilations can be interpreted both as gestures of social exclusion and as a compromise between the Roman punitive tradition and Christian moral requirements that limited the death penalty.[122] The torture of prisoners' bodies was gradually abandoned in the 9th century, except for a significant episode when the body of the rebel Thomas the Slav was dismembered in 823. After the 8th century, the Empire went on the offensive, and emperors increased the number of triumphal ceremonies during which the bodies of prisoners were treated according to a model that appeared in the period of transition that was the subject of this presentation.

Bibliography

Sources

CHRONICON PASCALE (284-628 AD), ed. by MICHAEL WHITBY/MARY WITHBY, Liverpool 1989.
EVAGRIUS SCHOLASTICUS, The Ecclesiastical History, ed. by MICHAEL WHITBY, Liverpool 2000.
MALALAS, JOHN, The Chronicle, ed. by ELIZABETH JEFFREYS et al., Melbourne 1986.
NIKEPHOROS PATRIARCH OF CONSTANTINOPLE, Short history, ed. by CYRIL MANGO, Washington D. C. 1990.
THEOPHANES CONFESOR, The Chronicle. Byzantine and Near Eastern History AD 284-813, ed. by CYRIL MANGO et al., Oxford 1997.
THEOPHYLACT SIMOCATTA, The History, ed. by MICHAEL WHITBY/MARY WHITBY, Oxford 1986.

---

122 BURY, 1958, II, p. 415.

Literature

ANASTOS, MILTON V., *Vox populi voluntas Dei* and the election of Byzantine Emperor, in: ID., Studies in Byzantine Intellectual History, London 1979, pp. 181-207.
BELL, CATHERINE, Ritual. Perspectives and Dimensions, New York et al. 1997.
BROWN, T. S., Urban violence in early medieval Italy: the cases of Rome and Ravenna, in: Violence and Society in Early Medieval West, ed. by GUY HALSALL, Woodbridge et al. 2002, pp. 76-86.
BROWNING, ROBERT, Justinian and Theodora, London 1971.
BURY, J. B., History of the Later Roman Empire from the Death of Theodosius I to the Death of Justinian, I-II, New York/London 1958.
CAMERON, ALAN, Circus Factions. Blues and Greens at Rome and Byzantium, Oxford 1976.
CANTARELLA, EVA, Il supplizi capitali in Grecia e a Roma, Milano 1991.
CHASSIN, L. M., Bélisaire généralissime byzantin (504-565), Paris 1957.
DAGRON, GILBERT, Naissance d'une capitale. Constantinople et ses institutions de 330 à 451, Paris 1974.
DOWNEY, GLANVILLE, Constantinople in the Age of Justinian, Norman 1960.
DVORNIK, FRANCIS, The Circus Parties in Byzantium. Their Evolution and their Supression, in: ID., Photian and Byzantine Ecclesiastical Studies, London 1974.
EVANS, J. A. S., The Age of Justinian. The Circumstances of Imperial Power, London et al. 1996.
ID., The "Nika" Rebellion and the Empress Theodoro, in: Byzantion LIV, 1 (1984), pp. 380-382.
GERO, STEPHEN, Byzantine Iconoclasm during the Reign of Constantine V with particular attention to the Oriental Sources, Louvain 1977.
GIL, JOSÉ, Metamorphoses of the Body, Minneapolis et al. 1998.
GREGORY, TIMOTHY E., *Vox populi*. A Popular Opinion and Violence in the Religious Controversies on the Fifth Century A. D., Columbus 1979.

GUILLAND, RODOLPHE, Études de topographie de Constantinople Byzantin, Amsterdam 1969.
ID., Études sur le Grand Palais de Constantinople, in: Byzantion, XXXIV (1964), pp. 329-346.
HALDON, JOHN, Warfare, State and Society in the Byzantine World (565-1204), London 2003.
ID., Byzantium in the Seventh Century. The Transformation of a Culture, Cambridge 1990.
HEAD, CONSTANCE, Justinian II of Byzantium, Madison et al. 1972.
JANIN, R., Constantinople byzantine. Développement urbain et répertoire topographique, deuxième éditions, Paris 1964.
JENKINS, ROMILLY, Byzantium. The Imperial Centuries (AD 610-1071), London 1966.
JONES, A. H. M., The Later Roman Empire (284-602). A Social, Economic and Administrative Survey, I, Oxford 1986.
KAEGI JR., WALTER EMIL, Heraclios. Emperor of the Byzantium, Cambridge 2003.
ID., Byzantine Military Unrest (471-843). An Interpretation, Amsterdam 1981.
ID., New evidence on the early reign of Heraclius, in: Byzantinische Zeitschrift 66, 2 (1973), pp. 308-330.
LENSKI, NOEL, The Reign of Constantine, in: The Cambridge companion to the Age of Constantine, ed. by NOEL LENSKI, Cambridge 2006, pp. 59-91.
LOMBARD, ALFRED, Constantin V, empereur des romains (740-775), Paris 1902.
MANGO, CYRIL, The Triumphal Way of Constantinople and the Golden Gate, in: Dumbarton Oaks Paper 54 (2000), pp. 173-188.
MCCORMICK, MICHAEL, Eternal Victory. Triumphal Rulership in Late Antiquity. Byzantium and the Early Medieval West, Cambridge 1986.
NICHANIAN, MIKAËL, De la guerre "antique" à la guerre "médiévale" dans l'Empire romain d'Orient. Légitimité impériale, idéologie de la guerre et révoltes militaires, in: Guerre et société au Moyen Âge. Byzance – Occident (VIIIe-XIIIe), ed. by DOMINIQUE BARTHÈLEMY/ JEAN-CLAUDE CHEYNET, Paris 2010, pp. 27-41.

OLSTER, DAVID MICHAEL, The politics of usurpation in the seventh century. Rhetoric and revolution in Byzantium, Amsterdam 1993.

RIVIÈRE, YANN, Le cachot et les fers. Détention et coercition à Rome, Berlin 2004.

SCHREINER, PETER, Réflexions sur la famille imperiale à Byzance (VIIIe-Xe siècles), in: Byzantion LXI, 1 (1991), pp. 181-193.

SHLOSSER, FRANZISKA E., The Reign of the Emperor Maurikios (582-602). A Reassessment, Athens 1994.

STRATOS, ANDREAS N., Byzantium in the Seventh Century, I-V, Amsterdam 1968, 1975, 1978, 1980.

SUMMER, GRAHAM V., Philippicus, Anastasius II and Theodosius III, in: Greek, Roman and Byzantine Studies, 17, 3 (1976), pp. 287-294.

TREADGOLD, WARREN, Byzantium and Its Army (284-1081), Stanford 1995.

ID., Seven Byzantine Revolutions and the Chronology of Theophanes, in: Greek, Roman and Byzantine Studies 31, 2 (1990), pp. 203-227.

"One man slashes, one slays, one warns, one wounds": Injury and Death in Anglo-Scottish Combat, c.1296-c.1403

IAIN MACINNES

Taken from a verse written after the battle of Bannockburn (1314) by a captured English poet, the text quoted in the title reflects the cut and thrust of medieval combat.[1] For all that there is recognition of the violent nature of combat there has been, however, relatively little discussion of the impact of war on the medieval warrior.[2] A lack of a substantial amount of archaeological evidence means that medieval historians are forced to look elsewhere in an attempt to uncover the types of injuries suffered by contemporary combatants and their ability to survive them. Chronicles and other literary sources are particularly rich sources of information for such an investigation as accounts of warfare, including detailed descriptions of battles, skirmishes and sieges, were popular episodes within these works. Indeed for some writers, providing accurate accounts of warfare satisfied the demands of their readers. For 'chivalric chroniclers' the whole intention was to "ensure that they included as full and correct as possible a list of the major participants and the deeds which

---

1 BOWER, 1987-98, vi, p. 375.
2 For recent considerations of this topic, see MACINNES, 2015, pp. 102-27; WOOSNAM-SAVAGE/DEVRIES, 2015, pp. 27-56; GELDOF, 2015, pp. 57-80; SKINNER, 2015, pp. 81-101.

they performed."³ While not all chroniclers fit neatly into the category of chivalric writers, there is little doubt that chivalric culture influenced many writers to the extent that warfare was something recorded carefully within their works. In such a literary environment it should be unsurprising, therefore, that descriptions of combat in these works were far more realistic than may be expected.⁴ Chronicle accounts of fourteenth-century Anglo-Scottish warfare are particularly detailed in their depiction of combat and include numerous examples of injuries given and sustained by English and Scottish warriors. This paper will provide a survey of some of these accounts, examining the types of injuries involved, the areas of the body most effected, and the ability – where such is possible to discern – of these men to survive the injuries they suffered.

Head and Facial Injuries

Despite the development by the fourteenth century of increasingly complex and sophisticated head protection, for the military elite at least, the head, and in particular the face, appear to have remained vulnerable to injury.⁵ In particular Scottish soldiers in this period were exposed to the growing English use of the longbow and therefore to injuries caused by arrows.⁶ As Thomas de Barri reflected when discussing the Otterburn Campaign (1388), "the archer stretching his bow was in no mood to be sparing, / sharpening the pointed darts of his arrows to cause a bitter wound."⁷ Massed archery fire in particular affected the Scots during several defeats in the fourteenth century. At Dupplin Moor (1332) "the Scots were defeated chiefly by the English archers, who so blinded and wounded the faces of the first division of the Scots by an incessant discharge of arrows, that they could not support each other."⁸ Less than a year later at Halidon Hill (1333) the Scots "were so grievously wounded in the face and blinded by the host of English archery [...] that they were

---

3   GIVEN-WILSON, 2004, p. 102.
4   DEVRIES, 2004, pp. 1-15.
5   RICHARDSON, 2011, pp. 311-4; SOUTHWICK, 2006, pp. 5-77.
6   KARGER et al., 2001, pp. 1550-1555.
7   BOWER, 1987-98, vii, p. 427.
8   LANERCOST, 1913, p. 270.

helpless, and quickly began to turn away their faces from the arrow flights and to fall."[9] Although at Neville's Cross (1346) they were said to have lowered their heads so that the missile fire deflected off their helmets, several notable Scots received arrow wounds, including the king himself who suffered two wounds to the face.[10] English barber surgeons were successful in removing one of these, but the other supposedly remained lodged in his head for several year after the battle.[11] Later examples demonstrate that, even towards the end of the fourteenth century, arrows continued to cause injury to many notable Scots, even though they were surely the best armed of their fellow warriors. David Lindsay, earl of Crawford, lost an eye at Otterburn (1388).[12] Archibald Douglas, fourth earl of Douglas, was similarly blinded in one eye at Homildon Hill (1402).[13] For most of the men named here their injuries were survivable and some, like Douglas, would go on to receive further injury in later confrontations. Not all were so fortunate. The Scottish knight William Lundie was shot in the face by a crossbow bolt at Otterburn and, about three months later, died as a result of his wounds.[14] Arrow wounds were not suffered, however, solely by Scottish warriors. Although Scottish archery was generally seen as inferior to the English longbow, sieges often involved the use of archers to pressure those defending towns and castles. During the Scottish capture of Roxburgh Castle the castellan, Guillemin de Fiennes, was apparently killed by archery fire.[15] Roger Horsley, the English constable of Berwick Castle, lost an eye to an arrow during the Scottish siege of the town in 1318.[16] Although in reference to a different type of missile weapon, Thomas Gray wrote that his father was hit in the face by the bolt from a springald during the English siege of Stirling Castle (1303). Knocked out by the blow, Gray *senior* was assumed to be dead until he woke up not long before his planned burial.[17]

---

9   IBID., p. 279.
10 BAKER, 1889, p. 88; GRANT, 1998, p. 29; HARDY, 1998, pp. 112-31.
11 BOWER, 1987-98, vii, pp. 259-61; PENMAN, 2004, pp. 138f.
12 BOWER, 1987-98, viii, p. 19.
13 IBID., p. 49.
14 BOWER, 1987-98, vii, p. 419.
15 BRUCE, 1997, pp. 384-6. See also SCALACRONICA, p. 51.
16 GRAY, 1907, p. 58.
17 IBID., 1907, pp. 25f.; PURTON, 2006, pp. 85-8.

While such notable examples demonstrate that missile fire could indeed cause injury, even to the best-armoured men on the battlefield, the examples of Scottish suffering under massed archery fire suggest that these attacks were more of an "impediment" than they were fatal.[18] Describing the battle of Ben Cruachan (1308), Barbour wrote that James Douglas and his men softened up their opponents by "wounding them with swift arrows" before finishing off their enemy at close quarters with swords.[19] At Bannockburn the Scots suffered from the "horrible shower" of steady English archery fire which left "tokens behind them that needed medical treatment."[20] While incredibly dangerous, and capable of causing troops to bunch together with potentially deadly results, such examples do suggest that the quality of armoured equipment was sufficient to ensure that death did not immediately result from an arrow wound. This is validated by Bower's comment about the Scots at the Homildon Hill (1402). Under withering English archery fire the Scots were described as being "smothered [...] with arrows [which] made them bristly like a hedgehog."[21] This in itself does not necessarily appear to have been deadly, although the arrows that pinned their hands to their spears were likely of greater concern. Arrowhead design may have been adapted over time to produce slimmer points that allowed for penetration between chainmail links.[22] This could account for injuries such as some of those described above, although with plate armour increasingly replacing mail during this period it would have affected the rank and file soldiers more than the military elite. This might then explain the lethal impact of such concentrated fire experienced by the Scots at Dupplin Moor (1332). Here men tried to escape the incessant discharge of arrows by turning inward, which only resulted in their deaths in the resultant press where "many died [...] without a wound in the collision of bodies, the friction of armour, and the stumbling of horses as they were crushed against each other."[23] Even without examples like Dupplin, the longbow remained a dangerous weapon and men could be killed as a result of a

---

18 For a twelfth-century crusade example of such injuries, see MITCHELL et al., 2006, pp. 152, 150.
19 BRUCE, 1997, p. 364.
20 IBID., p. 482.
21 BOWER, 1987-98, viii, p. 47.
22 MITCHELL, 2004, p. 177; JESSOP, 1996, pp. 192-205.
23 BOWER, vii, pp. 77-9.

number of variables, including "the type of bow used, the velocity of flight, the design of arrowhead and the part of the body injured", as well as simple (mis)fortune.[24]

The head was exposed to other forms of injury unrelated to missile fire. In spite of the protection provided by bascinets and helmets it was likely still at risk. Indeed it may have been deliberately targeted in close-quarter combat as a means of more quickly incapacitating an opponent in situations where blows to other protected parts of the body proved ineffective.[25] What resulted was effectively blunt force trauma to the head. Barbour's account of the battle of Methven (1306) suggests just such an occurrence in a confrontation between Christopher Seton and Philip Mowbray. Both men were mounted when Seton struck Mowbray with a blow "that caused him to reel dizzily, although he was [a man] of great strength; [Mowbray] would have fallen straight to the ground had he not been propped up by his steed."[26] Several years later, following his adoption of Bruce/Scottish allegiance, Mowbray was injured in similar fashion at the battle of Faughart (1318). Barbour wrote that he was "knocked senseless in the fight" and dragged off the battlefield by two enemies who took him for ransom. Mowbray recovered his senses while being carried from the field and was able to escape his captors.[27] Such examples, and the already-mentioned case of Thomas Gray *senior*, show the dangers inherent in blows to the head. For those less well-armoured than the chivalric elite, blows to the head were more likely to be fatal. Evidence from a series of excavated bodies relating to the Danish battle of Visby (1361) demonstrates that a majority of those killed as a result of blade injuries died as a result of wounds inflicted to the head.[28] It was perhaps at greatest risk following defeat when soldiers fleeing the battlefield on foot were often chased down by mounted victors, where blows from above were often likely fatal.[29] This appears to have been the experience of Scottish soldiers following their defeats at Halidon Hill (1333) and Neville's Cross (1346). At Halidon in particular the English

---

24 MITCHELL, 2004, p. 156.
25 POWERS, 2005, p. 10; MITCHELL, 2004, p. 117.
26 BRUCE, 1997, pp. 100-2.
27 IBID., p. 672.
28 THORDMAN et al., 1939, i, pp. 160-92; MITCHELL, 2004, p. 110.
29 For discussion of possible evidence of men killed while fleeing the battlefield, see KJELLSTRÖM, 2005, pp. 23-50.

"pursued [the fleeing Scots] on horseback, felling the wretches as they fled in all directions with iron-shod maces."[30] Sieges too provided a dangerous environment in which head injuries were likely, although in this case it was the attackers who were more in danger of suffering such injury. During the English siege of Berwick (1319) the Scottish defenders struck "their foes so hard with stones that they left many lying [there], some dead, some hurt, some passed out."[31] Similarly at the siege of Dunbar (1338) some English attackers were killed by a stone thrown from a siege engine that "dashed [their] heads […] to pieces."[32]

Even the types of head protection that did exist may have proved insufficient when dealing with certain blows, or those from particular weapons. Barbour's description of the battle of Bannockburn (1314) states that the Scots "gave such blows with axes that they split heads and helmets."[33] Although it may appear that comments such as these are little more than literary hyperbole, to emphasise the strength of Scottish warriors, the possibility of an axe blow in particular penetrating a helm is suggested by Robert I's killing of Henry Bohun in the same battle. In this example the Scottish king struck the onrushing English knight with an axe "with such great force that neither hat nor helmet could stop the heavy clout that he gave him, so that he cleaved the head to his brains."[34] Moreover, descriptions such as these appear relatively common in contemporary sources, where it was often used to depict the heroic strength of the writer's heroes. Barbour wrote of James Douglas that "he cleft the skulls of so many that none alive can tell of them."[35] Mimicking to an extent his feat of strength at Bannockburn, Barbour also relates that Robert I was capable of committing similar injury to various men during his career.[36] That reality could reflect such literary depictions is suggested by the case of William Ramsay who perished as a result of wounds sustained in a border tournament against Henry of Lancaster (c.1342). His injury occurred when he "was pierced by a lance through

---

30 LANERCOST, 1913, pp. 279f., 341.
31 BRUCE, 1997, p. 648.
32 BOWER, 1987-98, vii, p. 129.
33 BRUCE, 1997, p. 488.
34 IBID., p. 450.
35 IBID., p. 60.
36 IBID., pp. 116-8, 220-2.

his helmet and brain."[37] Ramsay's case is particularly interesting because one Scottish source claims that he was in fact able to recover from the injury sustained and did not in fact die.[38] Archaeological evidence provides examples of individuals who were able to survive quite severe head trauma. Contemporary surgery, where available, could treat such wounds and in such instances broken skull fragments were extracted to relieve pressure on the brain caused by fractures. That treatment like this was available to more than just the elite is also suggested by archaeological evidence.[39] Archaeology also provides examples of men who survived quite serious head injury to fight (and die) another day.[40] For those who survived it was likely the depth of the wound that proved all-important. Even then men could still perish, not as a direct result of the wound but as a consequence of post-injury or post-operative infection.[41]

The Torso and Extremities

Injuries to the body are, in comparison, less common in chronicle accounts than those to the head. Interestingly this appears to replicate archaeological evidence, although the lack of finds relating to these injuries is likely the result of decomposition of the soft tissue most affected by such wounds.[42] Armour and other forms of protective equipment should, of course, have ensured that blows and penetrative strikes to the torso were blocked or prevented from being fatal. Chronicle examples provide numerous instances when this was, and was not, the case. In Thomas Gray's account of the murder of John Comyn by Robert Bruce, Comyn's uncle is said to have "struck [Bruce] with a sword in the

---

37 BOWER, 1987-98, vii, p. 137.
38 WYNTOUN, 1872-9, ii, pp. 443f.
39 MAYS, 2006, p. 101.
40 POWERS, 2005, p. 12; WILKINSON/NEAVE, 2003, pp. 1343-48. For detailed consideration of the remains of numerous individuals relating to a late medieval battle, see FIORATO et al., 2007.
41 ROKSANDIC et al., 2007, p. 639; MITCHELL, 1999, pp. 335-7; POWERS, 2005, p. 10.
42 MITCHELL, 2004, p. 108.

breast, but he being in armour, was not wounded."[43] The assumption here would appear to be that, if properly equipped, a warrior had less to fear from similar attacks. Other chroniclers and writers take a similar approach and reinforce the reality that the armoured nature of their protagonists ensured their survival in armed conflict. In his *Bruce*, John Barbour creates a series of vignettes in which Robert I is repeatedly placed in a position of fighting alone against groups of armed enemies. The fact that he wins all of these encounters demonstrates Bruce's bravery and military prowess. The examples also, however, acknowledge the additional virtue of the king's military preparedness. In one example, faced by a group of men guarding a ford, Bruce "was protected in armour [and therefore] did not need to fear their arrows."[44] In a similar encounter "the king was placed in such straits there, that he had never been so [badly] placed before, and but for the armour that he wore, he would have been dead, without a doubt."[45] And in another instance the king was struck by a man with an axe but sustained no apparent injury as a result of being well-armoured.[46] The author also took advantage of such tales to reinforce the dangers of warriors finding themselves in situations when they were unprepared and underequipped. Facing three men armed with bows and arrows, Bruce "had a great fear of their arrows because he was without armour."[47] On this occasion the king resorted to words over actions and appealed to chivalric virtue. He argued that his enemies should face him like men with swords, rather than killing him from afar with arrows. This they did and were defeated as a result. Although Bruce won the encounter, the dangers of going into battle without being fully prepared were obvious.

Other examples similarly highlight the dangers of combat for those ill-equipped to participate in it. In Barbour's description of the Scottish capture of Roxburgh Castle (1314), the first man over the walls was Simon Ledhouse. There he fought with two sentries. According to Barbour, Ledhouse won the encounter because he "was armed and strong" while at least one of his opponents "was unarmed [...] and had

---

43 GRAY, 1907, p. 30.
44 BRUCE, 1997, p. 230.
45 IBID., p. 268.
46 IBID., pp. 220-2.
47 IBID., p. 278.

nothing to stop the blow [he received]."[48] Chronicler recognition of the effectiveness of armour for those who had its protection was so prevalent that they were at times apparently forced to construct their tales with an eye both to the reality of conflict and to the desired effect of emphasising the qualities of their heroes. So, for example, Walter Bower described William Douglas of Nithsdale as being "so strong that whomsoever he had stuck with a blow of his mace or sword or a thrust of his lance fell dead to the ground."[49] At first glance this appears to be a normal description of a heroic Scottish military figure. Bower, however, also felt the need to include the caveat that when faced by those "protected by some kind of armour" Douglas instead caused the enemy to "[fall] on his back scarcely half alive."[50] The emphasis on Douglas's strength and prowess remains, but Bower recognised the reality that even a figure such as he was not superhuman. The emphasis on realism in this depiction of events reinforces the idea that chroniclers often wrote of conflict in a way that warriors themselves would recognise as lifelike and that their descriptions of armour, weaponry, injury and death in combat are more representative of 'real life' than may be expected. A final example helps to emphasise this point. Walter Bower, in his description of the battle of Dunbar (1296), provides an account of the knight Walter Siward. Although an Englishman by birth, Siward fought on the Scottish side at Dunbar. Having escaped the battlefield the knight was killed by his own servant who "stabbed the sorrowing master in the back with a lance, and throwing him off his horse to the ground, immediately slaughtered his unsuspecting and defenceless master with his sword."[51] The obvious implication in this episode is that the knight's armour was sufficient to ensure that the spear-thrust was not fatal. What it did instead was force the knight to the ground where his heavy armour restricted his movements and likely stopped him from being able to raise himself. In this largely defenceless position he was open to attack by the servant who, with his sword, could provide the killer blow.[52]

---

48 IBID., p. 382.
49 BOWER, 1987-98, p. 411.
50 IBID.
51 IBID., p. 73.
52 Descriptions of battle do suggest that quite often the Scottish infantry would attack English horses to bring down the well-armoured knights. According

The protection provided by armour was not, however, all-encompassing and as much as chroniclers often appear to assume that armour would protect the body, they paradoxically also create literary motifs around occasions when armour failed to perform its function. For example they often describe injuries sustained in the melee in quite spectacular fashion, such as the description that "blood burst out of [...] mail-coats."[53] Barbour in particular uses this phrase, or variations thereof, quite frequently.[54] Writing of the battle of Roslin (1302), Bower commented that "[the English] attack was so heavy and savage that many had their armour pierced and were deprived of their lives."[55] Another example relates to the Scottish knight John Stewart who, at the battle of Connor (1315), "was wounded in the body there, by a spear which pierced right sharply."[56] The impact of spear thrusts, or blows from mounted warriors' lances, was often related in chronicle accounts to torso injuries, some of which resulted in death. Examples include the injury suffered by William Douglas of Liddesdale at the skirmish at Crichton (*c*.1337). Here "his body [was] transfixed with a lance, [and] he barely escaped from the hands of his enemies; but fortunately he recovered quickly."[57] A similar injury that resulted in fatal consequences was suffered by two warriors at the skirmish at Burgh Muir (1335). A Scottish man-at-arms, Richard Shaw, fought with a foreign knight in which both "drove their horses on with their spurs, and at a gallop they each transfixed the body of the other with their lances, and thus with a mortal wound fell dead to the ground."[58] A particularly bizarre fatality involves the example of William Keith at the siege of Stirling Castle (1337). The Scottish chronicler Andrew Wyntoun provides the fullest account of this

---

    to chroniclers, those who were brought down in such fashion were often killed (see, for example, BRUCE, 1997, p. 434).
53 BRUCE, 1997, p. 98.
54 See for example, IBID., p. 476.
55 BOWER, 1987-98, vi, p. 295.
56 BRUCE, 1997, p. 554.
57 BOWER, 1987-98, vii, p. 139. The translation of Wyntoun words things slightly differently, stating that 'Dowglas wes strykyn throw the body; /Bot he lywyd efftyr in gud hele' (WYNTOUN, 1872-9, ii, p. 448).
58 BOWER, 1987-98, vii, p. 113. Bower's tale has more than a suggestion of being invented. In the aftermath of the skirmish both warriors were stripped of their armour and the foreign knight was apparently discovered to be a woman.

incident. He describes Keith climbing the castle wall only to be struck by a stone thrown from the battlements. Borne from the ladder by the stone, Keith's lance appears to have struck the ground first "and stekyd hym on his awyn spere: / and off that wounde sone deyde he."[59] The unfortunate nature of Keith's death may explain its prominence in this chronicle. Despite the dangers to attackers inherent in siege warfare, this was a particularly curious example and one that emphasised that, no matter how well-armed, death was always a possibility for those who fought. Even those events which mimicked war could be dangerous, and in some examples fatal. The dangers of tournament fighting are apparent in two examples. In the first, Patrick Ramsay and Richard Talbot fought a series of tilts on the border in the 1340s. According to Bower the English knight "was run through by Sir Patrick's lance, and after confession breathed his last."[60] Wyntoun's account, however, goes into far more detail about this encounter, describing two separate clashes between this pair. In the first tilt Talbot was struck by Graham's lance which pierced a double layer of plate and penetrated an inch or more into Talbot's chest. Having survived this injury, the two clashed again the following day and on this occasion Talbot was killed when he was run through by Graham's lance.[61] In the second example an English chronicle accounts that John Dunbar, earl of Moray, died from wounds received at an English tournament. Notably he was said to have suffered broken ribs. While a fall from his horse in the fight could have resulted in such an injury, it is also possible that Moray's horse fell with him, as suggested in the chronicle account, and crushed the knight under its weight. The earl died as a result of his wounds on his return journey to Scotland.[62]

Beyond the torso, injuries to a warrior's extremities are even less prevalent in narrative accounts than those suffered to the body. This is likely a result of their relatively minor nature and the fact that they would have seldom been fatal. Paradoxically, however, their very nature may have also made them more common. Evidence from archaeological excavations suggests that injuries to the forearms – mostly taking the form of defensive injuries – and to the lower leg were amongst the most

---

59 WYNTOUN, 1872-9, ii, pp. 455f., 438; BOWER, 1987-98, vii, p. 131.
60 BOWER, 1987-98, vii, p. 139.
61 WYNTOUN, 1872-9, ii, pp. 444f.
62 BRUT, 1906-8, p. 348.

common recorded wounds alongside those to the skull.[63] In one historical example of such an injury it was actually good fortune for the recipient. William Keith, fighting in Spain with James Douglas and his companions on their quest to take Robert I's heart on crusade, was forced to spend the day in his quarters because "his arm was broken in two."[64] Barbour does not make clear how Keith came by this injury, but it ensured his absence from the skirmish with Muslim forces at Teba in which Douglas and the rest of the Scots were almost all killed. Other injuries to the extremities were suffered by men such as the English knight Anthony Lucy. In the border skirmish at Dornock (1332), Lucy was injured in the hand and foot, as well as in the eye, but was said to have recovered well from all his wounds.[65] William Douglas of Liddesdale similarly suffered an injury from which he was able to recover, but one which was potentially more serious. During the siege of Perth (1339) Douglas was "seriously wounded [...] in the thigh with a bolt from a crossbow."[66] He was able to make a suitable recovery, but as the previous example of William Lundie suggests, crossbow injuries could easily prove fatal. Liddesdale was injured again around 1341, although in a very different scenario. In this instance he was fighting in a border tournament against Henry of Lancaster, earl of Derby. In the first tilt Douglas "brak his spere; And a sclys off the schafft, that brak, In till his hand a wounde can mak."[67] Demonstrating his personal chivalric qualities, Derby called a halt to proceedings after this occurrence, likely because Douglas's injury precluded him from fighting to his full potential thereafter. At the battle of Glen Brerachan (1392), David Lindsay of Glen Esk – who was mounted at the time – was injured by a sword stroke that cut through his stirrup and boots into his foot and "straik the Lyndesay to the bane."[68] Evidence from the Visby battlefield demonstrates that similar injuries were quite common and it has been suggested that such blows – whether

---

63 MITCHELL, 2004, pp. 116f.
64 BRUCE, 1997, p. 766.
65 LANERCOST, 1913, p. 278.
66 BOWER, 1987-98, vii, p. 143. Bower went on to say of this occurrence that "the besiegers were upset by the great degree of malice in this action", although it is unclear why this particular action was filled with more malice than any other.
67 WYNTOUN, 1872-9, ii, p. 441.
68 IBID., pp. 59f.

to mounted or foot soldiers – were intended "to bring the opponent to the ground before finishing him off."[69] Injuries to the leg were certainly more likely to occur when a mounted warrior, such as Lindsay, fought enemies who were fighting on foot.[70] Further injuries to extremities were inflicted by missile weapons. At Homildon Hill (1402), as already discussed, English archers poured fire into the ranks of the stationary Scottish divisions, "transfixing the hands and arms of the Scots to their own lances. By means of this very harsh rain of arrows they made some duck, they wounded others, and killed many."[71] The number of injuries caused by such an attack must have been enormous, but as the chronicler makes clear not all were fatal. Far more dangerous was the fact that the Scots could not withstand such an assault indefinitely and resorted to ill-disciplined flight where attacks such as those described above likely resulted in far greater casualties.

Conclusion

This article has provided a brief consideration of evidence contained within literary and chronicle sources and its usefulness for studies of the impact of war on the warrior. Examples of the types of injuries sustained, the parts of the body most affected and the lethality or survivability of such injuries, provide detailed evidence of the warrior's bodily experience of combat. That the head was perhaps a more likely target than the torso points to deliberate tactics in one-to-one combat that focused on incapacitating the enemy as quickly as possible. Injury to the head as a result of less precise forms of warfare in the form of massed ranks of archers are also understandable in terms of angle of fire and 'accidental' injuries through weak points such as helmet visors. Importantly, examples collated from written sources appear to align largely with existing archaeological evidence which can be used to provide corroboration for descriptions of injuries sustained, and the warriors' ability to survive such wounds. Indeed, further and more detailed analysis of available sources offers the opportunity to study such

---

69 THORDMAN et al., 1939, pp. 171-8; MITCHELL, 2004, pp. 111, 117.
70 MITCHELL, 2004, p. 117.
71 BOWER, 1987-98, viii, p. 47.

themes in far greater depth than has been attempted up to this point. The Anglo-Scottish conflict provides a particularly good focus for such an examination, spanning as it did the majority of the fourteenth century and coming at an important point in the development of tactics, strategy, military organisation and both offensive and defensive military equipment. Considering the focus in many works on the Hundred Years War, the Scottish Wars of Independence present a valuable comparative example against which to consider the accepted maxims regarding warfare in this period. For example, casualty lists of Scottish nobles killed in battle in the fourteenth century seem disproportionately high. Conventions of ransom and chivalric conduct should, in theory at least, have ensured that a larger number were spared, if for no other reason than that such prisoners were valuable commodities. If noble prisoners were not able to survive the battlefield as easily as their fellows in the Anglo-French conflict, then what does this suggest about the nature of Anglo-Scottish warfare?[72] Does it imply that Scotland's nobles were less well-protected than their contemporaries elsewhere? Were they more likely to suffer injury and death in the flight that resulted from numerous Scottish battlefield defeats? Or were they perhaps less likely to have access to sufficient quality medical care to ensure their survival post-battle? These questions are beginning to receive some consideration, but far more could be undertaken to better understand the nature of warfare in this period and, in particular, the Scottish warrior experience.[73] Incorporating the themes of injury and lethality into such analysis provides an under-utilised perspective on the physical impact of warfare on the individual and therefore points towards a more realistic understanding of contemporary conflict. The complementary use of archaeological and historical sources allows comparison of the depiction and the physical remains of combat and reaffirms medieval literary sources as an essential resource in understanding not only the mentality of the age, but also the physicality of the medieval period. Considering the modern developments in the study of military history more widely, these sources and

---

72 For discussion of the rules of ransom and their use in the Hundred Years War, see AMBÜHL, 2013.
73 For recent discussion of some of these questions, see MACINNES, 2015, pp. 102-27; MACINNES, 2016 (forthcoming); MACDONALD, 2013, pp. 179-206.

approaches offer exciting opportunities for the study of medieval warfare generally, but also in particular for lesser-studied and under-sourced periods of conflict.

Bibliography

Sources

ANON., The Brut or Chronicles of England, ed. by FRIEDRICH W.D. BRIE, London, 1906-8.
ANON., The Chronicle of Lanercost, 1272-1346, ed. by HERBERT E. MAXWELL, Glasgow 1913.
LE BAKER, GEOFFREY, Chronicon Galfridi le Baker de Swynebroke (Rolls Series), ed. E.M. THOMPSON, Oxford 1889.
BARBOUR, JOHN, The Bruce, ed. by ARCHIBALD A.M. DUNCAN, Edinburgh 1997.
BOWER, WALTER, Scotichronicon, ed. by DONALD E.R. WATT et al., Aberdeen 1987-98.
GRAY, THOMAS, Scalacronica, ed. by Herbert E. Maxwell, Glasgow 1907.
WYNTOUN, ANDREW OF, The Orygynale Cronykil of Scotland, ed. by David Laing, Edinburgh 1872-9.

Literature

AMBÜHL, RÉMY, Prisoners of War in the Hundred Years' War. Ransom Culture in the Late Middle Ages, Cambridge 2013.
DEVRIES, KELLY, The Use of Chronicles in Recreating Medieval Military History, in: The Journal of Medieval Military History 2, ed. by BERNARD S. BACHRACH et al., Woodbridge 2004, pp. 1-15.
FIORATO, VERONICA et al. (eds.), Blood Red Roses. The Archaeology of a Mass Grave from the Battle of Towton AD 1461, Oxford 2007.
GELDOF, M.R., "And to describe the shapes of the dead". Making Sense of the Archaeology of Armed Violence, in: Wounds and Wound Repair in Medieval Culture (Explorations in Medieval Culture 1), ed. by LARISSA TRACY/KELLY DEVRIES, Leiden 2015, pp. 57-80.

GIVEN-WILSON, CHRIS, Chronicles. The Writing of History in Medieval England, London 2004.
GRANT, ALEXANDER, Disaster at Neville's Cross. The Scottish Point of View, in: The Battle of Neville's Cross 1346, ed. by DAVID ROLLASON/MICHAEL PRESTWICH, Stamford 1998, pp. 15-35.
HARDY, ROBERT, The Military Archery at Neville's Cross, 1346, in: The Battle of Neville's Cross 1346, ed. by DAVID ROLLASON/MICHAEL PRESTWICH, Stamford 1998, pp. 112-31.
KARGER, BERND et al., Arrow Wounds: Major Stimulus in the History of Surgery, in: World Journal of Surgery 25 (2001), pp. 1550-1555.
KJELLSTRÖM, ANNA, A Sixteenth-Century Warrior Grave from Uppsala, Sweden: the Battle of Good Friday, in: International Journal of Osteoarchaeology 15 (2005), pp. 23-50.
MACDONALD, ALASTAIR .J., Courage, Fear and the Experience of the Later Medieval Scottish Soldier, in: Scottish Historical Review, 92,2 (2013), pp. 179-206.
MACINNES, IAIN A., Heads, Shoulders, Knees and Toes: Injury and Death in Anglo-Scottish Combat, c.1296-c.1403, in: Wounds and Wound Repair in Medieval Culture (Explorations in Medieval Culture 1), ed. by LARISSA TRACY/KELLY DEVRIES, Leiden 2015, pp. 102-27.
MACINNES, IAIN A., Scotland's Second War of Independence, 1332-1357, Woodbridge 2016 (forthcoming).
MAYS, SIMON A., A Possible Case of Surgical Treatment of Cranial Blunt Force Injury from Medieval England, in: International Journal of Osteoarchaeology 16 (2006), pp. 95-103.
MITCHELL, PIERS D., Medicine in the Crusades: Warfare, wounds and the medieval surgeon, Cambridge, 2004.
MITCHELL, PIERS D., The Integration of the Palaeopathology and Medical History of the Crusades, in: International Journal of Osteoarchaeology 9 (1999), pp. 333-343.
MITCHELL, PIERS D. et al., Weapon Injuries in the 12th Century Crusader Garrison of Vadum Iacob Castle, Galilee, in: International Journal of Osteoarchaeology 16 (2006), pp. 145-155.
PENMAN, MICHAEL, David II, East Linton 2004.
POWERS, NATASHA, Cranial Trauma and Treatment: A Case Study from the Medieval Cemetery of St. Mary Spital, London, in: International Journal of Osteoarchaeology 15 (2005), pp. 1-14.

PURTON, PETER, The myth of the mangonel. Torsion artillery in the Middle Ages, in: Arms and Armour 3,1 (2006), pp. 79-90.

RICHARDSON, THOM, Armour in England, 1325–99, in: Journal of Medieval History 37,3 (2011), pp. 304-20.

ROKSANDIC, MIRJANA et al., Death in the Line of Duty: Late Medieval Burials at the Site of Lepenski Vir, Serbia, in: International Journal of Osteoarchaeology 17 (2007), pp. 635-642.

SKINNER, PATRICIA, Visible Prowess?: Reading Men's Head and Face Wounds in Early Medieval Europe to 1000 CE, in: Wounds and Wound Repair in Medieval Culture (Explorations in Medieval Culture 1), ed. by LARISSA TRACY/KELLY DEVRIES, Leiden 2015, pp. 81-101.

SOUTHWICK, LESLIE, The Great Helm in England, in: Arms & Armour 3,1 (2006), pp. 5-77.

THORDMAN, BENGT et al. (eds.), Armour from the Battle of Visby, 1361, 2 vols, Stockholm, 1939.

WILKINSON, CAROLINE/NEAVE, RICHARD, The Reconstruction of a Face Showing a Healed Wound, in: Journal of Archaeological Science 30 (2003), pp. 1343-48.

WOOSNAM-SAVAGE, ROBERT C./DEVRIES, KELLY, Battle Trauma in Medieval Warfare: Wounds, Weapons and Armor, in: Wounds and Wound Repair in Medieval Culture (Explorations in Medieval Culture 1), ed. by LARISSA TRACY/KELLY DEVRIES, Leiden 2015, pp. 27-56.

Willing Body, Willing Mind: Non-Combatant Culpability According to English Combatant Writers, 1327-77

TREVOR RUSSELL SMITH

It is often stated that people in the Middle Ages accepted war and its commonplace violence against non-combatants with fatalism. They argue that because attacking non-combatants was a pragmatic way to conduct war people had no reason to object.[1] Accordingly, devastation found widespread acceptance amongst English writers during periods of success, such as Edward III's reign (1327-77).[2] Late-medieval war is also sometimes seen as a mark of brutality, especially in contrast with the seemingly less violent ideals of chivalry and Christianity.[3] However, it is rarely asked what combatants thought of their own actions. Indeed, some claim that the many surviving letters by combatants "tell us little about the men who wrote them", while ignoring their careful use of rhetoric entirely.[4]

In this essay I challenge these notions by exploring English combatants' presentation of devastation and attacks against non-combatants during the wars of Edward III.[5] First I investigate how

---

1   The key proponents are ALLMAND, 1971, p. 181; ALLMAND, 1999, p. 264; STRICKLAND, 1996, pp. 291-329. This view has gone largely unchallenged in the works of military historians.
2   As, for example, argued by COX, 2014, p. 13.
3   MCGLYNN, 2008.
4   BARBER, 2013, p. 23.
5   All documents are interpolated in cited chronicles unless noted otherwise, and all translations are my own. I use the terms "combatant" and "non-

combatants justify their bellicosity by elevating non-combatants to equal combatant status. I then consider how combatants sidestep the issue of representing non-combatant victims of devastation through the use of short formulaic phrases and paying more attention to exciting actions like skirmishes and battles. I conclude by showing how combatants expressed a keen interest in the ethical problems of attacking non-combatants.

During Edward III's reign there are few examples of English writers trying to rationalise defeat and setback, as they were rare. More often they write of their successes, such as the battles of Halidon Hill (1333), Sluys (1340), Crécy (1346), Neville's Cross (1346), and Poitiers (1356), and the sieges of Berwick (several), Caen (1346), and Calais (1346-47).[6] The English people suffered relatively little in these conflicts compared to their enemies, especially the French.[7] Accordingly, writings by English combatants hold rather unique views on war. The French perspective is different because their people suffered considerably from war. Their writings complain loudly, but they have already been studied in detail and are beyond the scope of the present essay.[8]

Many English combatants during the fourteenth century wrote about war in personal correspondence, newsletters, and, sometimes, longer texts. For example, Edward III, his son Edward of Woodstock (later called the Black Prince), Walter Bentley, Bartholomew Burghersh, Henry of Lancaster, John Wingfield, and others, wrote letters to major figures or cities to be disseminated throughout the country in the mid-fourteenth century.[9] Many of these were intended to be read at church

---

combatant" throughout for simplicity. For difficulties of terminology (e.g. fighter, knight, soldier, squire), see PRESTWICH, 1996, pp. 12-18.

6   English chroniclers were more interested in examining victories than defeat, as is evident from the far more numerous surviving letters on successes.

7   See for example KING, 2002; HUGHES, 1994.

8   See for example the French friar Jean de Venette's critical presentation of various actions against non-combatants, particularly those in 1360: VENETTE, 2011, pp. 226-46. But also see HEWITT, 1966, pp. 133-39; WRIGHT, 1998; CONTAMINE, 2003, pp. 452-68. Few fourteenth-century Scottish writings survive that comment on non-combatants.

9   On the mechanics of proclamations and news, see DOIG, 1998. Although these writings may not always have been personally penned by combatants, they consistently represent what the combatants intended to be written as is evident by comparing their attitudes with other writings by combatants. Because there has not been a comprehensive study and collection of military

services to people of all stations.[10] Combatants intended them to inform on military events, provide reassurance, sway opinion, and often to ask for supporting prayers from the people.[11] An unknown number of these letters are found in various collections, but the most important of them are interpolated directly by chroniclers into their texts, such as those by Adam Murimuth (*c.* 1325-47), Robert Avesbury (*c.* 1356), and John Tynemouth (*c.* 1347-50), as well as the anonymous *Lanercost Chronicle* (*c.* 1346), 1327-47 continuation of the *Anglo-Norman Prose Brut* (*c.* 1347), and *Gesta Edwardi Tertii* (*c.* 1340-77).[12] In other cases they were paraphrased or otherwise integrated into chronicles. English knights also produced more literary texts, such as Thomas Gray's *Scalacronica* (1357-62), a lengthy chronicle, and John Clanvowe's *The Two Ways* (1391), a penitential treatise.

I. Non-Combatants in Reality and Theory

In the later Middle Ages war was conducted through large-scale campaigns of devastation.[13] Armies routinely burned the countryside, pillaged towns, and attacked non-combatants during campaigns. They took what they could carry and burned the rest. The extent of devastation greatly increased as armies grew in size and emphasised mobility in the fourteenth century. English campaigns of devastation during the so-called Hundred Years War (1337-1453) were known particularly for their impact, so much so that they are given the distinguishing term *chevauchées* by scholars.[14] In these campaigns the English moved through enemy territory on a broad front so that they could destroy as much as possible while avoiding enemy forces and lengthy sieges. Some

---

letters during the later Middle Ages I cannot claim to have seen every text or compared all surviving versions, but see FOWLER, 1991.
10 See notes 51 and 52 below.
11 See HEWITT, 1966, pp. 159-65; J. TAYLOR, 1987, pp. 217-35; FOWLER, 1991; BARBER, 2013, pp. 23-26.
12 For texts discussed throughout see introductions to editions and J. TAYLOR, 1987.
13 On devastation, raids, and pillaging, see WRIGHT, 1998, pp. 26-79; ALLMAND, 1999.
14 For example in DEVRIES, 1991; FOWLER, 1991; PRESTWICH, 1996; ROGERS, 2000.

regions suffered annual devastation and took many years to fully recover.[15] It was advantageous for leaders to devastate territory because it allowed them to draw supplies from the land as they passed through, pay their men's wages with loot, destabilise local government, and undermine enemy political legitimacy, rather than confront enemy strength directly.[16]

There was a clear distinction in England, France, and Scotland between combatant and non-combatant during the later Middle Ages. This was largely because non-combatants were untrained and stood no chance against the well-equipped and experienced armies of the day.[17] Gratian, in his widely disseminated *Decretum* (*c.* 1150), lucidly declares that "pilgrims, preachers, clerics, monks, women, or the defenceless poor" should not be targeted in war.[18] The absence of significant change or addition to these prescriptions in later decretals and commentaries suggests that these categories of non-combatants remained valid to writers over the following two centuries.[19] Later English thinkers made similar proclamations in their own treatises, such as William Pagula (writing *c.* 1331-32), who states that "in time of war priests, monks, lay brothers, country folk going and returning, who are engaged in agriculture, ought have security".[20]

---

15 It is difficult to discern the reality of war from chronicles, or intention from results. For an evaluation of the effects of devastation based predominantly on records rather than narratives, see ROGERS, 2002.

16 HEWITT, 1966, pp. 93-110. See also ROGERS, 1994; ROGERS, 2000, which promote a theory that English military leaders conducted devastation in order to draw the opposing army into battles that were advantageous to the English. However, the strategic intentions of devastation are drawn from rhetorical narratives and far from objective.

17 Large-scale professional militias were more common in the German and Italian states, the Low Countries, and Switzerland. They were rare and mostly ineffectual in England, France, and Scotland: GUNN, 2010; WRIGHT, 1998, pp. 62-70; DEVRIES, 2008, pp. 55f.

18 GRATIAN, 1959, C. 24 q. 3 c. 25 (p. 997): "peregrinos, uel oratores cuiuscumque sancti, siue clericos, siue manachos, uel feminas, aut inermes pauperes".

19 RUSSELL, 1975, pp. 161, 186. See also KEEN, 1965, pp. 189f.

20 PAGULA, 1891, p. 132: "tempore guerre debent securitatem habere presbiteri, monachi, conversi mercatores, rustici euntes et redeuntes, in agriculturam existentes".

English narrative sources also envision untrained non-combatants as unfit for enduring war. The *Long Anglo-Norman Prose Brut* (written 1333-35) describes the English non-combatants that move to resist the 1319 Scottish invasion as "monks, priests, friars, and canons as well as laymen. Alas! what sorrow and what a shame, for the English farmers who knew nothing of war were killed there".[21] In several fourteenth-century English texts, David II, king of the Scots, is said to invade England in 1346 in the expectation that, because all of Edward III's knights and soldiers were fighting in France, there remained in the country only various categories of non-combatants: "monks and canons, friars and priests, swineherds and shepherds, cobblers and skinners".[22] As is evident from the texts described above, there is a clear distinction between combatants and non-combatants that diffused widely through preaching and other means in fourteenth-century England. These sources and other chronicles list categories of non-combatants, who are inherently innocent and exempt, in order to portray attacks against them as immoral.[23]

The common English practice of devastation was sometimes at odds with justifications for going to war. The Hundred Years War, principally fought between England and France, was founded on the English claim

---

21 Anglo-Norman Prose Brut, 1995, pp. 237f.: "moignes, prestres, Ffreres & chanoun come Seculers [...] Allas, quelle dolour & quelle Damage, qar les Engleis housbonde qe rien ne sauoient de Guerre illoeqes furent tuez".
22 Anonimalle Chronicle, 1970, pp. 25f.: "moignes et chanouns, freres et prestres porchers et berchers, suers et pelters". See categories of non-combatants similarly invoked in the same episode in AN Prose Brut Continuation, 1307-77, fol. 177v; AN Prose Brut Continuation, 1327-47, fol. 196v; Brut, 1906-08, p. 299; Chronicon de Lanercost, 1839, p. 348; DENE, fols 93r-93v; READING, 1914, p. 102; the poems "Letre de Dauid le Bruys" and "Tractatus belli apud Crucem", edited in MINOT, 1914, pp. 112-14 and 127 (here lines 10-12, 38-40), 114-22 and 127-29 (here lines 102-06, 109-12). Nearly every contemporary English chronicle claims that either Philippe VI incited David II's invasion, that no resistance was expected, or both. These appear in a variety of forms, despite the claim that they "all carry the same meaning": ROGERS/BUCK, 1998, p. 54 n. 11. In these cases the addition of non-combatant categories adds a moral element to the episode.
23 See for example the particularly critical portrayal of David II's 1346 invasion of England in Chronicon de Lanercost, 1839, pp. 344-52; and analysis in SMITH, 2014.

to the French crown.[24] Some saw the contradictions in English kings enforcing their rights by attacking the people they claimed to rule. The poet John Gower highlights this problem in his *Confessio Amantis* (c. 1386-90) through the allegorical story of Athemas and Demephon, who are deprived of their lands and plan to exact vengeance by attacking their people in a particularly ruthless fashion.[25] But Gower challenges this strategy by asking "to what final conclusioun / thei woulde regne Kinges there, / if that no poeple in londe were?"[26] He concludes that it is better to use diplomacy because of the immoral and impractical nature of devastation.

II. Non-Combatants Bearing Arms

Representations of siege warfare clearly illustrate combatants' considerations of the ethical problems of non-combatant victims because they neatly compartmentalise the violence of war to one place over a period of time. The city as a whole is besieged and attacked instead of any individual components or persons. Combatants portray sieges as if they were made up solely of combat between legitimate combatants in contrast to the reality of non-combatants suffering from starvation and attack during the violent sacks that followed cities that were taken by force.[27]

---

24 Edward III claimed his right to the French throne in a widely publicised letter to the pope and college of cardinals in 1339. See the many copies surviving in contemporary chronicles: AN Prose Brut Continuation, 1327-47, fols 185r-188v; Chronicon de Lanercost, 1839, pp. 319-26 (a geneological table to support this claim is included after two more letters, on p. 330); Gesta Edwardi Tertii, 1882-83, pp. 140-47; MURIMUTH, 1889, pp. 91-100; TYNEMOUTH, fols 230v-232v. For other versions of the *Lanercost* genealogical table, see TYSON, 2008, pp. 93-98, 103-05; PAGAN, 2016, p. 163 n. 53; and generally also HEWITT, 1966, p. 163; JONES, 1979, pp. 25-28; C. TAYLOR, 2001. In reality there were other concerns which encouraged the conflict, but these rights are given precedence in English chronicles.
25 GOWER, 1900-01, bk 3 lines 1781-86 (vol. 1 p. 274).
26 GOWER, 1900-01, bk 3 lines 1816-18 (vol. 1 p. 275).
27 See HEWITT, 1966, pp. 118-23; WRIGHT, 1998, pp. 96-116; CONTAMINE, 2003, pp. 207-26, 342-50.

Combatant writers commonly portray non-combatant casualties of sieges as having willingly fought against the English. When Edward III describes the defenders of Caen in 1346 he includes among them "the commons, armed and capable of defence" and again, when listing casualties, as "a great number of commons".[28] He explicitly states that the common people (i.e. non-combatants not trained for war) who had taken up arms to fight against his army were amongst the victims. This letter was widely circulated and copied in a variety of forms, but in every one of them these terms are preserved intact.[29]

At Caen Burghersh similarly lists non-professionals fighting as combatants when he states that the "commons of the country and the city, who had decided to have held the said city against the king, my lord, and all his power" were in the French force.[30] The Augustinian Canon, Henry Knighton, integrates into his *Chronicle* (*c.* 1379-97) a version of this letter translated into Latin that has the non-combatants take up arms by describing them as "citizens and countrymen, who disposed themselves to hold the city against King Edward", and when casualties as "burghers, truly, and the commons and rabble".[31] His version makes explicit the

---

28 In his letter to the chancellor, treasurer, and other members of his council in London, edited in FOWLER, 1991, pp. 83f.: "communes armez et defensables", "communes grant nombre"; see also note 43 below.
29 See for example: to the archbishop of York, in Chronicon de Lanercost, 1839, pp. 342f (here 342).: "communes armes et defensables", "communes grant noumbre"; a similar version, but integrated into the text without salutations, in Anonimalle Chronicle, 1970, pp. 19f. (here 20): "communes armes et defensables", "communes graunt noumbre"; to London and changed into third-person, edited in FROISSART, 1867-77, vol. 18 pp. 286f. (here 296): "communes armés et defensables", "communes graunt nombre". This letter was reused and continued in Edward III's letter to Thomas de Lucy later that year, in a miscellany with many texts on the war (Oxford, Bodleian Library, MS Ashmole 789, fols 148r-148v), edited in COXE, 1842, pp. 351-55 (here 352): "comunes armes et defensables", "communes grant noumbre" . See also FOWLER, 1991, p. 91 n. 87.
30 Burghersh's letter to the archbishop of Canterbury, in Murimuth, 1889, pp. 202f. (here 202): "comuns de pais et de la ville, les queux se avoient ordeyne daver tenuz la dite ville encountre le roi mon seignur et tot soun poair"; see also note 72 below.
31 KNIGHTON, 1995, pp. 54, 56: "ciuium et compatriotarum, qui disposuerant se tenuisse ciuitatem contra regem Edwardum", "De burgensibus uero et communibus ac plebeis, capti sunt et mortui circiter .v. millia".

meaning of *communes* as amateurs drawn from the city's populace, rather than any sort of less-wealthy professional combatant.

Michael Northburgh similarly portrays non-combatants who take up arms as combatants at Caen in his newsletter. Initially he describes "a great quantity of men of arms were in the city" fighting against the English.[32] However, he also includes non-combatants amongst the captured and killed, in perhaps questionable places: "there were killed knights, squires, and other people of the city in great quantities, in the streets, houses, and in the gardens".[33]

Combatants portray what were clearly large numbers of formerly non-combatants as casualties, some perhaps unarmed in reality, as if they had been evenly matched combatants. In reality, however, the capture of Caen was more of a sack, as is reported by the eyewitness account of the *Acta bellicosa* (*c*. 1346-49):

> "Everywhere [the English] killed by the sword all those caught. But those who had taken refuge in houses, the strong and powerful, having discerned so many of their people dead, and nothing except death for them to be imminent, surrendered themselves captive to their pursuers, but the footmen of the English army, did not accept any for ransom, neither from nobles nor average men, and cut them down for no reason."[34]

---

32 Northburgh's newsletter, in AVESBURY, 1889, pp. 358-60 (here 359): "graunt foisoun dez gentz darmes fusrent deinz la ville"; translated into Latin in MURIMUTH, 1889, pp. 212-14 (here 213): "galeatis et armatis aliis erat plena"; see also note 62 below. Murimuth misidentifies Northburgh, Edward III's counselor, as the king's confessor. Northburgh conveys the king's attitudes in his two newsletters because of his closeness to the king through the campaign. Some reports by English non-combatants during campaigns take similar attitudes to those of combatants because their writings are similarly meant as propaganda. See CARLSON, 2012, p. 39.

33 In AVESBURY, 1889, pp. 358-60 (here 359): "mortz chivalers, esquiers, et autres gentz de la ville graunt foisoun, en lez rues, mesouns, et es gardines"; translated into Latin in MURIMUTH, 1889, pp. 212-14 (here 214): "sunt occisi milites et armigeri et alii, in hortis, domibus, et plateis jacentes"; see also note 62 below.

34 Acta bellicosa, 1894, p. 166: "omnes deprehensos undique gladio perimiebant. Sed qui domibus confugerant, valentes et majores, tantam cernentes mortalitatem sue nacionis, et nil aliud nisi mortem eisdem imminere, ipsos prosequentibus se captivos reddebant, sed pedestres

However, combatant writers make no suggestions that any people were killed outside of combat. They thereby suggest that those killed were licit targets because they had willingly fought against the English. Combatants deliberately ignore the reality of Caen, which they surely knew of or witnessed themselves, and in their letters they turn the sack into a willing contest fought solely between combatants.

Combatant writers focus on the actions of their men rather than any elements of the siege of Caen itself, brief though it was. They ignore the besieging force's culpability in forcing the city-dwellers into the role of combatants. Equally, combatant writers describe what may have been non-combatant victims of the sack as if they had been combatants. They clearly sidestep the ethical issues in the supposedly accepted "right of storm", wherein everything and everybody in a fortified place taken by force were at the will of the conquerors.[35] But some non-combatant writers found these actions troubling. For example, Jean Froissart emotionally condemns Edward of Woodstock's 1370 sack of Limoges:

> "there is none so hard a heart, if he had been at Limoges and he thought himself on God, who would not have wept tenderly over the great suffering that took place there, for more than three thousand persons: men, women, and children, were there killed and beheaded that day. God have their souls, for they were indeed martyrs!"[36]

Anglorum exercitus tam proceres quam mediocres, nulla admissa redempcione, in frustra concidebant". See also the first-hand account of Richard Wynkeley, Edward III's confessor, in his letter to the Prior and Convent of the Blackfriars, London, in MURIMUTH, 1889, pp. 215-17 (here 215), 245-48 (an expanded version integrated in London, British Library, Cotton Nero D X); the first part of which is also in AVESBURY, 1889, pp. 362f. (here 362).

35 See KEEN, 1965, pp. 119-33, esp. 122f. n. 3 (where he notes that the right of storm is found in narratives and not legal texts); STRICKLAND, 1996, pp. 222-24.

36 FROISSART, 1869-1975, vol. 7 p. 250 (§ 666): "Il n'est si durs coers, se il fust adonc à Limoges et il li souvenist de Dieu, qui ne plorast tenrement dou grant meschief qui y estoit, car plus de trois mil personnes, hommes, femmes et enfans, y furent deviiet et decolet celle journée. Diex en ait les ames, car il furent bien martir!" ("B" recension), see also vol. 7 pp. 249-53 (§ 666-67) for other details of the sack and pp. 427-29 for slight "A" recension variants. The "Amiens" and "N" recensions present different but equally critical

In contrast, English combatant writers only indirectly suggest that there might have been non-combatants present at Caen, and only in so much as they were not immune from violence because they took up arms and willingly attacked English forces.

Non-professionals are not shown as, nor implied to be, forced to fight in battles in combatant writings.[37] Instead, they willingly become combatants and are made out to be fair opponents for the professionals in English armies. Some of these apparent skirmishes seem to be descriptions of devastation that are altered so that their victims instead willingly resist. For example, Gray describes an attack on the land as the English "had a great fight, in a fury like war, with the local peasants who were there killed and defeated".[38] In a similar fashion Northburgh, narrating the English army's march from Poissy to Calais in his 1346 newsletter, repeatedly describes non-combatants taking up arms to fight against the English: "there came a great number of men of arms with the commons of the country and of Amiens, well armed. And the earl of Northampton and his men issued upon them so that there were killed more than 500 of our enemies", the English "killed a great abundance of the commons of France and of the city of Paris and others of the country, [who were] well armed, of the army of the king of France', and the English attacked "the commons of the country, who were assembled and well-armed, and they defeated and killed 200 and more".[39] The people of the French countryside are not shown to be merely defending their homes and farms against devastation, but rather as actively seeking out the English to fight. Northburgh describes the non-combatants as "well-armed" and includes them amongst the combatants in every case in order to portray them as enemies that are worthy to fight and kill.

---

versions of the sack: FROISSART, 1991-98, vol. 4 pp. 111f.; FROISSART, 1867-77, vol. 17 pp. 501f.
37 See WRIGHT, 1998, pp. 80-83.
38 GRAY, 2005, p. 102: "ils auoint vn graunt puynez au fure de guere od lez paysens enuyroun, qi furount illoeqes mortz et descoumfitz".
39 In AVESBURY, 1889, pp. 367-69 (here 367f.): "vindrent gentz darmes a graunt nombre od les comunes du pais et de Amyas, bien armez. Et le counte de Northamptone et ses gentz issirent sur eaux, issint qe fusrent mortz plus qe D. de noz enemys", "tuerent graunt plente de comunes de Fraunce et de la ville de Paris et aultre du pais, bien armez, del host de roy de Fraunce", "issiront sour les comunes du pais, qe fusrent assemblez et bien armez, et lez desconfiteront et occirount CC. et plus".

Combatant writers directly discuss all aspects of warfare except non-combatants. Edward III, in his 1347 letter to the archbishop of Canterbury, instead of including such details as non-combatants suffering in sieges, focuses on the challenge his men faced by French forces that attempted to lift the English siege of Calais. He repeatedly mentions his desire for a combat between champions to decide the siege's outcome, and once the French propose a fight on even terms he states that "we accepted their offer and took up the battle willingly", but the French "began to change their offers and to speak of the city all anew, as if ignoring the battle" and avoid the confrontation. Edward III is eager to equate this to defeat, as he claims that the French depart the confrontation "as if defeated".[40] Many other English non-combatant writers mention this episode to suggest the French were cowardly, not confident in their own abilities, and therefore their actions weakened their right to rule France.[41]

English combatant writers are keen to portray their leaders as bravely seeking battle whenever possible. Gray consistently claims that English forces move towards the enemy for battle and, in one case while campaigning in France in 1360, explicitly states that they "had traversed as much of France as was in their ability, seeking battle, to prove their lord's rights".[42] During the 1346 Normandy campaign, Edward III states he and his army will "hasten towards our adversary, wherever that he might be from one day to another, as best as we can".[43] Wingfield claims that Edward of Woodstock, during his 1355 campaign in southern France, eagerly turned his army to attack the French force upon news of

---

40 In AVESBURY, 1889, pp. 391-93 (here 393): "nous acceptasmes lour offre et prendissoms le bataille volunters", "comencerent de varier en lour offres et de parler de la ville tut novele, auxi come entrelessant la bataille", "auxi com descomfit".
41 See for example Edward III's willingness to remove his siege-works to allow the French army to better approach for a pitched battle, only for the French to flee in the night before the battle in KNIGHTON, 2005, p. 82. See similar portrayals of this episode that link the French departure with cowardice in LE BAKER, 1889, pp. 90f.; Brut, 1906-08, p. 300; READING, 1914, p. 104.
42 GRAY, 2005, p. 188: "ou auoint enuyrounez le plus de Fraunce en qanqe en lour fust, querant batail, dauoir derenez le droit lour siris".
43 In his letter to the chancellor et al. in London, edited in FOWLER, 1991, pp. 83f. (here 84): "hastier devers nostre adversaryer, queu parte q'il soit de jour en autre, tant come nous purrons"; see also notes 28 and 29 above.

its approach.[44] Many English challenges to enemy leaders are interpolated in chronicles, such as Edward III's challenge to Philippe VI in 1340.[45] In this letter Edward III states his desire to avoid Christian bloodshed and offers many options for his adversary to meet him in battle. However, Philippe refuses because, he claims, the letter was not addressed to him, King Philippe VI of France, but "to the so-called Philippe of Valois", a pejorative in English diplomatic writing.[46] In all of these examples the enemy either accepts the challenge but fails to show, or makes weak excuses as to why they are not obliged to fight, in order to portray the English as brave and confident in their claims and their enemies as cowards in their clearly propagandistic writings.[47]

Writings by combatants are crafted to fulfil certain objectives depending on what sort of audience was intended. If writing for a military audience, combatants emphasise the achievement of their men and their martial prowess. Edward III, writing to Edward of Woodstock in 1342, claims that his achievements are "held a great success for our war" and elsewhere focuses on the difficult challenges he overcame.[48] Similarly, in his 1339 letter to Woodstock, Edward III repeatedly focuses on his expectation that the French will meet him in battle.[49] However, when writing for an audience of churchmen, combatants focus on divine will and prayer rather than the particulars of war. Edward III's letter to Woodstock describing the battle of Sluys in 1340 focuses on military aspects: "our said enemies had assembled their ships in a most strong array and they put up a most noble defence all day and the night after",

---

44 In his letter to the bishop of Winchester, in AVESBURY, 1889, pp. 439-43 (here 441); see also notes 54 and 70 below.
45 In MURIMUTH, 1889, pp. 110f.; AVESBURY, 1889, pp. 314f.; translated into Latin in TYNEMOUTH, fol. 235v; also translated into Latin and paraphrased in Chronicon de Lanercost, 1839, p. 334.
46 In MURIMUTH, 1889, pp. 112-14 (here 112): "au dite Philippe de Valoys"; AVESBURY, 1889, pp. 315f. (here 315): "al dit P(helipe) de Valeis"; TYNEMOUTH, fols 235v-236r (here 235v): "philippo de ualesio"; Chronicon de Lanercost, 1839, p. 334: "quia litera non fuerat sibi tanquam regi Franciae directa".
47 See also CONTAMINE, 1979, pp. 71-74; STRICKLAND, 1998, pp. 320-26.
48 In AVESBURY, 1889, pp. 340-42 (here 340): "quele chose homme tient une graunt esploit a nostre guerre".
49 In AVESBURY, 1889, pp. 304-06; paraphrased and translated into Latin in KNIGHTON, 2005, pp. 16-18.

with the result the dead littered the coast of Flanders.[50] In contrast, his letter to the archbishop of Canterbury on the same battle focuses on giving thanks and prayer without focusing on martial glory by claiming that "our hope was Christ himself, and God allowed us to prevail", along with several other similar passages.[51] Equally, in his 1333 letter to the archbishop of York describing his victory against the Scots at Halidon Hill, Edward III minimises military glory and instead focuses on divine will and prayer.[52] These two perspectives, on either divine will or human agency, appealed to different audiences and were clearly understood by combatant writers in their selective rhetoric.

III. Formulaic Representation and Absence of the Non-Combatant

Writing about devastation was problematic because the events were not easily or accurately concentrated into a single description, as in reality they were carried out continuously throughout campaigns that often lasted months. It is difficult to convey the scale, duration, and extent of the destruction in a manner that does not seem excessive or critical. Writings by English non-combatants describe devastation in simple, short, and formulaic phrases, such as "they invaded and burned up Galloway, and led away spoil and cattle", or "Cumberland and other

---

50 Edited in NICOLAS, 1827, pp. 200f.: "nos ditz enemys qi avoyent assemble lours niefs en moult fort array et lesqu'x fesoient ml't noble defens tut cel iour et la noet ap's [...] se gissent les corps mortz et tut pleyn de lieux sr la costere de fflaundres".
51 In AVESBURY, 1889, pp. 312-14 (here 313): "ipse spes nostra Christus Deus [...] nos praevalere concessit"; also in AN Prose Brut Continuation, 1327-47, fols 192r-193r; in Tynemouth's *Historia aurea* variant in GUISBOROUGH, 1848-49, vol. 2 pp. 357-59 (not in primary Tynemouth manuscripts). See also Edward III's letters asking for prayer before campaigns and after victories, similarly devoid of martial language, such as that to the archbishop of York, 1338, in Gesta Edwardi Tertii, 1882-83, pp. 135f.; to his bishops, 1342, in TYNEMOUTH, fols 240v-241r; to the archbishop of Canterbury after the start of his 1346 campaign, edited in FROISSART, 1867-77, pp. 285f. See also HEWITT, 1966, pp. 160-65.
52 In Gesta Edwardi Tertii, 1882-83, pp. 116-18.

areas were devastated by slaughter and blaze".[53] Combatants employ this language in their own writings, such as "they burned and destroyed Plaisance and all the country around", "they ravaged and destroyed all the country of Astarac", "they put to fire and destruction all the country of Commingues", and "they put to fire and destruction several *bonnes villes* in the country of Lisle".[54] These are terse and often only use one or two short phrases to represent devastation that lasted throughout an entire campaign.[55] Hewitt, without considering the moral implications, claims that these formulaic phrases were understood by readers as shorthand that referred to the violent details of raids.[56] However, these consistently subdued representations of unsavoury acts are intentional and should not be dismissed.

There are clear reasons for the varying levels of attention to the violence of war in texts. Sometimes this seems to be because non-combatants do not care about devastation in their own writings.[57] However, in many cases this is because the events were distant and relatively unimportant to the writers.[58] For example, the *Lanercost Chronicle*, written in either the Lanercost Priory or Carlisle, gives a narration of David II's 1346 invasion of northern England that is three

---

53 Chronicon de Lanercost, 1839, pp. 269, 341: "invaserunt Galwithiam et combusserunt, et spolia et pecora abduxerunt", "Cumberlande [...] caede et incendio devastantes", also 259f., three times on 272, 278f., 279, 281f., 282f., 285f., 286f., 287, twice on 288, 290f., 291, 291f., 292, 292f., 293, 335, twice on 341. See also SMITH, 2014.
54 Wingfield's letter to the archbishop of Winchester, 1355, in AVESBURY, 1889, pp. 439-43 (here 440): "laad ars et destruit [Pleasance] et tut la pays environ", "gasty et destruit tout le pays [de Astrik]", "lez fist ardre et destruire et tout le pays [de Comenge]", "fist ardre et destruire plusors bones villes [en la countee de Lylle]"; see also notes 44 above and 70 below.
55 See for example the consistent usage by GRAY, 2005, pp. 10, 16, 18, 20, twice on 36, 40, 42, 68, 80, 86, 88, twice on 96, 98, 100, 114, 118, 122, 124, twice on 126, twice on 128, 132, 134-41 (many in Lelands abstract), 152, 160, 166, 170, twice on 172, 176, 178, 182, 184, 186, 188, 194, twice on 196, 202.
56 HEWITT, 1966, p. 102.
57 Briefly considered by HEWITT, 1966, pp. 97, 100-02, 114f., 121-23.
58 Their lack of attention was not because they were not aware of what happened. Non-combatants were informed by widely-circulated newsletters and other testimony.

times as long as that for Edward III's 1346 Normandy campaign.[59] The southern clerk, Geoffrey le Baker, represents the two campaigns in an equally disproportionate fashion, but with more attention to the campaign in France.[60] For combatant writers, devastation did not act as mere background information, noise, or colour. They directed and witnessed devastation first hand throughout the course of campaigns. Combatant writers focus on what their armies do, rather than on simple news itself. Sometimes they include considerable details of their armies' movements through the countryside, such as Edward III's day-to-day report of part of his 1339 campaign.[61] By focusing on action, when armies attack the land, combatant writers suggest that they are acting and conducting some form of war rather than manoeuvring aimlessly. This focus on actions is skewed, however, considering that battles, skirmishes, and sieges were historically rare, especially in proportion to the raids conducted daily throughout campaigns of devastation. Overall, this fulfils newsletters' sometimes-stated objectives to earn financial and spiritual support from England by praising the actions of English armies and demonstrating progress.

Combatants do not state that people are attacked, but rather that the English are moving through the area or attacking an armed force. They were clearly aware of the reality of their campaigns and might simply think these details were implied in their descriptions. However, their consistent lack of such details suggests that it was thought unsavoury to discuss non-combatants as victims openly, especially in writings that were ostensibly meant to praise their own actions and receive acclaim. Sometimes they explicitly state that non-combatants are absent during devastation. During the 1346 Normandy campaign Burghersh reports that as the English advanced "there was not man nor woman of estate who dared to wait in towns, castles, or in the country through which the army passed, but all fled away" and Northburgh similarly states that

---

59 Chronicon de Lanercost, 1839, pp. 342-44 (Normandy), 344-52 (northern England).
60 LE BAKER, 1889, pp. 79-86 and 89-92 (Normandy), 86-89 (northern England).
61 Edward III's newsletter, 1339, in a miscellany of several documents (London, British Library, MS Cotton Caligula D III, fol. 25), edited in FROISSART, 1867-77, pp. 84-86. See also Wingfield's letter to Richard Stafford, 1356, in AVESBURY, 1889, pp. 445-47; and note 71 below.

when the English arrive at Barfleur they "thought to have found many people, but found none".⁶² Consequently, the English attacks in the early portion of the campaign are made to be without violence or opposition. Similarly, Edward of Woodstock reports that during his 1355 campaign in southern France "those who were in [the town of Samatan] left at the coming of our men".⁶³ Because these incidents are noted as being exceptional, they suggest that non-combatants were thought normally to be in the path of such attacks. Combatants' versions of events take this into account to suggest that their campaigns were less violent than normal.

Combatant writers omit the historically common suffering of non-combatants during sieges entirely. None of the combatant letters on Caen directly mention the killed as non-combatants, but always as armed defenders.⁶⁴ No mention is made of the commonly used trope of the besieged suffering from starvation during longer sieges, such as is described in grisly detail by the Middle English poem *Siege of Jerusalem* (c. 1370-89) and in much fourteenth-century historical writing.⁶⁵ Several writings by English non-combatants on the siege of Calais (1346-47) include such details in their own narratives.⁶⁶ Some, such as the poet Laurence Minot (writing in the mid-fourteenth century), link this suffering to Calais' role as a haven for raiders who attacked the English coast in order to suggest their suffering served as punishment for their involvement.⁶⁷ At least three letters by Edward III from the siege of

---

62 Burghersh's letter to the archbishop of Canterbury, in MURIMUTH, 1889, pp. 202f. (here 202): "il ny avoit home ne femme destat qe osa attendre en villes, chastels, ne en pays, la ou le oust passa, qe touz ne sen fuyrount"; see also note 30 above; Northburgh's newsletter, in AVESBURY, 1889, pp. 358-60 (here 358): "quidoient avoir trove plusors gentz, et troverent nulles a regard"; translated into Latin in MURIMUTH, 1889, pp. 212-14 (here 212): "credentes ibidem magnam hominum multitudinem invenisse; non tamen invenerunt aliquos respective"; see also notes 32 and 33 above.
63 In his letter to the bishop of Winchester, in AVESBURY, 1889, pp. 434-37 (here 434): "ceaux (qe) dedeinz estoient voideront a la venue de noz gentz"; see also note 72 below.
64 See notes 28-33 above.
65 Siege of Jerusalem, 2003, lines 1067-1100 (pp. 72-75).
66 See for example the many Latin and French texts that depict suffering at Calais, described and listed in DEVRIES, 1991, pp. 141-44, 158f., 170f. n. 71, 178 n. 158.
67 MINOT, 1914, poem 8 lines 1-16 (p. 27). See also HUGHES, 1994.

Calais survive, all of which are have various details except those on non-combatants or their suffering.[68] Gray only once mentions a city suffering from starvation amongst his nearly forty descriptions of sieges, but briefly and without comment.[69]

Combatants only praise attacks on non-combatants that are represented as such with qualifying conditions. Wingfield, during Edward of Woodstock's 1355 campaign in southern France, describes devastation eight separate times in contrast to the standard one or two mentions of devastation for an entire campaign found in other writings. He does this to emphasise the scale of the English army's devastation when he asserts that "there was never such loss or such destruction as there has been by this *chevauchée*", because he believes non-combatants readily contribute to the French war effort, "for the lands and good towns that are destroyed by this *chevauchée* found for the king of France more each year to maintain his war than did half of his realm".[70] His repeated descriptions of attacks on towns and the countryside, without mentioning non-combatants who were surely attacked in reality, make English actions all the more praiseworthy. In a letter from the following year Wingfield claims that the English army attacks the land in order "to destroy their supplies" rather than for its own sake.[71] In both letters Wingfield portrays non-combatants as contributing to war and therefore

---

68 All of these letters date from 1347. Two with unknown addressees are edited in FROISSART, 1867-77, vol. 18 pp. 301f.; and another to the archbishop of Canterbury, in AVESBURY, pp. 391-93.

69 GRAY, 2005, p. 136 (for suffering at the 1346-47 siege of Calais, but this may be inaccurate as the original portion of this text is missing and only Leland's abstract survives), 38-42, 42, 44, 46, 48-52, 62, 72, 86, twice on 100, 110, 116, 118, 120, 124, 128, 130, 142, 148, three times on 156, 164, three times on 166, twice on 172, twice on 174, 176, twice on 178, twice on 182, 184, 196. I do not include in this count the Creation-1272 portion of the text because it is largely based on an amalgamation of Tynemouth's *Historia aurea* and, especially for 1100-1272, an Anglo-Norman *Brut*.

70 In his letter to the bishop of Winchester, in AVESBURY, 1889, pp. 439-43 (here 442): "y nont unqes tiel part eu tiel destruccion come il aad eu a ceste chivachee. Car les pays et lez bones villes qe sount destruits a ceste chivache trova a roy de Fraunce plus chescun an a maintenir sa guerre qe ne fist la moite de soun roialme"; see also notes 44 and 54 above. On this concept see ROGERS, 2000, pp. 323-34; HEWITT, 1966, pp. 50-74; KEEN, 1965, pp. 139f.

71 In his letter to Richard Stafford, in AVESBURY, 1889, pp. 445-47 (here 447): "pur destruire lours vives"; see also note 61 above.

implies that attacking them is strategically sensible and praiseworthy. Woodstock, during his 1355 campaign in southern France, gives a more humanitarian purpose to devastation when he claims it was meant to relieve allied lands and people from attack.[72] These justifications are meant to show that non-combatants willingly contributed to war, although indirectly, and were therefore licit targets.

IV. Ethical Sensitivities

Combatants were not ignorant of the ethical problems of war as is shown by their rationalisations and preferred representation as knights fighting in idealistic wars that were devoid of non-combatant victims.[73] The English resort to devastation only because the French refuse to fight openly, according to John Fastolf, when he states that the king of England

> "hathe offered unto his adversaries, as a goode Cristen prince, that alle menne of Holy Chirche, and also the comyns and labourers of the reaume of Fraunce [...] that the werre in eithere partie shuld be (and) rest alonly betwixt men of werre and men of werre, the whiche offre the said adversarie have utterly refused, and be concluded to make theire werre cruelle and charpe, without sparing of any parsone."[74]

Devastation clearly had no place in an ideal war. But war was rarely, if ever, practiced without devastation before Richard II (r. 1377-99) and Henry V (r. 1413-22).[75] Some texts, such as the *Acta bellicosa* and

---

72 In his letter to the bishop of Winchester, in AVESBURY, 1889, pp. 434-37 (here 434); see also note 63 above.

73 See for example writings that omit devastation entirely in favour of skirmishes, battles, and sieges: Lancaster's newsletter, 1346, in AVESBURY, 1889, pp. 372-74; Bentley's letter to "reverent piere en Dieu", 1352, in AVESBURY, 1889, pp. 416f.; Burghersh's letter to John Beauchamp, 1356, edited in COXE, 1842, pp. 369f.

74 Edited in STEVENSON, 1861-64, vol. 2 pp. 575-85 (here 581). Note however that he wrote his letter in the early-fifteenth century. This ideal of war fought solely between combatants also prevailed in fourteenth-century English romance.

75 See for example their ordinances that prohibit devastation: CURRY, 2011; CURRY, 2008.

William Dene's *History of Rochester* (*c.* 1350), suggest that Edward III attempted to restrain his men during his 1346 campaign in Normandy.[76] However, the majority of contemporary English texts that describe the campaign fail to mention such restraint. Many of these writings draw upon newsletters that would have surely included such details if they had actually occurred.[77] None of the letters by combatants suggest any attempts at restraint in their campaigns.[78] Therefore, suggestions of restraint by chroniclers are likely rhetorical rather than a reflection of reality. This is further borne out by the historical extent of devastation and the elaborate descriptions by contemporary writers, some of whom were eyewitnesses.

Occasionally English combatants were bothered by these acts in relation to their ideals. Gray laments this disproportionate suffering by stating that "the people bear the burden of the sins of kings" in his conclusion to the *Scalacronica*.[79] He was aware of the ethical issues in the conduct of war, especially as they contrasted with justifications. However, the attitudes in his presentation of war are inconsistent and he makes no other moral commentary on the suffering of non-combatants.

---

76 Acta bellicosa, 1894, p. 160; DENE, fol. 91r. This is unquestioningly accepted as historical reality by many, such as ROGERS, 2000, pp. 238-40; AYTON, 2005, p. 62.

77 See the many contemporary English chronicles that describe the campaign and battle of Crécy, often in great detail: many are given in LIVINGSTON/DEVRIES, 2015, pp. 248-50 (*Anonimalle Chronicle*), 198 (Anonymous of Canterbury's *Chronicle*), 158-64 (le Baker's *Chronicle*), 198 (*Chronicon brevis*, fairly brief), 86-88 (*Lanercost Chronicle*), 148-50 (Continuation "A" of Higden's *Polychronicon*), 134-36 (Dene's *History of Rochester*), 198-200 (*Eulogium historiarum*), 192 (Leland's abstract of Gray's *Scalacronica*), 140-44 (variant of Murimuth's *Continuatio chronicarum*), 212 (Reading's *Chronicles*), 140 (Tynemouth's *Historia aurea*); but in addition see AN Prose Brut Continuation, 1307-77, fols 175r-176r; AN Prose Brut Continuation, 1327-47, fols 195v-196v; St Albans "A" Continuation of Higden's *Polychronicon*, 1343-77, fol. 294r (some similarities to Continuation "A", but greatly expanded); Long Kirkstall Abbey Chronicle, fols 82v-83v; Northern Latin Brut, pp. 66f (similar to *Anonimalle Chronicle* and *Lanercost Chronicle*); and the many other terse or short chronicles that remain unedited.

78 See notes 28, 29, 30, and 68 above; as well as Edward III's letter to the mayor and bailiffs of Newcastle, edited in FROISSART, 1867-77, vol. 18 pp. 289f.

79 GRAY, 2005, p. 194: "le poeple port coup dez pecchez dez roys".

Edward III, in his 1328 letter asking for peace, laments the suffering and destruction of war: "the massacres, misfortunes, crimes, destruction of churches, and countless evils, which by misfortune of this manner of wars, have in many ways affected subjects of both kingdoms".[80] Instead of simply stating that non-combatants are targeted in devastation, he recognises that their suffering can be lamentable. Both of these cases show combatants perceiving non-combatants as innocent rather than as licit targets.

Some English combatants recognised the problems of English military conduct. Others felt it unacceptable and joined convents in penance for their bloody lives.[81] A few even vehemently criticise their own acts during war in their writings. Clanvowe dismisses the conduct of war and pursuit of worldly chivalry entirely: "byfore God alle vertue is worsshipe and alle synne is shame. And in þis world it is euene þe reuers, ffor þe world holt hem worsshipful þat been greete werrey ours and fiȝteres and þat distroyen and wynnen manye loondis [...] and in lyuyng in eese, sloupe, and many ooþere synnes".[82] He claims that leading the knight's life, with all its violent excess and greed, was a sure way to Hell, and conversely, that avoiding it was the way to Heaven. Clanvowe explicitly condemns the actions that made up devastation when expounding on the Commandments: "þoo þat sleen any man in þouȝt, in woord, or in deede, þei breken þe fifthe comaundement [...] alle þoo þat robben or stelen, taaken by maistrie, or be extorcoun, or by any gyle, or falsheede here neiȝebores goodis, þei breken þe seuenþe comaundement".[83] He based his text on sermons in both form and language, which further illustrates his intention for it to be read as a moralistic lesson.[84]

Combatants' presentation of war often became the *de facto* version of events and understanding of the common conditions of war. Sometimes they clearly influenced other writers' attitudes, such as the representation

---

80   In Chronicon de Lanercost, 1839, p. 262: "caedes, occasiones, scelera, ecclesiarum destructiones et mala innumerabilia, quae hujusmodi occasione guerrarum regnicolis utriusque regni multipliciter contingebant".
81   See the examination of knights considering the morality of their actions by KAEUPER, 2009, pp. 12, 14, 19, 23f., 34.
82   CLANVOWE, 1975, p. 69.
83   CLANVOWE, 1975, p. 74.
84   For sermon composition and structure, see ROSS, 1940, pp. xliii-lv.

of war in Knighton's *Chronicle*. At other times, however, writers clearly disagreed with them, such as when the writer of the *Lanercost Chronicle*, after the interpolated letter of Edward III that focuses on English military achievements, gives only a simple description of the noteworthy battle of Crécy, in which Edward III "engaged in a grave battle and overcame his adversary, as the Lord concedes", but "not by human, but by Divine power, was it ended".[85] When combatants' letters are included in chronicles they commonly take the place of the chroniclers' own version of events. This then prevents other writers from voicing their own, possibly dissenting, opinions, as is evident in the presentation of Edward III's Normandy campaign in 1346 in the document-laden chronicles of Murimuth and Avesbury.[86] Therefore, the differences between writings by combatants and those non-combatants who had access to such documents are sometimes blurred

Conclusions

Chivalric and bellicose attitudes were appealing representations of the ethically problematic warfare conducted in the later Middle Ages. Combatants were not simply mindless, patriotic, and pugnacious brutes, ignorant of these issues, but instead carefully produced writings to promote their perspectives in light of these ideals. They justify their actions to both themselves and their audiences by portraying war as palatable and praiseworthy with a clear awareness that some might perceive their acts as unsavoury.

Combatant writers rationalised their campaigns by portraying their victims as willing contributors to war. In skirmishes, battles, and sieges they always portray those killed as having willingly fought and on equal terms to the professional English armies. They quietly ignore the fact that many killed in these events were unarmed and, in all respects, exempt from attack. Instead, they focus on the challenge of these events and the

---

85 *Chronicon de Lanercost*, 1839, p. 344: "conserto gravi proelio, suum adversarium vicit, Domino concedente", "non humana sed Divina potentia consummatum". Compare with the other representations of Crécy in note 77 above.
86 MURIMUTH, 1889, pp. 198-218; AVESBURY, 1889, pp. 357-69, 384-87, 390-402.

laudable display of martial prowess. The human victims of devastation are mostly ignored by combatant writers in favour of formulaic language and details of more exciting actions. Sometimes devastation is justified because the goods and people destroyed contributed to the enemy's ability to wage war, or through other pragmatic pretexts. Non-combatants are portrayed in combatants' writings as licit targets because they are shown willingly choosing to involve themselves in war.[87]

This military perspective was meant for wide-ranging public consumption. There was a general interest in military affairs, so much so that most surviving English sermon collections include *exempla* on contemporary, classical, and biblical war.[88] Therefore, it was not too difficult to convince the common man to accept the conduct of war if it was presented in the particularly distorted fashion of combatant writings because it seems morally acceptable, exciting, and praiseworthy, just like these sermons were.

However, these notions of non-combatant culpability are rarely found together or explicitly stated, especially before the fifteenth century. It should not be assumed that everybody agreed with them as part of a sophisticated philosophy against non-combatant rights. The notion of "total war" is a modern one and should not be retroactively applied by piecing together disparate sources. Enemy non-combatants were not always assumed to be licit targets or perceived as part of an entirely hostile group that was "the enemy", or rebels, especially in writings by non-combatants. In many cases it is evident that combatants could see non-combatants differently from these common representations. More rarely they actively questioned the legitimacy of their own actions.

We cannot accept the current evaluation of combatants' brutal disregard for non-combatants or, more generally, the perception of war by English writers during Edward III's reign. Knights did not revel in killing and were cautious about how their conduct might be criticised. The issues were far more complex, especially through time and place, and the perspective of combatants during the later Middle Ages deserves further attention. There was a rich and varied dialogue on the nature of

---

87 All of these elements are combined in the newsletter by an anonymous English combatant at the 1340 siege of Tournai, in DENE, fols 85v-86v.
88 See for example the many sermons in BRINTON, 1954, but note that nearly every sermon collection has such stories. See also SHERWOOD, 1980, pp. 287-301.

non-combatants in the large body of English writings, and combatants recognised and engaged with these issues through the rhetoric they carefully employed in their writings.

Bibliography

Sources

Acta bellicosa, in: JOSEPH MOISANT (ed.), Le Prince Noir en Aquitaine, 1355/56-1362/70, Paris 1894, pp. 157-74.

The Anglo-Norman Prose "Brut", ed. and trans. by MARCIA LUSK MAXWELL, unpublished PhD thesis, Michigan State University 1995 [Long Anglo-Norman Prose Brut, from 1 of 16 manuscripts only].[89]

Anglo-Norman Prose Brut Continuation, 1307-77 [unedited: Oxford, Corpus Christi College, MS 78, fols 164v-189r].[90]

Anglo-Norman Prose Brut Continuation, 1327-47 [unedited: London, British Library, MS Cotton Tiberus A VI, fols 184r-199r].[91]

The Anonimalle Chronicle, 1333 to 1381, ed. by V. H. GALBRAITH, rev. ed., Manchester 1970.

AVESBURY, ROBERT, De gestis mirabilibus Regis Edwardi Tertii, in: Adae Murimuth; Robertus de Avesbury (Rolls Series 93), ed. by EDWARD MAUNDE THOMPSON, London 1889, pp. 279-471.

LE BAKER, GEOFFREY, Chronicon, ed. by EDWARD MAUNDE THOMPSON, Oxford 1889.

BRINTON, THOMAS, Sermons, 1373-1389, ed. by MARY AQUINAS DEVLIN (Camden Third Series 85-86), 2 vols, London 1954.

The Brut, or the Chronicles of England, ed. by FRIEDRICH W. D. BRIE (Early English Text Society 131, 136), 2 vols, London 1906-08 [Brutus-1333 portion is a translation of the Long Anglo-Norman

---

[89] See DEAN/BOULTON, 1999, no. 46 (pp. 32f.); manuscript list corrected by Oldest Anglo-Norman Prose *Brut*, 2006, p. 51 n. 192.

[90] See DEAN/BOULTON, 1999, no. 49 (p. 34). The 1346 Neville's Cross invasion (on fols 176v-178r) is edited and translated in ROGERS/BUCK, 1999, pp. 74-77.

[91] See DEAN/BOULTON, 1999, no. 48 (p. 34), although they erroneously put the end date at 1346. The 1346 Neville's Cross invasion (on fols 196v-197v) is edited and translated in ROGERS/BUCK, 1999, pp. 72-75.

Prose Brut into Middle English, along with a sometimes derivative 1333-77 continuation, and many others afterwards].

Chronicon de Lanercost, MCCI-MCCCXLVI, ed. by JOSEPH STEVENSON, Edinburgh 1839.

CLANVOWE, JOHN, The Two Ways, in: Works, ed. by V. J. SCATTERGOOD, Cambridge 1975, pp. 57-80, 86-89.

COXE, HENRY OCTAVIUS (ed.), The Black Prince, London 1842.

DENE, WILLIAM, History of Rochester [unedited: London, British Library, MS Cotton Faustina B V, fols 2r-101r].[92]

FROISSART, JEAN, Chroniques, ed. by SIMÉON LUCE et al., 15 vols, Paris 1869-1975 [Book I "B" recension in vols 1-8 with "A" variants in notes].

ID., Chroniques, Livre I. Le manuscrit d'Amiens, Bibliothèque municipale no. 486, ed. by GEORGE DILLER, 5 vols, Genève 1991-98.

ID., Oeuvres, ed. by KERVYN DE LETTENHOVE, 25 vols, Bruxelles 1867-77 [*Chronicles*, Book I "N" recension in vol. 17].

GAILBRAITH, V. H. (ed.), Extracts from the *Historia aurea* and a French "Brut", 1317-47, in: English Historical Review 43 (1928), pp. 203-17.

Gesta Edwardi Tertii, in: Chronicles of the Reigns of Edward I and Edward II, ed. by WILLIAM STUBBS (Rolls Series 76), 2 vols, London 1882-83, vol. 2 pp. 93-151 [1327-77 continuation of Bridlington Chronicle].

GOWER, JOHN, Confessio Amantis, in: English Works, ed. by G. C. MACAULAY (Early English Text Society, Extra Series 81-82), 2 vols, London 1900-01, vol. 1 pp. 1-519, vol. 2 pp. 1-480, 495-550.

GRATIAN, Decretum, ed. by EMIL FRIEDBERG/AEMILIUS LUDWIG RICHTER, 2nd ed., Graz 1959.

GRAY, THOMAS, Scalacronica, 1272-1363, ed. and trans. by ANDY KING (Surtees Society 209), Woodbridge 2005.

GUISBOROUGH, WALTER OF, Chronicle, ed. by HANS CLAUDE HAMILTON, 2 vols, London 1848-49.

---

[92] The 1340 siege of Tournai (on fols 85v-86v) is edited and translated in ROGERS, 1998; the 1346 battle of Crécy (on fols 92r-92v) is edited and translated in LIVINGSTON/DEVRIES, 2015, pp. 134-37; the 1346 Neville's Cross invasion (on fols 93r-93v) is edited and translated in ROGERS/BUCK, 1998, pp. 76-79.

KNIGHTON, HENRY, Chronicle, 1337-1396, ed. and trans. by G. H. MARTIN, Oxford 1995.
LIVINGSTON, MICHAEL/DEVRIES, KELLY (eds.), The Battle of Crécy. A Casebook, Liverpool 2015.
Long Kirkstall Abbey Chronicle [unedited: Oxford, Bodleian Library, MS Laud misc. 722 (SC 1174), fols 38v-88r].[93]
MINOT, LAURENCE, Poems, ed. by JOSEPH HALL, 3rd ed., Oxford 1914.
MURIMUTH, ADAM, Continuatio chronicarum, in: Adae Murimuth; Robertus de Avesbury, ed. by EDWARD MAUNDE THOMPSON (Rolls Series 93), London 1889, pp. 3-276.
NICOLAS, NICHOLAS HARRIS (ed.), A Chronicle of London, from 1089 to 1483, London 1827.
Northern Latin Brut [unedited: Durham, Cathedral Library, MS B.ii.35, pp. 1-68; also in one other MS].[94]
The Oldest Anglo-Norman Prose *Brut* Chronicle, ed. and trans. by JULIA MARVIN, Woodbridge 2006.
PAGULA, WILLIAM, De speculo Regis Edwardi III. Seu tractatu quem de mala regni administratione, ed. by JOSEPH MOISANT, Paris 1891.
READING, JOHN, Chronica, 1346-1367, in: Johannis de Reading et Anonymi Cantuariensis, ed. by JAMES TAIT, Manchester 1914, pp. 99-186.
ROGERS, CLIFFORD J. (ed. and trans.), An Unknown News Bulletin from the Siege of Tournai in 1340, in: War in History 5 (1998), pp. 358-66.
ROGERS, CLIFFORD J./BUCK, MARK C. (eds. and trans.), The Scottish Invasion of 1346, in: Northern History 34 (1998), pp. 51-82.
ROSS, WOODBURN O. (ed.), Middle English Sermons (Early English Text Society 209), London 1940.
The Siege of Jerusalem, ed. by RALPH HANNA/DAVID LAWTON (Early English Text Society 320), Oxford 2003.
St Albans "A" Continuation, 1343-77, of RANULF HIGDEN, Polychronicon [unedited: Cambridge, Corpus Christi College, MS 6, fols 305r-310r; also in two other MSS].[95]

---

93 See J. TAYLOR, 1952.
94 The 1346 Neville's Cross invasion is edited in OFFLER, 1984, pp. 57-59.
95 See GALBRAITH, 1927, pp. 390-95.

STEVENSON, JOSEPH (Ed.), Letters and Papers Illustrative of the Wars of the English in France during the Reign of Henry the Sixth, King of England (Rolls Series 22), 2 vols, London 1861-64.
TYNEMOUTH, JOHN, Historia aurea [unedited: London, Lambeth Palace Library, MSS 10-12; also in two other primary MSS, and several others as continuations of other chronicles].[96]
VENETTE, JEAN DE, Chronique, ed. and trans. [into French] by Colette Beaune, Paris 2011.

Literature

ALLMAND, CHRISTOPHER, The War and the Non-Combatant, in: The Hundred Years War, ed. by KENNETH FOWLER, London 1971, pp. 163-83.
ID., War and the Non-Combatant in the Middle Ages, in: Medieval Warfare, ed. by MAURICE KEEN, Oxford 1999, pp. 259-69.
AYTON, ANDREW, The Campaign, in: The Battle of Crécy, ed. by ANDREW AYTON/PHILIP PRESTON, Woodbridge 2005, pp. 35-107.
BARBER, RICHARD, Edward III and the Triumph of England. The Battle of Crécy and the Company of the Garter, London 2013.
CARLSON, DAVID R., John Gower. Poetry and Propaganda in Fourteenth-Century England, Woodbridge 2012.
CONTAMINE, PHILIPPE, La guerre au Moyen-Âge, 6th ed., Paris 2003.
ID., L'idée de guerre à la fin du Moyen Âge. Aspects juridiques et éthiques, in: Comptes rendus de séances de l'Acadeémie des Inscriptions et Belles-Lettres 123 (1979), pp. 70-86.
COX, RORY, John Wyclif on War and Peace, London 2014.
CURRY, ANNE, Disciplinary Ordinances for English and Franco-Scottish Armies in 1385. An International Code?, in: Journal of Medieval History 37 (2011), pp. 269-94.
DEAN, RUTH J./BOULTON, MAUREEN B. M., Anglo-Norman Literature. A Guide to Texts and Manuscripts, London 1999.

---

96 A variant as a 1327-46 continuation of another chronicle is edited in GUISBOROUGH, 1848-49, vol. 2 pp. 297-426; with differences from the three primary manuscripts noted and edited in GALBRAITH, 1927, pp. 396-98; GALBRAITH, 1928, pp. 208-15.

ID., The Military Ordinances of Henry V. Texts and Contexts, in: War, Government and Aristocracy in the British Isles, *c*. 1150-1500, ed. by CHRIS GIVEN-WILSON et al., Woodbridge 2008, pp. 214-49.

DEVRIES, KELLY, Hunger, Flemish Participation and the Flight of Philip VI. Contemporary Accounts of the Siege of Calais, 1346-47, in: Studies in Medieval and Renaissance History n.s. 12 (1991), pp. 129-81.

ID., Medieval Mercenaries. Methodology, Definitions and Problems, in: Mercenaries and Paid Men. The Mercenary Identity in the Middle Ages, ed. by JOHN FRANCE, Leiden 2008, pp. 43-60.

FOWLER, KENNETH, News from the Front. Letters and Despatches of the Fourteenth Century, in: Guerre et société en France, en Angleterre et en Bourgogne, XIVe-XVe siècles, ed. by PHILIPPE CONTAMINE et al., Villeneuve d'Ascq 1991, pp. 63-92.

DOIG, JAMES A., Political Propaganda and Royal Proclamations in Late Medieval England, in: Historical Research 71 (1998), pp. 253-80.

GAILBRAITH, V. H., The *Historia aurea* of John, Vicar of Tynemouth, and the Sources of the St Albans Chronicle, 1327-1377, in Essays in History Presented to Reginald Lane Poole, ed. by H. W. C. DAVIS, Oxford 1927, pp. 379-98.

GUNN, STEVEN, War and the Emergence of the State. Western Europe, 1350-1600, in: European Warfare, 1350-1750, ed. by FRANK TALLETT/D. J. B. TRIM, Cambridge 2010, pp. 50-73.

HEWITT, H. J., The Organization of War under Edward III, 1338-62, New York 1966.

HUGHES, MICHAEL, The Fourteenth-Century French Raids on Hampshire and the Isle of Wight, in: Arms, Armies and Fortifications in the Hundred Years War, ed. by ANNE CURRY/MICHAEL HUGHES, Woodbridge 1994, pp. 121-44.

JONES, W. R., The English Church and Royal Propaganda during the Hundred Years War, in: Journal of British Studies 19 (1979), pp. 18-30.

KAEUPER, RICHARD, Holy Warriors. The Religious Ideology of Chivalry, Philadelphia 2009.

KEEN, MAURICE, The Laws of War in the Late Middle Ages, London 1965.

KING, ANDY, "According to the Custom Used in French and Scottish Wars". Prisoners and Casualties on the Scottish Marches in the Fourteenth Century, in: Journal of Medieval History 28 (2002), pp. 263-90.

MCGLYNN, SEAN, By Sword and Fire: Cruelty and Atrocity in Medieval Warfare, London 2008.

OFFLER, H. S., A Note on the Northern Franciscan Chronicle, in: Nottingham Medieval Studies 28 (1984), pp. 45-59.

PAGAN, HEATHER, Trevet's *Les cronicles*: Manuscripts, Owners and Readers, in: The Prose *Brut* and Other Late Medieval Chronicles. Books Have Their Histories. Essays in Honour of Lister M. Matheson, ed. by JACLYN RAJSIC, ERIK KOOPER, AND DOMINIQUE HOCHE, Woodbridge 2016, pp. 149-64.

PRESTWICH, MICHAEL, Armies and Warfare in the Middle Ages. The English Experience, New Haven 1996.

ROGERS, CLIFFORD J., By Fire and Sword. *Bellum hostile* and "Civilians" in the Hundred Years' War, in: Civilians in the Path of War, ed. by MARK GRIMSLEY/CLIFFORD J. ROGERS, Lincoln 2002, pp. 33-78.

ID., Edward III and the Dialectics of Strategy, 1327-1360, in: Transactions of the Royal Historical Society 6th ser. 4 (1994), pp. 83-102.

ID., War, Cruel and Sharp. English Strategy under Edward III, 1327-1360, Woodbridge 2000.

RUSSELL, FREDERICK H., The Just War in the Middle Ages, Cambridge 1975.

SHERWOOD, FOSTER H., Studies in Medieval Uses of Vegetius' *Epitoma rei militaris*, unpublished PhD dissertation, University of California at Los Angeles 1980.

SMITH, TREVOR RUSSELL, Ethics and Representation of War in the *Lanercost Chronicle*, 1327-46, in: Bulletin of International Medieval Research 20 (2014), forthcoming.

STRICKLAND, MATTHEW, Provoking or Avoiding Battle? Challenge, Judicial Duel, and Single Combat in Eleventh- and Twelfth-Century Warfare', in: Armies, Chivalry and Warfare in Medieval Britain and France, ed. by MATTHEW STRICKLAND, Stamford 1998, pp. 317-43.

ID., War and Chivalry. The Conduct and Perception of War in England and Normandy, 1066-1217, Cambridge 1996.

TAYLOR, CRAIG, Edward III and the Plantagenet Claim to the French Throne, in: The Age of Edward III, ed. by J. S. BOTHWELL, Woodbridge 2001, pp. 155-69.

TAYLOR, JOHN, English Historical Literature in the Fourteenth Century, Oxford 1987.

ID., The Kirkstall Abbey Chronicles (Thoresby Society 42), Leeds 1952.

TYSON, DIANA B., Three Short Anglo-Norman Texts in Leeds University Library, Brotherton Collection MS 29, in: Nottingham Medieval Studies 52 (2008), pp. 81-112.

VALE, MALCOLM, War and Chivalry. Warfare and Aristocratic Culture in England, France and Burgundy at the End of the Middle Ages, Athens 1981.

WRIGHT, NICHOLAS, Knights and Peasants. The Hundred Years War in the French Countryside, Woodbridge 1998.

Body Techniques of Combat: The Depiction of a Personal Fighting System in the Fight Books of Hans Talhofer (1443-1467 CE)

ERIC BURKART

If we turn to "bodies in battle" in the Middle Ages, the question how fighters of the past actually used their bodies in combat is a quite obvious one. Unfortunately, it is difficult to answer. Only very few medieval sources document movements in a way that would allow a detailed reconstruction. Additionally, the interpretation of these sources greatly involves the interpreter's own perception of her body and movement, a knowledge that is usually subconscious and difficult to communicate to a (reading) scientific community. From the point of view of cultural history, this hermeneutic framework and the resulting communicational gap is crucial to any scientific approach towards medieval "techniques of the body".[1]

The most promising historical documents concerning body techniques of combat are the late medieval and early modern fight books.[2] In this contribution, I shall focus on a series of five 15th century manuscripts ascribed to the fencing master Hans Talhofer. These treatises will serve as a case study to discuss the communication strategies of medieval fight books and the connection between the

---

1 MAUSS, 1979; MALLINCKRODT, 2008; SPATZ, 2015.
2 LENG, 2008; BOFFA, 2014.

integrated didactic images and the embodied knowledge of their makers.[3]

Apart from the hermeneutic set up, there is yet another factor that renders a study on body techniques of combat rather difficult. Interpersonal physical violence is a human practice that is documented throughout the history of mankind. Yet, the violent action itself is volatile and only its material traces can be subject to a historical inquiry. At the same time, violence is one of the most powerful symbols in human culture. Both the act of converting imagined or experienced violence in textual, pictorial or other representations *and* the act of interpreting these representations therefore highly depend on the respective contemporary discourses.

While the discursive structures of the Middle Ages are the primary concern of modern historians, their own society's discourses and their subjective attitudes towards violence in combat are not as commonly reflected upon.[4] Modern narratives on how violence is and was conducted are nevertheless omnipresent in today's media and exert a distinct influence on historians. They can be found in the news, in books, movies, plays, TV documentaries, video games and so forth. The way in which violence is depicted and narrated here is an object of study on its own. Not having conducted detailed research on this matter yet, I shall only try to highlight one aspect that seems rather obvious, yet nevertheless important for our historical perspective. It concerns the distinction between real and fictional violence on the one hand and the emotional impact of just and unjust violence on the other.

Highly simplified, most of today's narratives tend to distinguish between the just act of violence conducted by the active protagonist and cruel acts of unjust violence against innocent victims.[5] The first scheme dominates most of today's fictional narratives and is perhaps best impersonated by the hero of an action movie. The second is omnipresent in the news and other reports on real violence such as war atrocities or murder. Their main difference is the audience's degree of identification with the violent protagonists and with the harmed victims.

---

3   The contribution is largely based on a German paper on Hans Talhofer. For more detailed information on each of the manuscripts see BURKART, 2014.
4   GROEBNER, 2007.
5   Wolfgang Sofsky distinguishes between the active (and violent) "Körper" and the passive "Leib" that is harmed. See SOFSKY, 2005, p. 31.

To keep the desired ethnographic perspective, historians have to be highly aware of these modern, yet timeless narrative schemes. To tell (hi)stories you will mostly need protagonists. However, if these protagonists are medieval knights or fencing masters, some modern authors seem to adopt a rather admiring perspective. The narrative scheme of fictional, heroic violence in combination with romanticist images of knights in shining armour or Shakespearean villains thus affects the way in which modern models of the past are constructed. As the present contribution is also dealing with fencing masters and their knightly clients, it has to be made clear that these are not the heroes of our story. They simply were premodern violence professionals which have left interesting treatises documenting their physical skills as well as their style of self-fashioning. In contrast, the real protagonists of this paper are the fight books themselves. They emerged in a social context where academics or other people highly skilled in the use of media cooperated with these violence professionals. The central question of this contribution therefore is: how did these people try to represent a complex fighting system using texts and depictions?

To answer this question I shall first introduce the five surviving manuscripts. Subsequently, the terms "fight book" and "fighting system" will be discussed to address the process of transition from a subjective embodied knowledge to the written and depicted documentation of a didactic system. I hereby rely on the works of Michael Polanyi[6] and a series of three articles written by Jan-Dirk Müller, who first treated the medial transition from practical fighting to speech and from speech to writing in a series of articles in the 1990s.[7] I shall combine these observations with Polanyi's concept of "tacit knowing" and finally suggest possible situations of reception, for which the fight books of Hans Talhofer once were created.

---

6   POLANYI, 1958; POLANYI, 1966.
7   MÜLLER, 1992a; MÜLLER, 1992b; MÜLLER, 1994.

The Fight Books of Hans Talhofer

Between 1443 and 1467 CE, five extensive illuminated manuscripts were composed which depict a broad spectrum of armed and unarmed fighting techniques in large-sized drawings.[8] The treatises explicitly link these techniques to the fencing master Hans Talhofer. Four of them contain pictorial representations of Talhofer, who is displayed as author of the described fighting system (see fig. 1).

Yet the biography of the historic Hans Talhofer (also: Talhoffer, Dalhofer) remains a desideratum and further research is urgently needed. He is traceable in the sources between 1433 and 1482 and seems to have been a member of the German fencing fraternity "brotherhood of our dear lady and pure Virgin Mary and the Holy and warlike heavenly prince Saint Mark", also referred to as the "Marx brothers". This guild-like organisation was the first of its kind to receive an imperial privilege by Frederick III in 1487, granting it the exclusive right of promoting a fighter to the rank of "master of the long sword". For this purpose, the fraternity members met once a year in Frankfurt to elect their captain and to examine the candidates in various styles of fighting.[9]

As many facts about Talhofer's biography are still unknown, previous researchers tried to deduce several features of his personality from the manuscripts. Especially Hans-Peter Hils, one of the few early

---

8   The five surviving 15th century manuscripts that were probably created during Talhofer's lifetime will below be denoted by abbreviations referring to the city of the holding institution: TG – Gotha, Universitäts- und Forschungsbibliothek Erfurt/Gotha, Chart. A 558; TK – Königseggwald, Gräfliches Schloss, Hs. XIX, 17-3; TB – Berlin, Kupferstichkabinett der Stiftung Preußischer Kulturbesitz, 78 A 15; TKø – København, Kongelige Bibliotek, Thott 290 2°; TM – München, Bayerische Staatsbibliothek, Cod. icon. 394a. Cf. LENG, 2008, pp. 35–62. TG and TK have been published as facsimile-editions: HERGSELL, 1889; KÖNIGSEGG-AULENDORF/SCHULZE 2010. The scans of TKø and TM are available online: TKø (http://www.kb.dk/erez4/fsi4/fsi.swf?pages_server=http://www.kb.dk/erez4&pages_dir =online_master_arkiv_5/non-archival/Manus/VMANUS/2009/maj/thott-2_290, 05.03.2016); TM (http://nbn-resolving.de/urn:nbn:de:bvb:12-bsb00020451-7, 05.03.2016).
9   On Hans Talhofer and his manuscripts see HILS, 1983; HILS, 1985c, pp. 161-183; HILS, 1985a; HILS, 1986; HILS, 1995; KEIL, 1995; STANGIER, 2009; JAQUET, 2013, vol. I, pp. 196-207.

researchers on fight books who published a doctoral thesis on the subject in 1985, identified several figures in the treatises (in addition to those explicitly denominated) as self-representations of the fencing master. In manuscript TK, he also saw a retrospective documentation of an actual judicial combat[10] fought between the addressee of the treatise and his anonymous enemy. I have argued for a more sceptical reading of these manuscripts.[11] The figures in question are not marked as representations of the author and fencing master, contrary to those figures in the same treatises that are explicitly denominated by a caption or identified by Talhofer's coat of arms. The fight books are furthermore not naturalistic depictions of real fights, but highly normative documents that present an ideal way of fighting according to a didactic system.

To understand the content of Talhofer's treatises, it is important to first introduce fight books as a genre of specialised technical literature that originated around the beginning of the 14th century. According to Daniel Jaquet's definition, I designate any written account on theory and practice of armed and unarmed combat with or without depictions as a fight book.[12] However, the contemporary late medieval term "fechtbuch" should not hide the fact that the early 14th and 15th century fight books in particular form a very heterogeneous corpus of sources with distinct addressees and communication strategies. The larger part has to be attributed to a pragmatic context of use, yet there are some surviving copies that were designed for princely courts and their demand for prestigious objects. Mere text manuscripts without any depictions exist, but they are an exception. The usually included drawings are often of inferior quality, which supports the assumption of a pragmatic context of use for a large part of these manuscripts.[13]

Thus, the situations of reception of the fight books have to be conceptualised in a very broad and open manner, leaving it to a detailed dissection of the concrete evidence to determine its intended purpose(s).

---

10 NEUMANN, 2010; NEUMANN, 2012. See also the contribution of Daniel Jaquet in this volume.
11 I tried to correct some persisting errors regarding the number of pictorial self-representations of Talhofer and the deduced conclusions on his personality in my abovementioned article BURKART, 2014.
12 JAQUET, 2013, vol. I, pp. 18–20.
13 LENG, 2008, pp. 1–5.

The spectrum encompasses combinations of a pragmatic recording of concrete body techniques for practitioners[14] to the documentation of princely status by showing affinity to martial culture and the display of splendour through prestigious illuminations.

The five 15th century manuscripts linked to Hans Talhofer fit very well into this spectrum of possible purposes. All manuscripts have in common that they depict a large number of fighting techniques for various situations. The curriculum comprises judicial combat in armour with spear, long sword and dagger, judicial combat with large shields and clubs or swords, judicial combat of a woman against a man, armoured fighting with staff weapons, unarmoured combat with sword and small shield (*Buckler*), techniques with single handed and single edged blades (*langes Messer*, long knife), unarmed combat, fighting with daggers, mounted techniques with various weapons and spontaneous situations of self-defence.

Talhofer's fight books can be grouped in different ways, depending on the applied criteria. Two of them, TG (ca. 1443/1448) and TKø (1459), were probably personal manuscripts owned by Talhofer himself to serve as compendia and as archetypes for the other manuscripts.[15] They are the only treatises to contain versified teachings of Talhofer's influential predecessor, the martial arts teacher Johannes Liechtenauer, whose fighting system is traceable in fight books from the late 14th to the 17th century.[16] TG and TKø also collect other useful information apart from fighting techniques, such as texts on divination or depictions of military and other technical equipment from the Bellifortis tradition.

Two other manuscripts are so congruent in their overall structure and most of the drawings that one might think of some sort of serial production. TK and TB (ca. 1451) also depict various sets of techniques, but they especially focus on the preparation of noblemen for a judicial combat in full armour.[17] The addressees of the manuscripts are furthermore represented as combatants in the drawings and are identified by their coat of arms and their denomination in the captions. These personalised treatises seem to document the martial education of

---

14 A good example ist the manuscript 3227a from the Germanisches Nationalmuseum in Nuremberg. See BURKART, 2016.
15 BURKART, 2014, pp. 276-279, 286-292.
16 WIERSCHIN, 1965; HILS, 1985b; HILS, 1985c; LENG, 2008, pp. 5-22.
17 BURKART, 2014, pp. 279-286.

a certain Luthold von Königsegg (TK) and the brothers David and Buppelin vom Stain (TB), who are depicted as disciples alongside master Talhofer.

The latest manuscript TM (before 1467) shares common and distinct features with these two groups.[18] The quality of the drawings and the broad spectrum of depicted techniques are similar to Talhofer's personal treatise TKø. Yet, TM is the only manuscript executed in vellum and contains neither varia nor text paragraphs. Apart from a representation of Talhofer on the last folio, no figures are specified by denomination. However, the coat of arms of the first possessor Eberhard im Bart (1445-1496), count and later duke of Württemberg, was inserted after the completion of the manuscript in 1467. Although TM does not illustrate the process of martial formation of a depicted addressee, it certainly belongs to the group of fight books in the possession of one of Talhofer's disciples. Another indication strengthening this reading is an entry in the accounts of Eberhard im Bart. In the account book for the years 1467-1469, the undated payment of a certain sum to a "Talhofer" is mentioned, who is listed among the simple servants ("lön der einspendig knecht").[19]

Another important aspect of fight books is the situational context for which the described fighting techniques were suitable. Interpersonal violence as human practice is always governed (yet not determined) by social norms.[20] If we thus look at the depicted techniques and try to deduce the situations for which they seem suitable and which (explicit and implicit) norms of fighting seem to be in force, we obtain further information on the social context of the respective fighting system. Talhofer's system, as it is depicted in the five manuscripts, was not

---

18 BURKART, 2014, pp. 293-297.
19 Stuttgart, Hauptstaatsarchiv, A 602 Nr 286 = WR 286, fol. 21r. Online: http://www.landesarchiv-bw.de/plink/?f=1-22511, (03.04.2016). I would like to thank Jens-Peter Kleinau (Frankfurt a.M.) for pointing me at this entry.
20 From the perspective of social constructivism, norms are closely related to identities. See CANCIAN, 1975, pp. 135–159. A survey on the connection between norms of fighting and the related identities of social groups thus seems promising. For this perspective see several contributions in the proceedings of the international conference "Agon und Distinktion. Soziale Räume des Zweikampfes zwischen Mittelalter und Neuzeit": ISRAEL/ JASER, 2015.

designed for a playful or sport-like context of use. It seems to aim at serious fights and situations of extreme and life threatening violence. The manuscripts especially focus on the situational context of the violent, but explicitly regulated judicial combat (see fig. 2) and also cover spontaneous situations of self defence against better armed assailants.[21]

Terms and Concepts: Fighting Systems and Communication Strategies for Tacit Knowledge

If we now return to the initial question of how fighters of the past used their bodies in battle, we first have to look at the type of information actually documented in the fight books. Hans Peter Hils stated that TK was the retrospective documentation of an actual judicial combat fought between Luthold von Königsegg and his unknown adversary.[22] The comparison of TK with the other manuscripts, especially with TB, makes this assumption highly questionable.[23]

Fight books neither document real events nor a past fighting practice. On the contrary, I would argue that they contain descriptions of didactic systems designed for the documentation and transmission of fighting skills. These systems are usually authorised by the evocation of a master such as Hans Talhofer or Johannes Liechtenauer, who is presented as their founder.[24] In the fight books, the practical knowledge and skill attributed to such authoritative figures works as a mean to certify the described system itself and to prove its effectiveness in combat. This context also explains the striking attempts of self-fashioning in many fight books and the fact that some of them also contain means to cope with the contingent outcome of actual fights (such as the short divinatory manuals inserted in TG and TKø).

---

21 See especially TKø, fols. 76v, 77r and TM fol. 121v.
22 HILS, 1983, pp. 102, 116.
23 BURKART, 2014, p. 283.
24 BAUER, 2014.

To address the relationship between past fighting practices and the content of the fight books, I would like to propose the following terms: Firstly, we have to distinguish between

- actual *fighting practice* in contingent confrontations between two or more opponents
- *body techniques of combat* as ideal-types of movements in combat that are often denominated to facilitate communication and
- *fighting systems* as didactic selections and combinations of certain sets of favoured body techniques.

These three items can be understood as elements of what I would like to call a *culture of fighting*. Based on a knowledge-oriented definition of culture[25], the term culture of fighting also comprises the contemporary symbolic orders that organise the subjective realities of the fighters and thus enable and restrict their action. A fighting system is therefore a very complex phenomenon, both on a technical as well as on a social level.[26] On a technical level, it is a selection of techniques that enables its practitioners to prevail in a situation of interpersonal violence. Yet, the concrete structure of a specific system is based on multiple factors: What is the anticipated situation of combat (sportive competition, military confrontation, ritualised duel, spontaneous self-defence, etc.)? What likely threats are identified (unarmed attackers, fights with bladed weapons, with guns/projectile weapons, against multiple opponents)?

---

25 RECKWITZ, 2012, pp. 84-90.
26 Scientific research on cultures of fighting has recently become more and more popular within academia. In 2011 the interdisciplinary *Commission for Martial Arts & Combat Sports* (Kommission Kampfkunst & Kampfsport) was founded within the *German Association for Sports Science* (Deutsche Vereinigung für Sportwissenschaft – dvs). Two years later, the independent academic journal *Acta Periodica Duellatorum* (APD) published its first volume dedicated to Historical European Martial Arts studies. Then, in 2015, the interdisciplinary journal *Martial Arts Studies* was founded by Paul Bowman and Benjamin Judkins. The scientific approach towards martial arts – in this article I prefer to use the wider term cultures of fighting – has much benefitted from the stimuli of cultural studies (BOWMAN, 2015), religious studies (BERG/PROHL, 2014; BERG, 2015), cultural history/Kulturwissenschaft (WETZLER, 2014; WETZLER, 2015) and anthropology (FARRER/WHALEN-BRIDGE, 2011) to mention just a few publications.

How are the physical and mental prerequisites of the practitioners conceptualised? What equipment is required to use the system? How much time is available for the formation of practitioners? Based on these and other settings in combination with strategic and tactical considerations, a specific system is intentionally designed, evolves naturally or is adapted within a given historical culture of fighting.[27] But, being a cultural phenomenon, these selections of techniques and strategies are based on a specific mind-set that symbolically organises the world of the practitioners and establishes distinct patterns of meaning. The main frame of a fighting system is therefore a set of assumptions on the nature of combat itself. It is a model for reality, reduced in complexity and formulated in the terms of a struggle between success and defeat, or – life and death. That is why studies on fighting systems from a historical, transdisciplinary and transcultural perspective promise very interesting insights in the specific cultures in which they emerged.

Fight books as medial attempts to codify fighting systems are yet facing a twofold paradox. First of all, fights are contingent situations. At least two individuals are struggling for physical superiority and the conservation of their particular corporal integrity. As the reactions of an opponent are ultimately unpredictable, a fighting system cannot guarantee what its practitioners are usually longing for – a strategy that secures the personal superiority and integrity in all possible situations. The specific system can therefore only be a codification of ideal-type solutions to ideal-type threats. It serves as a didactic tool to reduce complexity and to facilitate communication. By the use of a system, the contingent situation of combat thus becomes describable and manageable for the practitioners.

The second paradox is related to the communication of subjective skill in contrast to objective knowledge. Following the works of Michael Polanyi, the fighting skills of competent instructors such as Hans Talhofer represent a form of "tacit knowing" that is bound to

---

27 See the contribution of Daniel Jaquet in this volume. His description of judicial combat illustrates, how a specific fighting system was created just for these occasions and how it was promoted by late medieval fencing masters.

personal experience and cannot be fully verbalised.[28] Thus, it should not be possible to satisfactorily describe the art of fighting with written or spoken words as Polanyi states:

> "Rules of an art can be useful, but they do not determine the practice of an art; they are maxims, which can serve as a guide to an art only if they can be integrated into practical knowledge of the art. They cannot replace this knowledge. [...] An art which cannot be specified in detail cannot be transmitted by prescription, since no prescription for it exists. It can be passed on only by example from master to apprentice. This restricts the range of diffusion to that of personal contacts."[29]

Fighting techniques as techniques of the body[30] are socially transmitted and acquired through complex processes of implicit and explicit learning. At a basic level, fighters of the past were socialised into certain ways of using their bodies in combat. For this type of learning, descriptions and depictions were irrelevant. The only thing that mattered was skill and personal contact with other skilled fighters to allow learning by imitation. However, if we look at the fight books, we are confronted with a specialised technical language and elaborated medial attempts to codify technical skills. We are thus looking at the remaining traces of explicit learning. Experienced fighters or professional instructors condensed their skills into certain concepts of how techniques of the body worked and made attempts to describe this knowledge within the fight books.

---

28 An example given by Polanyi is the skill to ride a bycicle. The capability to keep one's balance when starting represents a body technique that can only partially be explained by description or demonstration. First of all it has to be experienced with one's own body. Only through this experience the technique becomes a form of personal knowledge that is bound to the individual experience of body movement and that cannot be described by just explaining the physical mechanisms at work (as a form of explicit knowledge). POLANYI, 1958, pp. 49f. Nearly all aspects of martial formation face the same difficulties.
29 POLANYI, 1958, pp. 50, 53.
30 In his article first published in 1935, Marcel Mauss defines the term as "the ways in which from society to society men know how to use their bodies" (MAUSS, 1979, p. 70).

The communication structures of these treatises were first analysed by Jan-Dirk Müller in the above mentioned series of articles.[31] He identifies three key elements used in medieval fight books: shortened and encrypted mnemonic verses, descriptions in prose and drawn depictions. According to Müller, the didactic tradition seems to have had its origin in orally transmitted verses used by fencing masters to structure the formation of their students. These verses were meanwhile or afterwards secured by writing them down as *zedel* (note, derived from Latin *schedula*). They mainly consisted of specialised technical terms and were intentionally shortened and encrypted to ensure that only initiates could understand them.[32] The central part, i.e. the actual information about fighting techniques and strategies, therefore had to be present outside of the verses in the person of an already skilled practitioner or teacher. The verses only served as mnemonic anchors that helped to memorise and organise practical knowledge.[33]

In the medieval sources, the verses mainly survived in combination with an interpreting glossation.[34] In the text, the glosses fulfil the function a competent teacher would have fulfilled in a face-to-face

---

31 See note 7.
32 A good example is the presumably oldest version of those verses in a late 14th century commonplace book: "Das ist der text in deme her nennet dy fuenff hewe (...). Das ist von deme Czornhawe: Der dir oberhawet / czornhaw ort deme drewet. Wirt her is gewar / nym is oben ab ane vaer." (This is the text in which he [Liechtenauer] mentions the five strikes [...]. This is about the wrath-strike: An opponent who attacks you with a strike from above / he will be threatened by the point of your wrath-strike. Does he realize it / take it up above without any danger.) Nürnberg, Germanisches Nationalmuseum, Hs. 3227a, fol. 23r.
33 Talhofer's personal fight books for example contain copies of the verses of Johannes Liechtenauer (TG, fol. 18r-20v; TKø, fol. 2r-7v). But TKø and the manuscript for Luthold von Königsegg also present Talhofer's own short verses mimicking the style of the Liechtenauerian system (TKø, fol. 1rv; TK, fol. 1v).
34 See again the commonplace book from Nuremberg: "Glosa: Hie merke und wisse das lichtenawer eyn oberhaw slecht von der achsel heisset den czornhaw. Wen eym itzlichem in syme grymme und czorne zo ist im keyn haw als bereit als der selbe." (Glosa: Here you should note and know that Lichtenauer calls a simple strike from above coming directly from the shoulder a wrath-strike. As anyone in his grim and wrath uses this strike instinctively.) Nürnberg, Germanisches Nationalmuseum, Hs. 3227a, fol. 23v.

situation. Like the fencing master, the glosses interpret the encrypted verses and translate them into a concrete description of body movements in prose. While the verses only work as a reference to knowledge of movements, knowledge they do not contain themselves, the glosses do include more detailed information about the referenced techniques. Just as a written fixation of the didactic verses in form of a *zedel* could have preserved the text and relieved the memory of teachers and students alike, the written glossation also relieves the memory of a practitioner by linking the mnemonic anchors in the verses with textual descriptions of movements and techniques.

Another possibility to represent fighting techniques is the use of didactic images. Like the glossation, the images contain a lot more information on the referenced techniques than the verses. Some fight books, such as one copy of the system of long knife fighting attributed to Hans Lecküchner[35], combine images, verses and descriptions in prose. In the case of Talhofer's manuscripts, the images are only accompanied by short captions. They usually denominate the depicted action but seldom add further information on the execution of the technique. Only very few images are serial and depict stages of one motion or a sequence of motions. The main part of the drawings shows a crucial moment in the execution of an action. The single picture therefore works as a symbol for a complex fighting technique (see fig. 3).

I therefore argue that, in comparison with the mere textual tradition of Johannes Liechtenauer, the images in Talhofer's treatises combine the mnemonic function of the verses with the explanatory function of the glosses. The copies of Liechtenauer's verses in the personal manuscripts TG and TKø show that the system of Talhofer was closely connected to or even originated in the teachings of Johannes Liechtenauer. However, a glossation of the mnemonic verses is missing entirely in all of Talhofer's manuscripts. Instead, the image takes up the task to transmit the actual information on the movements.[36]

Especially the high-quality drawings of the latest manuscript TM activate their reader's motor imagery (see fig. 4). However, compared to the Liechtenauerian glosses, the almost uncommented images are not

---

35 LENG, 2008, pp. 73-77.
36 MÜLLER, 1992a, p. 271.

capable of transmitting tactical information and of linking complex motion sequences.[37] With the quite exact depiction of bodily postures, the image has more to offer than the text. Yet, like the intentionally encrypted mnemonic verses of Liechtenauer, the images of Talhofer require the possession of prior specialised knowledge (i.e. the interpreter is already a skilled fighter who knows Talhofer's system) to be understood as representations of complex fighting techniques. Another option would be the presence of an expert who is able to provide the necessary explanations and demonstrate and correct the movements. Like the verses of Liechtenauer, the images of Talhofer should therefore be primarily understood as mnemonic references for a (tacit) knowledge of motor skills that the contemporary interpreters already possessed.

The key to understand Talhofer's fight books is therefore the conceptualisation of the situation of reception for which they once were created. My point is that they were not designated for a communication *through* the book between absentees, but that they should serve as a medium for a communication *about* the book between attendees. The pictorial representations of the addressees in TK and TB as well as the entry in the accounts of Eberhard im Bart suggest that these young nobles were personally trained by Hans Talhofer. If this is correct, the transmission of skills would have taken place in a face-to-face situation of practical instruction. Consequently, the surviving fight books merely played an auxiliary role. They served – just as Liechtenauer's encrypted verses for the initiates of his system – as mnemonic anchors to recapitulate the already learned lessons. Instead of resorting to verses for the organisation of practical knowledge, Talhofer uses the more evident image. The acquired fighting skills of his students thus become "(re)presentable". The illuminated fight books document that their addressees must be reckoned as competent fighters and disciples of the fencing master Talhofer. The book therefore also serves as an objectivation of the symbolic capital of master and apprentice alike.

---

37 MÜLLER, 1994, pp. 371-374.

Conclusion: What Fight Books tell us about Bodies in Battle

Interpreting the late medieval fight books of Hans Talhofer as representations of moving bodies in battle has proven quite challenging, if not impossible. The images – as well as the encrypted verses in the Liechtenauerian tradition – only refer to embodied knowledge which they themselves do not (or only partially) transmit. A successful understanding and an adequate reconstruction of the depicted techniques would therefore require the explanations of a skilled contemporary expert.

Following the works of Michael Polanyi, we can furthermore conclude that media referring to fighting systems are always incomplete. They have to be, because the implicit knowledge or tacit knowing to which they refer cannot be fully verbalised or depicted. So, despite the late medieval tendencies to theorise and document fighting systems, the communicational gap between the skilled practitioner and its audience persists. This is perhaps best illustrated by a citation from one of the first glossators of the Liechtenauerian verses written around the year 1389:

"Also note this and know that one cannot truly and meaningfully speak or write about fighting. Yet you can show and demonstrate it with the hand. Therefore open up your senses and consider it even more. And practise it the more in training, so the easier you will remember it in serious fights. As practice is better than art, because practice might prove useful without art, but art will not prove useful without practice."[38]

---

38 "Auch merke das / und wisse das man nicht gar eygentlich und bedewtlich von dem fechten mag sagen und schreiben ader aus legen / als man is wol mag czeigen und weisen mit der hant. Dorumme tu of dyne synnen und betrachte is deste bas. Und ube dich dorynne deste mer yn schimpfe / zo gedenkestu ir deste bas in ernste. Wen ubunge ist besser wenne kunst / denne ůbunge tawg wol ane kunst aber kunst tawg nicht wol ane ůbunge." Nürnberg, Germanisches Nationalmuseum, Hs. 3227a, fol. 15r.

If we take this one step further, we see that what is documented in the fight books is neither skill nor a volatile fighting practice. The fight books primarily contain auxiliary means of communication that enable practitioners to talk about *their* subjective skills. Fight books can therefore – no matter whether they use mnemonic verses, a textual description of body movements in prose or drawings – only refer to practical know-how that they do not contain themselves. With regard to bodies in battle, they remain tacit. However, they tell us a lot about the ways in which people imagined battle and tried to prepare for it by organising their embodied knowledge.

Illustrations

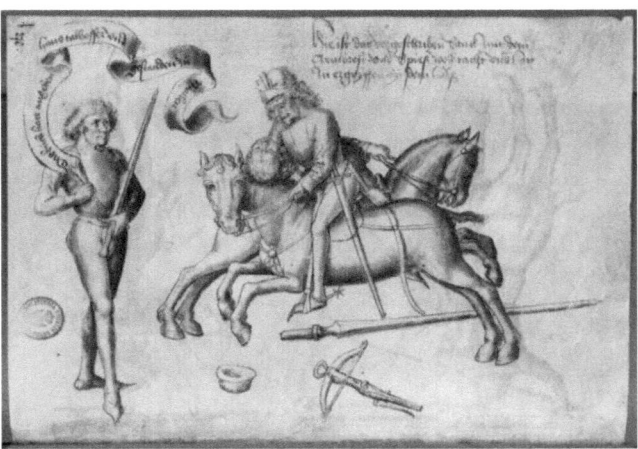

Fig. 1: Hans Talhofer, Fechtbuch, 1467. Bayerische Staatsbibliothek München, Cod.icon. 394 a, fol. 136v, urn:nbn:de:bvb:12-bsb00020451-7

Body Techniques of Combat

Fig. 2: Hans Talhofer, Fechtbuch, 1467. Bayerische Staatsbibliothek München, Cod.icon. 394 a, fol. 38r, urn:nbn:de:bvb:12-bsb00020451-7

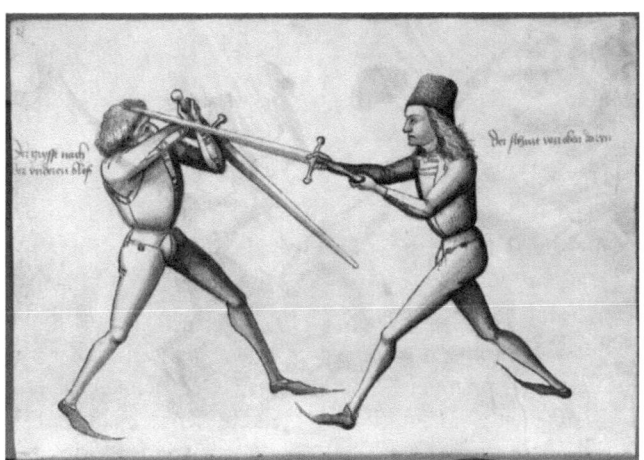

Fig. 3: Hans Talhofer, Fechtbuch, 1467. Bayerische Staatsbibliothek München, Cod.icon. 394 a, fol. 12r, urn:nbn:de:bvb:12-bsb00020451-7

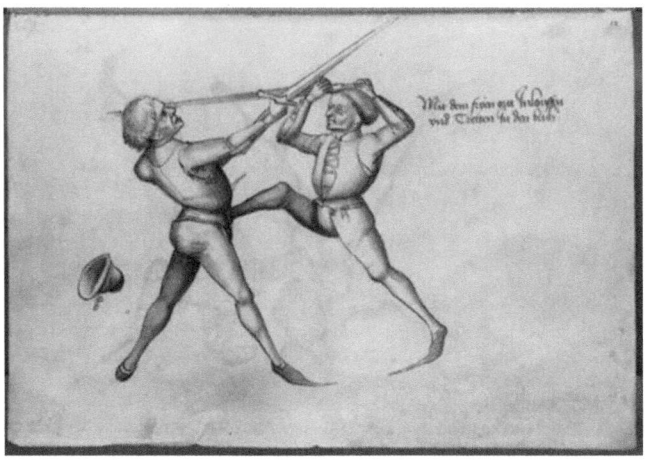

Fig. 4: Hans Talhofer, Fechtbuch, 1467. Bayerische Staatsbibliothek München, Cod.icon. 394 a, fol. 7v, urn:nbn:de:bvb:12-bsb00020451-7

Bibliography

Literature

BAUER, MATTHIAS JOHANNES, "Einen Zedel fechter ich mich ruem / Im Schwerd vnd Messer vngestuem". Fechtmeister als Protagonisten und als (fach-)literarisches Motiv in den deutschsprachigen Fechtlehren des Mittelalters und der Frühen Neuzeit, in: Zweikämpfer: Fechtmeister – Kämpen – Samurai (Das Mittelalter. Perspektiven mediävistischer Forschung 19/2), ed. by UWE ISRAEL/CHRISTIAN JASER, Berlin 2014, pp. 302-325.

BERG, ESTHER, Martial Arts, Medien und Materiale Religion. Kampfkunst als Gegenstand religionswissenschaftlicher Forschung, in: Religion in Ex-Position. Eine religionswissenschaftliche Ausstellung (Universitätsmuseum Heidelberg – Kataloge 11), ed. by CARINA BRANKOVIĆ et al., Heidelberg 2015, pp 78-81.

BERG, ESTHER/PROHL, INKEN, 'Become your Best'. On the Construction of Martial Arts as Means of Self-Actualization and Self-Improvement, in: JOMEC Journal 5 (2014). http://www.cardiff.ac.uk/jomec/jomecjournal/5june2014/Berg_Prohl.pdf, (12.04.16).

BOFFA, SERGIO, Les manuels de combat. Fechtbücher et Ringbücher (Typologie des sources du Moyen Âge occidental 87), Turnhout 2014.

BOWMAN, PAUL, Martial Arts Studies. Disrupting Disciplinary Boundaries (Disruptions), London 2015.

BURKART, ERIC, The Autograph of an Erudite Martial Artist. A Close Reading of Nuremberg, Germanisches Nationalmuseum, Hs. 3227a, in: Late Medieval and Early Modern Fight Books. Transmission and Tradition of Martial Arts in Europe (14th-17th Centuries) (History of Warfare 112), ed. by DANIEL JAQUET et al., Leiden 2016, pp. 451-480.

ID., Die Aufzeichnung des Nicht-Sagbaren. Annäherung an die kommunikative Funktion der Bilder in den Fechtbüchern des Hans Talhofer, in: Zweikämpfer: Fechtmeister – Kämpen – Samurai (Das Mittelalter. Perspektiven mediävistischer Forschung 19/2), ed. by UWE ISRAEL/CHRISTIAN JASER, Berlin 2014, pp. 253-301.

CANCIAN, FRANCESCA, What are Norms? A Study of Beliefs and Action in a Maya Community, London 1975.

FARRER, DOUGLAS/WHALEN-BRIDGE, JOHN (eds.), Martial Arts as Embodied Knowledge. Asian Traditions in a Transnational World, Albany 2011.

GROEBNER, VALENTIN, Schock, Abscheu, schickes Thema. Die Kulturwissenschaften und die Gewalt, in: Zeitschrift für Ideengeschichte 1/3 (2007), pp. 70-83.

HERGSELL, GUSTAV (ed.), Talhoffers Fechtbuch (Gothaer Codex) aus dem Jahre 1443. Gerichtliche und andere Zweikämpfe darstellend, Prag 1889.

HILS, HANS-PETER, Reflexionen zum Stand der hauptberuflichen Fechter des Späten Mittelalters unter Berücksichtigung historischer Rechtsquellen, in: Würzburger Fachprosa-Studien. Beiträge zur mittelalterlichen Medizin-, Pharmazie- und Standesgeschichte aus dem Würzburger medizinhistorischen Institut (Würzburger medizinhistorische Forschungen 38), ed. by GUNDOLF KEIL, Würzburg 1995, pp. 201-215.

ID., "Kempen unde er Kinder ... de sin alle rechtelos". Zur sozialen und rechtlichen Stellung der Fechtmeister im späten Mittelalter, in: Zusammenhänge, Einflüsse, Wirkungen. Kongressakten zum ersten Symposium des Mediävistenverbandes in Tübingen, 1984, ed. by JOERG FICHTE et al., Berlin 1986, pp. 255-271.

ID., "Der da sigelos wirt, dem sleht man die hant ab". Zum Stand der hauptberuflichen Fechter nach mittelalterlichen Rechtsquellen, in: Zeitschrift der Savigny-Stiftung für Rechtsgeschichte, Germanistische Abteilung 102 (1985a), pp. 328-340.

ID., Liechtenauer, Johannes, in: Die deutsche Literatur des Mittelalters/ Verfasserlexikon, 2nd ed., vol. 5 (1985b), pp. 811-816.

ID., Meister Johann Liechtenauers Kunst des langen Schwertes (Europäische Hochschulschriften. Reihe 3: Geschichte und ihre Hilfswissenschaften 257), Frankfurt am Main et al. 1985c.

ID., Die Handschriften des oberdeutschen Fechtmeisters Hans Talhoffer, in: Codices manuscripti 9-3 (1983), pp. 97-121.

ISRAEL, UWE/JASER, CHRISTIAN (eds.), Agon und Distinktion. Soziale Räume des Zweikampfs zwischen Mittelalter und Neuzeit (Geschichte, Forschung und Wissenschaft 47), Berlin/Münster 2015.

JAQUET, DANIEL, Combattre en armure à la fin du Moyen Âge et au début de la Renaissance d'après les livres du combat. Thèse de doctorat, Université de Genève 2013.

KEIL, GUNDOLF, Talhofer, Hans, in: Die deutsche Literatur des Mittelalters / Verfasserlexikon, 2nd ed., vol. 9 (1995), pp. 592-595.

KÖNIGSEGG-AULENDORF, JOHANNES ZU/SCHULZE, ANDRÉ (eds.), Der Königsegger Codex. Die Fechthandschrift des Hauses Königsegg (HS XIX, 17-3), Darmstadt 2010.

LENG, RAINER, Fecht- und Ringbücher (Katalog der deutschsprachigen illustrierten Handschriften des Mittelalters, Bd. 4/2, Lfg. 1/2, Stoffgr. 38), München 2008.

MALLINCKRODT, REBEKKA VON (ed.), Bewegtes Leben. Körpertechniken in der Frühen Neuzeit (Ausstellungskataloge der Herzog-August-Bibliothek 89), Wiesbaden 2008.

MAUSS, MARCEL, Body Techniques, in: ID., Sociology and psychology. Essays, transl. by Ben Brewster, London et al. 1979, pp. 95-123.

MÜLLER, JAN-DIRK, Hans Lecküchners Messerfechtlehre und die Tradition. Schriftliche Anweisungen für eine praktische Disziplin, in: Wissen für den Hof. Der spätmittelalterliche Verschriftungsprozeß am Beispiel Heidelberg im 15. Jahrhundert (Münstersche Mittelalter-Schriften 67), ed. by ID., München 1994, pp. 355-384.

ID., Bild – Vers – Prosakommentar am Beispiel von Fechtbüchern. Probleme der Verschriftlichung einer schriftlosen Praxis, in: Pragmatische Schriftlichkeit im Mittelalter. Erscheinungsformen und Entwicklungsstufen (Münstersche Mittelalter-Schriften 65), ed. by HAGEN KELLER et al., München 1992a, pp. 251-282.

ID., Zwischen mündlicher Anweisung und schriftlicher Sicherung von Tradition. Zur Kommunikationsstruktur spätmittelalterlicher Fechtbücher, in: Kommunikation und Alltag in Spätmittelalter und früher Neuzeit (Veröffentlichungen des Instituts für Realienkunde des Mittelalters und der Frühen Neuzeit 15), ed. by. HELMUT HUNDSBICHLER, München 1992b, pp. 379-400.

NEUMANN, SARAH, Der gerichtliche Zweikampf. Gottesurteil, Wettstreit, Ehrensache (Mittelalter-Forschungen 31), Ostfildern 2010.

NEUMANN, SARAH, Vom Gottesurteil zur Ehrensache? Deutungsvarianten des gerichtlichen Zweikampfes im Mittelalter, in: Das Duell. Ehrenkämpfe vom Mittelalter bis zur Moderne (Konflikte und Kultur – Historische Perspektiven 23), ed. by ULRIKE LUDWIG et al., Konstanz 2012.

POLANYI, MICHAEL, The Tacit Dimension. Chicago 1966.

ID., Personal Knowledge. Towards a Post-Critical Philosophy, Chicago 1958.

RECKWITZ, ANDREAS, Die Transformation der Kulturtheorien. Zur Entwicklung eines Theorieprogramms, 3rd ed., Weilerswist 2012.

SOFSKY, WOLFGANG, Traktat über die Gewalt. Frankfurt am Main 2005.

SPATZ, BEN, What a Body Can Do. Technique as Knowledge, Practice as Research, Abingdon 2015.

STANGIER, THOMAS, "Ich hab ein hertz als ein leb...". Zweikampfrealität und Tugendideal in den Fechtbüchern Hans Talhoffers und Paul Kals, in: Ritterwelten im Spätmittelalter. Höfisch-ritterliche

Kultur der Reichen Herzöge von Bayern-Landshut (Schriften aus den Museen der Stadt Landshut 29), Landshut 2009, pp. 73-93.

WETZLER, SIXT, Vergleichende Kampfkunstwissenschaft als historisch-kulturwissenschaftliche Disziplin. Mögliche Gegenstände, nötige Quellen, anzuwendende Methoden, in: Menschen im Zweikampf. Kampfkunst und Kampfsport in Lehre und Forschung (Schriften der Deutschen Vereinigung für Sportwissenschaft 236), Hamburg 2014, pp. 57-66.

WETZLER, SIXT, Martial Arts Studies as Kulturwissenschaft. A Possible Theoretical Framework, in: Martial Arts Studies 1 (2015), pp. 20-33.

WIERSCHIN, MARTIN, Meister Johann Liechtenauers Kunst des Fechtens (Münchener Texte und Untersuchungen zur deutschen Literatur des Mittelalters 13), München 1965.

Six Weeks to Prepare for Combat: Instruction and Practices from the Fight Books at the End of the Middle Ages, a Note on Ritualised Single Combats

DANIEL JAQUET

This contribution is following the first axis of the argumentation of the conference *Shaping Bodies for Battle*.[1] Several historians of medieval warfare complained about the lack of sources to delineate the training of men for battle,[2] as opposed to later periods, where a dedicated body of literature is available for the study of the soldiers' training.[3] However, in the specific context of late medieval ritualised single combat, including the various phenomena labelled as "judicial combat",

---

* I am thankful to Ariella Elema for her comments and corrections, and to Jens-Peter Kleinau for his research and collaboration on the texts of the appendices.
1 Underlying questions were formulated as follows: Which practices were used to make bodies fit for battle? What bodily techniques were taught and trained? What was seen as a fighter's ideal bodily appearance? How did fighters physically experience the shaping of their bodies?
2 For example, CONTAMINE, 2003, p. 364; KEEN, 1984, p. 238. See the recent contributions to this question in the very late 15th c. and early 16th c. in DERUELLE/GAINOT, 2013.
3 For a study of technical literature on the training of the soldier, see LAWRENCE, 2009.

some relevant information can be analysed to address the questions related to the preparation for battle, not only in narrative, but also in technical sources. These types of combat were indeed considered as "battle" (a dedicated form of warfare) in the late Medieval mind-set,[4] as they dealt with serious matters (*Ernst*) contrary to other forms of ritualised combat in a more playful fashion (*Schimpf*),[5] such as knightly games (tournaments, pas d'armes, jousts, etc.), or urban feasts including competitive sporting praxes (fencing schools, wrestling matches, mock battles, etc.). However, as argued in this contribution, all of those types of combats need to be studied together as part of the same phenomenon, diffracted by cultural habitus and societal contexts.

Therefore, I propose a study of selected instructions for the preparation for "judicial" combat found in the heterogeneous corpus of the Fight Books in the late Middle Ages,[6] which discuss not only knightly or princely single combats, but also those of the lower social strata. Moreover, I shall highlight three examples of those single combats for commoners out of a selected corpus of narrative, normative and pictorial documents in different geographical locations in the 15th c., in order to illustrate the instruction for combat found in the Fight Books. Both the relation of those fights and the technical content of the Fight Books also provide information about the fighting itself, which is less interesting for the purpose of this contribution. As a concluding point, the mutilation of the fighters as one common feature of the narration of the cases chosen can be highlighted in order to address issues concerning the representation of ritualised violence and about bodies in battle relevant for other interests in this volume.

---

4   For example, judicial combats are considered as such in the treatises of John of Legnano (1320-1383), Honorat Bovet (1340-1410), and Paris de Puteo (1410-1493). For a general discussion of these authors, see CAVINA, 2005, pp. 41-106.
5   For a comparison of those two types of circumstances in the perspective of ritualised combat, see JAQUET, 2016b and JASER/ISRAEL, 2014.
6   See the contribution of E. Burkart in this volume, as well as JAQUET, 2016a; BOFFA, 2014 and ANGLO, 2000.

Fighting for the truth, the proof of his cause or his honour

A widely accepted scholarly trend points out that the judicial duel or trial by battle tended to subside during the 15th c. to be replaced by the later duel of honour.[7] Recent works demonstrating that these forms of ritualised combat did indeed evolve, but with less rupture than was earlier believed have refined this postulate.[8] The point has been made that both temporal and spiritual powers attempted to limit the trial by combat as a lawful way of resolving conflicts, alongside the prohibition of the ordeal from the end of the 12th c. onward.[9] However, the aristocracy who still claimed to be entitled to resolve conflicts through ritualised combat as part of their hereditary and status privileges raised strong opposing voices.[10] The thirteenth and fourteenth centuries witnessed repeated prohibitions or limitations as authorities attempted to constrain those types of combat to very specific cases.[11] The practice of hiring a champion to settle legal grudges also appeared to decrease.[12] The late fourteenth century combats of Carrouges versus Le Gris[13] or Estravayer versus Grandson[14] are believed to be among the "last" trials by combat for the aristocracy and, if the often quoted passage of Olivier de la Marche[15] is to be trusted, would have fallen into disgrace by the

---

7 NOTTARP, 1956; MOREL, 1984.
8 CAVINA, 2003 and 2005; ISRAEL, 2008; HILTMAN/ISRAEL, 2007; ISRAEL/ORTALLI, 2009; NEUMANN, 2010; ELEMA, 2012; LUDWIG et al. (eds.), 2012.
9 MCAULEY, 2006, pp. 473-513.
10 STANGIER, 2009, pp. 75 and 78.
11 See the discussion about those circumventions in HILTMAN/ISRAEL, 2007, pp. 65-84 and TELLIER, 2012, pp. 107-121.
12 See the discussion about the historiography in JASER, 2014, pp. 380-406. See also ISRAEL, 2008, pp. 121-147.
13 GUENÉE, 1995, pp. 331-343 and PARAVICINI, 2016, pp. 23-84.
14 BERGUERAND, 2008.
15 [...] *car peu de gens vivans ont veu l'exécution de gaige de bataille, et a plus de soixante et dix an que, soubz ceste maison de Bourgongne, ne fut telle œuvre exécutée entre deux nobles hommes. Et moy qui ay demouré en ceste noble maison près de soixante ans, je ne veis de ma vie gaige de bataille.* Ed. PROST, 1878, p. 20. To be noted that this quote is only valid for aristocracy (entre deux nobles hommes). La Marche witnessed at least

end of the fifteenth century. However, "judicial combat" was still found in the 15th c. as a procedure codified in various customary laws, as an object of discourse in the heralds' compendia[16] and a direct application of the martial gesture in technical literature.

This apparent paradox is due to the problematic definition of those types of combat and the focus of scholarly research on the high strata of society. Indeed, the involvement of high aristocracy in the "old" trial by combat was exceptional during the fifteenth century,[17] even if it was still an object of discourse and provocation among princes.[18] Various customary laws had codified procedures for judicial single combat (lat: *duellum*, mfr: *gage de bataille*, mhd: *kampf*) for all social strata since the 13th c. (but mostly in the 14th c.),[19] mainly dealing with legal matters and procedures before the combat itself. These *consuetudines* also led to specialised *Kampfrecht*, especially in franchised cities during the second half of the 14th c., throughout the 15th c. and up to the middle of the 16th c.,[20] where details of the ritual before and during the combat

---

one judicial combat between commoners (Plouvier and Coquel, discussed below).

16 As defined by HILTMANN, 2011. See also his article with U. Israel on the specific correlation between those types of combat and his corpus of sources (HILTMANN/ISRAEL, 2007, pp. 65-84).

17 For example the case of the Earl of Ormond versus the Prior of Kilmayne in London in 1446 or Hector de Flavy versus Maillotin de Bours in Sedan in 1430 (see ELEMA, 2012, p. 161, note 79 and p. 312). See also the examples in the Holy Empire quoted from the dissertation of POSCHKO in JEZLER, 2014, p. 188.

18 See examples in VONES, 1996, pp. 321-332.

19 The best known examples among legal historian are Eike von Repgow, Sachsenspiegel (ed. ECKHARDT, 1972, Landgericht I, 63), or the Rechtsbuch Kaiser Ludwig von Bayern, 1346 (ed. VOLKERT, 2010). For the French kingdom, Philippe de Beaumanoir, Coutume du Beauvaisis. Also found as specialised treatises in the Italian peninsula, such as the anonymous *Summula de Pugna* or Roffredus of Benevento, *Summa de pugna*. This is however not exhaustive and there is no reference study on those consuetudines for the judicial combat taking in account all those geographical areas. For the Holy Roman Empire, see NEUMANN, 2010; for the French kingdom, see TELLIEZ, 2011 and CARBASSE, 1975, pp. 385-403; for Italy, see CAVINA, 2003.

20 See example quoted in FORTNER, 2007, pp. 10-22. For a more comprehensive discussion of the *Kampfrecht* in the South Germany, see LEISER, 1986, pp. 5-17. However, this phenomenon is not limited to the

itself were codified, including weaponry, clothing, the role and function of the different actors involved, etc. These single combats were settled by judicial courts, according to customary law and were fought on foot with long shields and either a wooden mace or a sword.[21] For example, the custom of Zwickau mid-14th c., drawing from material out of the *Sachsenspiegel*, advises that "All knights, valets (*knecht*) and merchants shall fight with a sword", while "Peasants shall fight with a wooden mace".[22]

Iconographical sequences depict such judicial single combats with the associated technical repertoire in several Fight Books of the 15th c.[23] For the purpose of this article, I shall focus on those attributed to Hans Talhoffer and Paulus Kal, two 15th c. fencing masters (*Schirm-, Fechtmeister*).[24] The preparation for judicial combat appears to have been part of their professional trade, according to the content of some of their written productions dedicated to the low and high aristocracy of the South Rhinelands.[25] Of particular interest are several passages

---

Holy Roman Empire, but stems to the kingdoms of England, France, Spain and many cities in the northern Italian peninsula.

21 In England and parts of France, another kind of weapon seems to have been customary: the *baculus cornutus*. See ELEMA, 2012, p. 249.

22 *Alle rittere, knechte und kauflüte sullen vechten mit dem swerte. / Alle gebüre sullen vechten mit kolben.* Zwickauer Rechtbuch 1348-1358, ed. PLANITZ, 1941, vol. II, 26, 6-8.

23 To be found in Fight Books attributed to Peter Falkner (Wien, Kunsthistorisches Museum, KK5012), Jorg Wilhalm (Augsburg, Universitätsbibliothek, Cod.I.6.2°.3 and Cod.I.6.2°.2; München, Bayerische Staatsbibliothek, Cgm 3711 and 3712), Paulus Hector Mair (Dresden, Sächsische Landesbibliothek, Hs Dresd. C93/94; München, Bayerische Staatsbibliothek, Cod. Icon.393 1/2; Wien, Österreichische Nationalbibliothek, Wien, Cod. 10825/10826) and in anonymous compendia (Paris, Musée National du Moyen Âge, Cl. 23842; Wolfenbüttel, Herzog August-Bibliothek, Cod. Guelf. 78.2 Aug. 2°). For a focus on the judicial combat between man and woman, I am preparing an article on the matter for the journal "Le Moyen Age" (forthcoming).

24 T. Stangier presents them as rivals, although there is no evidence that they were ever in contact. See STANGIER, 2009, pp. 79-93. For Talhoffer, see the historiographical review in BURKART, 2014, pp. 253-301. For Kal, see for instance WELLE, 1993, pp. 240-255.

25 For a discussion of the dedicatees, see STANGIER, 2009, pp. 79-93 and BURKART, 2014, pp. 253-301.

compiled in some of their compendia,[26] edited in appendix (1, A-C) and discussed below. Both masters dealt with knightly judicial combat (in armour on foot), judicial combat for commoners or burghers (including combat for a man against a woman). I shall concentrate on the second category of combat, which distinguishes between two technical repertoires: one involving a shield and sword – Swabian custom, the other a shield and mace – Franconian custom (see Fig. 1).[27]

---

26 References in appendix. Apart for those quoted, a large manuscript tradition is attributed to the authors, for description see LENG, 2008, 38.3 (Talhoffer) and 38.5 (Kal). There is however one manuscript misattributed to Talhoffer (38.3.7, which is in fact a copy of Kal) and the list of the copies is not exhaustive.
27 For a short and incomplete description of both customs, see FORTNER, 2007, pp. 19-22. See also some references in STANGIER, 2009, p. 75.

Six Weeks to Prepare for Combat

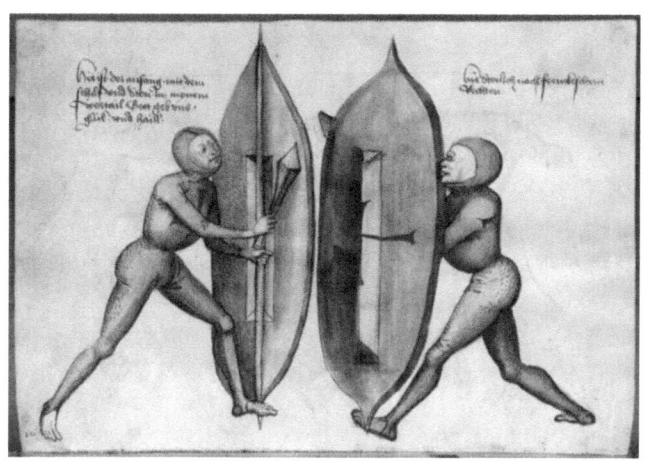

Figure 1: Franconian and Swabian customs
Legend: Hie ston Ich nach frenckeschem Rechten / Hie Ston Ich fry Nach Schwebischen Rechten. München, Bayerische Staatsbibliothek, Cod. Icon. 394a, ff. 53r and 65v.

The training of clients for "judicial" combat as a specific kind of trade for fencing masters

Both masters were well versed in the institutional underpinnings of those types of combat. Hans Talhoffer underlines that they still occurred within cities according to customary laws, although the *Decretals*[28] forbade those combats and emperors, princes and lords frowned upon them (A1). Stating that such endeavours are affairs of honour (*mütwill*),[29] he then lists the "legal" reasons to undertake such single combats: murder, treason, heresy, acts of betrayal towards one's lord, betrayal of one's given word when captured, fraud and the abuse of a women (A2). As Jezler noted, these causes are comparable to those forbidden and punished by contemporaneous tournament societies, as a means to maintain the noble ethos through social regulation.[30] This fact also highlights the similarity between the different forms of ritualised combat, of both serious and more playful varieties, touching upon different social strata.

Hans Talhoffer has several detailed insights for his client regarding the procedures of the ritual, before the combat (A3-A5) – including how to act in cases which may lead to the cancellation of the fight (A6-A7) – and at the start of the combat (A8-A9, A15-A16). Several of those procedures are also depicted in different versions of the Fight Books.[31]

As a professional in this field, Paulus Kal also compiled a list of items to be clarified with the court (including the judge, *urtailer*) by the master or his client in preparation for the combat (C1-26). This list is

---

28 Those are the Decretals of Raymond of Peñafort. After Pope Innocent III and the Fourth Lateran Council of 1215 prohibited clerics from attending or taking part in judicial duels, (*Constitutiones quarti Lateranensis una cum commentariis glossatorum*, ed. GARCIA, 1981, C.18), Pope Gregory IX issued Peñafort's Decretals in 1234 (IBID., X 3.50.9).
29 See the discussion of this matter in JAQUET, 2016b.
30 JEZLER, 2014, p. 189, ref. to pp. 66f.
31 Several iconographical cycles depicting the rituals before, during and after the combat, usually in the sections dedicated to the armoured combat on foot with swords and unarmoured combat on foot with judicial shield and sword or mace. For a description of the different versions of the works attributed to Hans Talhoffer, see BURKART, 2014, pp. 253-301.

reminiscent of the so-called *Questions,* which Geoffroy Charny addressed to his peers, the knights of the Order of the Star, one century earlier and which were related to procedural questions concerning the law of arms and practice in tourneying or jousting.[32] In Charny's case, the researcher would love to have the matching answers, but the analysis of such questions allows one at least to outline several praxeological elements by deductive analysis.

In terms of Kal's questions, the different actors and their roles during the combat can be deduced (C1) as follows: the adviser (*warner,* C2-3) interacts with court officials on behalf of the combatant; the listener (*lůsner,* C5, 8) is an assessor at court witnessing the combat; and the grid-warden (*grieswartl* C8-10) is the second of the combatant, allowed within the barriers and equipped with a staff. The combatant has the right to call his grid-warden to "pull the staff", so that the fighting is interrupted and each party can go to their rest-place (C7/C18). There is a respective example in the *Kampfrecht* of the city of Gelnhausen from 1360, where the combatant can call for the staffs three times.[33] Other details of relevance are, for example, how many maces the combatant can have (C13), what happens when he loses them inside or outside the circle, who is allowed to hand them back to him and when they are allowed to do so (C14-16). The conditions of defeat also require examination in detail (C17, 18, 24). For example, what is considered stepping out of or being pushed outside of the circle: "is it a hand, the body, a foot, the mace or the shield"? (C17). Final questions address issues about the crowd attending the fight, what regulation is there about the need to remain silent during the fight (C25) and what are the precautions taken to isolate the combatant from the crowd (C26)? Again, this is very similar to the regulations for tournaments or chivalric games, including single combat, which all attempt to regulate the reaction of the attending crowd.[34]

---

32 See KAUEPER/KENNEDY, 1996.
33 *So bit er fragen, wie dicke er den stangen begeren solle, so wird erteilt: dry stunt , diewyle sie sich nit begrifen haben, wan aber sie sich begryfen, so mag er ir keiner me begeren.* Hessisches Urkundenbuch, ed. HIRZEL, 1894. Credit for this finding goes to Jens-Peter Kleinau who published a blog article about it in 2013.
34 JEZLER, 2014, pp. 57-72. For a comparison between different rulesets, see RÜHL, 2001, pp. 193-208.

Concerning specialised weaponry and clothing, Kal and Talhoffer provide relevant information not only in the iconographic sequences depicting fighting techniques, but also in the text. Kal suggests inquiring about this subject before the fight (C19, C20). The Talhoffer compendium of 1459 comprises detailed (technical?) depictions of the clothing itself (107r), the maces (106v) and five different shields (104r-105v) with short written comments. Talhoffer also describes how the combatant should enter the barriers, with details on the clothing (A16) and the gesture performed for different parts of the rituals taking place prior to the fight.[35] Complementary details describing these outfits (discussed below) can be found in narratives and some normative texts of customary law.[36]

Physical training, diet of the combatant and the need for secrecy

According to Talhoffer, when the complaint has been lodged at the court in the appropriate manner (A3), "six weeks will be granted for his training days, and also four more days before his judgement, so that they can fight according to the custom of the land and the law" (A4). The training period of six weeks and the hiring of fencing masters are also found in customary law, for example in Münster-maifeld in 1372.[37]

---

35   Some of those rituals are also described in heraldic compendia. See ISRAEL/HILTMANN, 2007, pp. 65-84. Also of interest for anthropological studies of those rituals, outlined in the perspective of an historian, is OSCHEMA, 2011, pp. 142-161.

36   For example in 1446: *Alß dem scheffen ingeben yst, wie die zu dem kamp geschickt und gestalt sin sullen sin, hat der schieffe gewisset, sie sullen haben zum ersten eyn graen fyltzrocke, kogeln, hossen und schue; an eym ander zwen glych schilde, iglicher ein holczen kyckel und eyn hanthabe und sullen in wynden under dem kyne, zwen holtzen kepel glich eln lang, dryeecket hynden yen knop, und zwen henen degen glich eyner halben eln lang in eym fure and den spitzen gehert und die hencken by den uff die rechten sytten zu der hant um.* Landschreibereirechnung der Obergrafschaft (Landgericht Katzenelnbogen), DEMANDT, 1953, vol. 3, p. 2294. I thank Christine Reinle for having pointed out this source to me.

37   *halden sal vnvirderfflich ses wochen und dry tage, und yeme eynen meister gewinnen, der en kempen lere, und sal en halden, und daz alles dun der*

According to Talhoffer, both parties are bound by custom and the court not to break peace during this period under penalty of banishment (A4).

In the first compendium attributed to the master (1448), on the versos of the folios showing the technical sequence of the fighting gestures, an iconographical cycle illustrates the entire process of preparation for a judicial duel, from the hiring of the master outside of the city walls, to the preparation of the fighter up until the combat. This included such distractions as eating, listening to music, bathing, hunting, and time spent with his relatives, but also ritualised processes such as shaving, praying and anointing (App. 2).[38] One of the illustrations in the cycle depicts two physical exercises, which may have been part of the training: stone and javelin throwing. These exercises are also found in another of his Fight Books, dedicated to Luitold von Königsegg. It contains general rhymed advices given to one who cares about the "knightly values": he should "train during peace time by throwing stones and javelins, dancing and jumping, fencing and wrestling, mock jousting and tourneying and courting beautiful ladies".[39] The same book provides very rare information on physical training and diet in the context of preparations for a judicial combat:

> "He should especially get up early every day and hear a mass, then go back to his house, eat a loaf of St-John bread[40] and train for two hours. He shall not eat too much greasy food. After noon, he shall train two hours and at nightfall, before he lies down to sleep, he shall eat a slice of rye bread soaked in water. This makes for good breathing and a strong heart." (B2).

---

greue uff sine kost selber, ob der ghene der kuste nit enhat, der kemplich wirt angesprochen. Quoted in NEUMANN, 2010, p. 90, note 414. Other quotes regarding the hiring of fencing masters (*Bretons*) according to Norman customs in COULIN, 1906, p. 87. For English cases, see RUSSELLL, 1984, pp. 76-78.

38 See also STANGIER, 2009, p. 74.
39 [...] *vnd gedenck nach ritterschafft / mit freiden ueben / stein werffen vnd stang schueben / tantzen vnd springen / fechtten vnd ryngen / stechen vnd turnieren / schönen frawen hofieren.* Ed. SCHULZE, 2010, p. 23 (revised by the author).
40 Bread baked for the feast of St John (December 27). St John's wine and bread are common feature of medieval recipes (for St John blessed a poisonous glass of wine to render it harmless).

The master also underscores that he will evaluate his client to establish "whether he is weak or strong, choleric or gentle-minded, whether or not he has good breathing, and if he would work heartily" (A13). He should also know "how his top heats up if someone would quarrel or fight" (A14). On a side note, similar but more detailed advice based on humour theory and related to martial training is depicted in the fight book of Pietro Monte, written in the last decade of the 15th c., but published post-mortem in 1509.[41]

Talhoffer also notes that the client shall recognise the master as being trustworthy by the following qualities: pious, sober, righteous and protective, and his ability in the art of combat – "broadening the arsenal of techniques and knowledge about the art" (A12). Securing his trade, he warns against untrustworthy rivals, such as other fencing masters before him (and after him…).[42] He also insists on the need for secrecy: "Yet the combatant and the master shall guard that they let no man see them or the arsenal with which they work. And they both shall guard their doings from much of society; and say little of the fighting, so that no notice is made thereof." (A13)

This is, of course, crucial to the training for a judicial combat, but this kind of face-to-face instruction and need for secrecy is also emphasised by Fiore dei Liberi in other contexts. In his treatise from the very beginning of the 15th c., this master lists his students (among them knights) and explains that he trained them for deeds of arms (and for more serious matters). He then states that he has been "well paid" and that "he always taught this art in secrecy".[43] The monetary value of

---

41 For an introduction to this text, see FORGENG, 2014, pp. 107-114. The master also wrote a treatise on the "distinction of men", with long development on the physiological attributes related to physical exercise. See FONTAINE, 1991, p. 46.
42 A12. This kind of warning is found for example in the first witness of the *Zedel* of Liechtenauer at the end of the 14th c.; *Als man noch manche leychmeistere vindet dy do sprechen / das sy selber newe kunst vinden vnd irdenken vnd meynen das sich dy kunst des fechtens von tage czu tage besser vnd mere.* Ed. ZABINSKI, 2010, p. 130 (revised by the author).
43 *[…] di questi e d'altri i quali io fior ò magistradi io son molto contento perché io son stado ben rimunerato e ò aibudo l'onore e l'armore di miei scolari e di parenti loro digo anchora che questa arte io l'ò monstrado sempre ocultamente si che non glie sta presente alchuno.* Fiore de'i Liberi, Flos Duellatorum, 1409. RUBBOLI/CESARI, 2003, p. 25.

those secret teachings was also regulated in urban context within fencing guilds.[44]

Gouge the eye out: St William's miracle

Two of these judicial combats between commoners are described in chronicles of the 15th c. One in Valencienne (duchy of Hainault) in 1455 opposed Jacotin Plouvier, a burger of the town and Mahiot Coquel, a tailor from Tournai; another in London in 1456 opposed James Fisher, a tailor and fisherman, with Thomas Whitehorne, a man with no known profession and with reputation for robbery.[45] Both deadly combats are related in very crude terms and the chroniclers all made clear that they disliked this type of "improper" single combats.[46] The chroniclers give interesting details regarding the clothing and the weapons, supplementing information found in Fight Books and normative texts. For example, the combatants, whose hair and nails were cut, wore a tightly fitted garment made of leather[47], covered in grease "so that they could

---

44 For example in the Statutes of the Fencing Masters of Bruges in 1456: *Ende als van den verboorghene consten, te wetene ghewaepent te cechtene met haecsen end andersins, dat elc meester ende provoost boven dien van elcken leerlinghe zal moghen nemen dies hem ghebueren zoude moghen.* GALAS, 2011, p. 148. For a recent study on fencings guilds in the Lowlands, see GEVAERT/VAN NOORT, 2016, pp. 221-242.

45 Both case are studied in ELEMA, 2012, esp. pp. 1-5, 68, 135f., 234-237, 247-253, 266, 307-309, 313f., 318, 324-326. The sources for the first duel are *Chronique* de Mathieu d'Escouchy (DU FRESNE DE BEAUCOURT, 1863, vol. 2, p. 297-305); *Mémoire* d'Olivier de la Marche (PETITOT, 1825, vol. 2, p. 213-218); *Chronique* de Georges de Chastellain (KERVYN DE LETTENHOVE, 1864, vol. 3, p. 41-49); for the second one: *Gregory's Chronicle of London* (ed. GAIRDNER, 1876, pp. 199-202). For the first case, see also CAUCHIÈS, 1999, pp. 655-668 and LECUPPRE-DESJARDIN, 2016, pp. 181-197.

46 For example: [...] *tenoit en la bataille* [...] *plus honte que honneur* [...]. Olivier de la Marche, ed. PETITOT, 1825, p. 407; or the London chronicler: *.hyt ys to schamfulle to reherse alle the condyscyons of thys foule conflycte.* Ed. GAIRDNER, 1876, p. 200.

47 [...] *moste be clothyd alle in whyte schepys leter, bothe body, hedde, leggys, fete, face, handys, and alle.* IBID., p. 200. *Ilz avoient les testes raises, les piedz nuz, et les ongles coppez des mains et des piedz; et au regard du corps, des jambes et des bras, ilz estoient vestuz de cuyr bouilly,*

not grapple each other" and their hands were covered with ashes "so that they could handle their shield and mace".[48] The maces are all described as made of hardwood (medlar for d'Escouchy – *mellier bien nouteilleux* and de la Marche – *mesplier*; newly cut ash for Gregory – *grene hasche*).[49] None of the chronicles are illustrated during the 15th c. (some illustration are found in the 16th c.),[50] but the manuscript of a 15th c. chronicle from Brabant[51] illustrates a different duel, from 1236, depicting contemporaneous fashions for tightly fitted garments and maces (see fig. 2).

---

cousu estroictement sur leurs personnes. Olivier de la Marche, ed. PETITOT, 1825, p. 404.

48 [...] *deux bassins plains de gresse, dont les habillemens ... furent oingtz et engressez, affin que l'ung d'eulx ne peust prendre prinse sur l'autre.* [...] *deux bassins de cendres, pour oster la gresse de leurs mains, afin qu'ilz puissent mieulx tenir leurs escuz et leurs bastons.* IBID. p. 405.

49 The more detailed description in given in the Gregory's chronicle: "[...] and that they should have in their hands 2 maces of freshly cut ash, with bark being upon it, of 3 feet in length, and at the end ought to be a cudgel of the same[wood], provided that the addition adds any length at all." ([...] *grene hasche, the barke beynge a pon of iij fote in lenghthe and at the ende a bat of the same govyn owte as longe as the more gevythe any gretenys*). Gregory's chronicle, ed. GAIRDNER, 1876, p. 200. I thank Daria Izdebska for her help in translating that excerpt. This appears to be specific kind of mace, not to be compared with the ones used in France or Germany. See RUSSELL, 1983, pp. 432-442.

50 One illustration of the Coquel and Plouvier found in a 16th c. manuscript by A. Elema (Douai, Bibliotheque municipale MS 1183, ff. 188v-189r). Also to be noted that Paulus Hector Mair, compiler of a large anthology of the art of fighting in the middle of the 16th c. did also include illustrations of such fights, as well as copies of *Kampfrechten* and precise drawings of the shields, see note 61.

51 The redaction of this chronicle and the realisation of this manuscript constitute a complex case. The attribution to Jan van Boendale (Jan de Klerk) is dubious and one possible source for the relation of the duel is the chronicler Lodewijck van Vethem. The text has been edited by WILLEMS, 1837, pp. 26-32. I am grateful to Sergio Boffa for providing me with this information. He is currently preparing an article about this case.

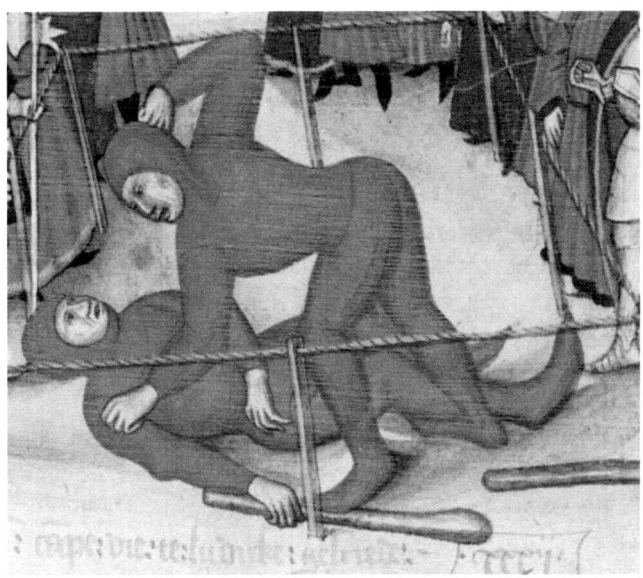

Figure 2: Judicial combat
Legend: Jan van Boendale, Brabantsche Yeesten, 1450-1480. Bruxelles, Bibliothèque royale, Ms IV 684, fol. 68.

The fight follows the same pattern in all these cases. Both combatants exchange a few blows and the fight proceeds to grappling and ends on the ground. All the written accounts describe very crude moves, including biting, scratching, breaking limbs and eye gouging. In the Whytehorne-Fisher case, one of the combatants bit the other in the private parts before the other bit the first man's nose and gouged his eye.[52] In the Plouvier-Coquel case, when both men wrestled on the ground, one gouged out both his opponent's eyes, and crushed his stomach with his knees while strangling him to death.[53] These

---

52 [...] *and bote hym by the membrys* [...] *and toke that fals peler by the nose with hys tethe and put hys thombe in hys yee. Gregory's Chronicle*, ed. GAIRDNER, 1876, p. 200.

53 [...] *car de ses mains et ongles lui creva les deux yeux de la teste et fist saillir dehors. Aveux clui estant sur son estomach a genoux lui creva le cœur et l'estrangla de ses mains puis le jetta hors desdictes lices.* Escouchy, ed. DU FRESNE DE BEAUCOURT, 1863, p. 297. See also for the eye gouging: [...] *Sy alla bouter son pousse de l'autre main en ses yeux et*

unchivalrous gestures are mentioned in the Fight Books' repertoire, but are usually – when described or referred to – labelled as "forbidden" or "secret". In connection to these, various regulations of the fencing competitions (*fechtschulen*) list these prohibited fighting techniques in the late 15th and 16th c.[54] As the statutes of the fencing guild of Bruges demonstrate,[55] those gestures were taught. One can also assume that they were part of the client's training in preparation for judicial combat. As a side note in the Plouvier-Coquel case, the master attributed to Mahienot Coquel is named "Hans" in the Chronique of Chastellain.[56] Of course, without other evidence, this is unlikely to be Hans Talhoffer.

Finally, one interesting common feature of the written descriptions of these combats is the eye gouging. A series of stained glass panels in the Saint William window of York Minster also illustrate this gesture (See fig. 3.).[57] This is related to one of the miracles in the *Vita* of Saint William of York (?-1154, canonised by Honorius III in 1227), here depicted as an early 15th c. judicial combat.[58] In this miracle, Ralph, falsely accused of breaking the king's peace, has to fight in a judicial combat. His eye is gouged out by his mightier opponent Besing. The sentence of the court is the loss of the other eye. The blind victim recovers his sight while visiting the tomb of Saint William. In addition to the *Vita*, the fact that all narrative accounts studied here include eye

---

y commença à fouiller dedens jusqu'au parfont tellement qu'il lui tirat les yeux hors jusques à pendre sur les joues. Chastellain, ed. KERVYN DE LETTENHOVE, 1864, p. 48. An additional manuscript of the chronique of Chastellain describes at length in very crude details the end of the combat (London, British Library, Additional Ms 54156, ed. DELCLOS, 1991, pp. 325-327).

54 For examples of those techniques and discussion of the connexion between Fight Books and fencing schools, see JAQUET, 2013.
55 See note 44.
56 *Or ont eu ces deux gens-icy par longue espace leurs maistres emprès eux, qui leur ont appris leurs envayes et deffenses, et tout ce en quoy il les espèrerent à sauver, et avoit Mahienot empès lui un nommé Hans, le meilleur qu'on savoit en nul pays,* [...] Chastelain, ed. KERVYN DE LETTENHOVE, 1864, p. 44. I thank Loïs Forster to have shared this passage with me.
57 FRENCH, 1999, pp. 70-73. Credit for this finding goes to A. Elema who mentions it in a note in her dissertation, see ELEMA, 2012, p. 255, n. 67.
58 Miracula 37, See NORTON, 2006, pp. 169-181 and 198-200.

gouging may point towards a topos for judicial combat.[59] However, this remains a postulate to be investigated by further studies, outside of the scope of this contribution.

Figure 3: The eye gouging
Legend: Stained glass panel of Saint William, detail. York Minster, 1414

Conclusion

This contribution highlights some of the benefits of further investigation of this type of judicial single combat for commoners in order to address issues related to the training of combatants as well as bodies in battle. As outlined by the different cases mentioned, these praxes occurred across the Western Europe at the end of the Middle Ages.[60] Further research may reveal that these were still practiced in the 16th c.[61] and certainly were not limited to the geographical boundaries

---

59 See the discussion about castration in combination with blinding as a Norman punishment in ELEMA, 2012, pp. 152-155.
60 The different examples in this contribution occurred in England, France, Germany, and the Low Countries.
61 In the context of the redaction of the Fight Books, the specialised sections about judicial combat and those about armoured combat on foot were still compiled up to 1570 (see JAQUET/WALCZACK, 2014). The Fight Books of Paulus Hector Mair (three versions between 1540-1550) would prove

of this contribution. These understudied single combats are indeed part of a greater phenomenon of ritualised combat, regulated by various norms and cultural habitus, most of the latter being tacit or implicit. The various forms of chivalric games – as models or ideals – also affect other types of sporting, competitive or ludic praxes involving all strata of the society, from the rural, to urban, and even to courtly contexts. The need to revise historiographical misconceptions about the apparent dichotomy between serious and playful context on one hand, and the vague definition of the different types of single combats (including judicial combats) on the other has been stated and calls for further research and case studies.[62]

By cross-analysing different types of sources, such as narrative descriptions, normative or legal sources and technical literature, the historian gains access to relevant information about the training (time spent, type of teaching, actors, even monetary value of the teachings), the rituals and material culture associated with these combats (procedures, gestures, weaponry, clothing) as well as actual details of the fighting itself. In the context of the studies of Historical European Martial Arts – and its main source: the Fight Books –, this type of investigation sheds new light on one of the many contexts of application of the martial gesture. If studied with a praxeological perspective, including comparison with other types of single combat in Western Europe at the end of the Middle Ages, it also sheds new light on the whys and wherefores about ritualised praxes of violence.

Bibliography

Sources

Chronique de Georges Chastellain: Les fragments du livre IV révélés par l'Additional Manuscript 54156 de la British Library, ed. by JEAN-CLAUDE DELCLOS, Genève 1991.

---

    interesting, since they also contain various *Kampfrechte* and sections dedicated to judicial combats (see note 50).
62 See for example JASER, 2016, pp. 221-242 and JAQUET, 2016b.

Chronique de Mathieu d'Escouchy, ed. by GASTON DU FRESNE BEAUCOURT, vol. 2, Paris 1863.

Constitutiones Concilii quarti Lateranensis una cum Commentariis glossatorum (Monumenta iuris canonici. Ser. A, Corpus glossatorum, 2), ed. by ANTONIUS G. GARCÍA Y GARCÍA, Città del Vaticano 1981.

Das Rechtsbuch Kaiser Ludwigs des Bayern von 1346 (Bayerische Rechtsquellen 4), ed. by WILHELM VOLKERT, München 2010.

Fiore dei Liberi, Flos duellatorum : manuale di arte del combattimento del XV. secolo, ed. by MARCO RUBBOLI/LUCA CESARI, Rimini 2002.

FRENCH, THOMAS, York Minster: The St. William Window (Corpus Vitrearum Medii Aevi Great Britain Summary Catalogue 5), Oxford 1999, pp. 70-73.

Hans Talhoffer, [Königsegg treatise], 1446-1459. Königseggwald, Gräfliches Schloss, Hs. XIX 17-3. ed. by ANDRÉ SCHULZE, 2 vols, Mainz 2010. See App. 1.

Hans Talhoffer, compendium (*Alte Armatur und Ringkunst*), 1459. Kobenhavn, Det Kongelige Bibliotek, Thott 290 2°. ed. by DIETER BACHMANN, s.d., online: http://schwertfechten.ch/quellen/hans-talhofer/talhofer-1459/, accessed 03.10.2015. See App. 1.

Hans Talhoffer, compendium, 1448. Gotha, Forschungsbibliothek, Hs Chart. A558.

Les mémoires de messire Olivier de la Marche (Collection complete des mémoires relatifs à l'histoire de France, 10), ed. by CLAUDE B. PETITOT, vol. 2, Paris 1825.

Oeuvres de Georges Chastellain, ed. by JOSEPH KERVYN DE LETTENHOVE, vol. 3, Brussels 1864.

Paulus Kal, compendium (*Allerley Kempf zur Rosz vnd Fuesz jn vnnd on harnisch*), ca. 1480. Wien, Kunsthistorisches Museum, KK5126. ed. by CARSTEN LORBEER et al., 2006, online: http://www.pragmatischeschriftlichkeit.de/transkription/edition_paulus_kal.pdf, accessed 03.10.2015. See App. 1.

Regesten der Grafen von Katzenelnbogen: 1060 - 1418, ed. by KARL E. DEMANDT, 4 vols., Wiesbaden 1953.

Schwabenspiegel: Kurzform. 1. Landrecht. 2. Lehnrecht (Monumenta Germaniae Historica. Fontes iuris Germanici antiqui, Nova series), ed. by KARL A. ECKHARDT, vol. 4, 1-2, Hannover 1972.

The Book of Chivalry of Geoffroy de Charny: Text, context and translation, ed. by RICHARD W. KAEUPER/ELSPETH KENNEDY, Philadelphia 1996.

Traicté de la forme et devis comme on faict les tournois par Olivier de la Marche, Hardouin de la Jaille, Anthonie de la Sale, etc, ed. by BERNARD PROST, Paris 1878.

Urkundenbuch zur Geschichte der Herren von Hanau und der ehemaligen Provinz Hanau, ed. by HEINRICH REIMER, vol. 3, Leipzig 1892.

WILLEMS, JAN FRANS, De Leuvensche kampvechter ten jare 1236, in: Belgisch museum voor de Nederduitsche tael- en letterkunde en de geschiedenis des vaderlands, vol. 1, Gent 1837, pp. 26-32.

William Gergory's Chronicle of London, in: The Historical Collections of a Citizen of London in the Fifteenth Century (Camden Society, New Series, 17), ed. by JAMES GAIRDNER, London 1876.

Zwickauer Rechtsbuch (Germanenrechte NF, Abt. Stadtrechtsbücher), ed. by HANS PLANITZ/GÜNTHER ULLRICH, Weimar 1941.

Literature

ANGLO, SYDNEY, The Martial Arts of Renaissance Europe, New Haven 2000.

BERGUERAND, CLAUDE, Le duel d'Othon de Grandson (1397). Mort d'un chevalier-poète vaudois à la fin du Moyen Âge, Lausanne 2008.

BOFFA, SERGIO, Les manuels de combat ("Fechtbücher" et "Ringbücher") (Typologie des sources du Moyen Âge occidental, 84), Turnhout 2014.

BURKART, ERIC, Die Aufzeichnung des Nicht-Sagbaren. Annäherung an die kommunikative Funktion der Bilder in den Fechtbüchern des Hans Talhofer, in: Das Mittelalter 19/2 (2014), pp. 253-301.

CARBASSE, JEAN-MARIE, Le duel judiciaire dans les coutumes méridionales, in: Annales du Midi 87/124 (1975), pp. 385-403.

CAUCHIÈS, JEAN-MARIE, Duel judiciaire et "franchise de la ville". L'abolition d'une coutume à Valenciennes en 1455, in: Mélanges Fritz Sturm, ed. by J.-F. GERKENS, Liège 1999, pp. 655-668.

CAVINA, MARCO, Il duello giudiziario per punto d'onore. Genesi, apogeo e crisi nell'elaborazione dottrinale italiana (secc. XIV-XVI), Torino 2003.

CAVINA, MARCO, Il sangue dell'onore: Storia del duello, Roma 2005.

CONTAMINE, PHILIPPE, La guerre au Moyen Âge, 6th ed., Paris 2003.

COULIN, ALEXANDER, Der gerichtliche Zweikampf im altfranzösischen Prozess, Berlin 1906.

DERUELLE, BENJAMIN/GAINOT, BERNARD (eds.), La construction du Militaire. Volume 1: Savoirs et savoir-faire militaires à l'époque moderne, Paris 2013.

ELEMA, ARIELLA, Trial by Battle in France and England, unpubl. P.hD. dissertation, University of Toronto 2012.

FONTAINE, MARIE-MADELEINE, Le condottiere Pietro Del Monte, Paris 1991.

FORGENG, JEFFREY L., Pietro Monte's Exercises and the Medieval Science of Arms, in: The Armorer's Art. Essays in honour of Stuart Pyhrr, ed. by DONALD J. LA ROCCA, Woonsocket 2014, pp. 107-114.

FORTNER, SARAH, "Kempflich angesprochen" über Kampfgerichte und Kampfrecht, in: Mittelalterliche Kampfesweisen, Bd. 3: Scheibendolch und Stechschild, ed. by ANDRÉ SCHULZE, Mainz 2007, pp. 10-22.

GALAS, MATT, Statutes of the Fencing Masters of Bruges (1456), in: Arts de combat. Théorie & Pratique en Europe – XIVe-XXe siècle, ed. by FABRICE COGNOT, Paris 2011, pp. 137-152.

GEVAERT, BERT AND VAN NOORT, REINIER, Evolution of Martial Tradition in the Low Countries: Fencing Guilds and Treatises, in: Late Medieval and Early Modern Fight Books. Transmission and Tradition of Martial Arts in Europe (14th-17th Centuries), ed. by D. JAQUET, K. VERELST and T. DAWSON, Leiden 2016, pp. 376-409.

GUENÉE, BERNARD, Comment le Religieux de Saint-Denis a-t-il écrit l'histoire? L'exemple du duel de Jean de Carrouges et Jacques le Gris (1386), in: Pratiques de la culture écrite en France au XVe siècle (Textes et études du Moyen Age 2), ed. by MONIQUE ORNATO/NICOLE PONS, Louvain-la-Neuve 1995, pp. 331-343.

HILTMANN, TORSTEN, Spätmittelalterliche Heroldskompendien: Referenzen adeliger Wissenskultur in Zeiten gesellschaftlichen Wandels (Frankreich und Burgund, 15. Jahrhundert) (Pariser historische Studien 92), München 2011.

HILTMANN, TORSTEN/ISRAEL, UWE, "Laissez-les aller." Die Herolde und das Ende des Gerichtskampfs in Frankreich, in; Francia 34/1 (2007), pp. 65-84.

ISRAEL, UWE, Wahrheitsfindung und Grenzsetzung. Der Kampfbeweis in Zeugenaussagen aus dem frühstaufischen Oberitalien, in: Quellen und Forschungen aus italienischen Archiven und Bibliotheken 88 (2008), pp. 121-147.

ISRAEL, UWE/ORTALLI, GHERARDO (eds.), Il duello fra medioevo ed età moderna: prospettive storico-culturali (I libri di Viella 92), Roma 2009.

JAQUET, DANIEL, "Personne ne laisse volontiers son honneur être tranché." Les combats singuliers "judiciaires" d'après les livres de combat, in: Armes et jeux militaires dans l'imaginaire (XIIe-XVe siècles), ed. by CATALINA GIRBEA, Paris 2016b (forthcoming).

ID., Le geste, le mot et l'image: La mise par écrit de l'art du combat à la fin du Moyen Âge (De Diversis Artibus, n.), Turnhout 2016a (forthcoming).

ID., Fighting in the Fightschools late 15c., early 16c., in: *Acta Periodica Duellatorum* 1 (2013), pp. 47-66.

JASER, CHRISTIAN, "Infamis etiam campio non esse potest." Kämpen in deutschen und italienischen Städten des Spätmittelalters zwischen Marginalität und Rechtspflege, in; Das Mittelalter 19/2 (2014), pp. 380-406.

JASER, CHRISTIAN, Ernst und Schimpf. Fechten als Teil städtischer Gewalt- und Sportkultur, in: Agon und Distinktion. Soziale Räume des Zweikampfs zwischen Mittelalter und Neuzeit, ed. by U. ISRAEL and C. JASER, Berlin 2016, pp. 221-242.

JASER, CHRISTIAN/ISRAEL, UWE, Einleitung. Ritualisierte Zweikämpfe und ihre Akteure, in: Das Mittelalter 19/2 (2014), pp. 241-248.

JEZLER, PETER, Gesellschaftsturniere – Die Turnierhöfe der deutschen Ritterschaft im Spätmittelalter, in: Ritterturnier. Geschichte einer Festkultur, ed. by PETER JEZLER et al., Luzern 2014, pp. 57-72.

KEEN, MAURICE H., Chivalry, New Haven/London 1984.

LAWRENCE, DAVID, The complete soldier (History of Warfare 53), Leiden 2009.

LECUPPRE-DESJARDIN, ÉLODIE, Le duel judiciaire dans les villes des anciens Pays-Bas bourguignons: privilège urbain ou acte de rébellion?, in: Agon und Distinktion. Soziale Räume des Zweikampfs zwischen Mittelalter und Neuzeit, ed. by U. ISRAEL and C. JASER, Berlin 2016, pp. 181-198.

LEISER, WOLFGANG, Süddeutsche Land- und Kampfgerichte des Spätmittelalters, in; Württembergisch Franken, 70 (1986), pp. 5-17.

LENG, RAINER et al., Katalog der deutschsprachigen illustrierten Handschriften des Mittelalters Band 4/2, Lfg. 1/2: 38: Fecht- und Ringbücher, München 2008.

LUDWIG, ULRIKE et al. (eds.), Das Duell – Ehrenkämpfe vom Mittelalter bis zur Moderne (Konflikte und Kultur – Historische Perspektiven 23), Konstanz 2012.

MCAULEY, FINBARR, Canon Law and the End of the Ordeal, in: Oxford Journal of Legal Studies 26/3 (2006), pp. 473-513.

MOREL, HENRI, La fin du duel judiciaire en France, in: Mélanges Henri Morel (Collection d'histoire des idées politiques 2), 1st publ. 1964, Aix-en-Provence 1989, pp. 175-243.

NEUMANN, SARAH, Der Gerichtliche Zweikampf: Gottesurteil, Wettstreit, Ehrensache (Mittelalter-Forschung 31), Ostfildern 2010.

NORTON, CHRISTOPHER, St. William of York, York 2006.

NOTTARP, HERMANN, Gottesurteilstudien, Muenchen 1956.

OSCHEMA, KLAUS, Toucher et être touché: l'emploi de gestes dans les batailles judiciaires et le façonnement des émotions dans la résolution des conflits, in: Médiévales (La chair des émotions. Pratiques et représentations corporelles de l'affectivité au Moyen Age) 61/2 (2011), pp. 142-161.

PARAVICINI, WERNER, Ein berühmter Fall neu betrachtet: das Gerichtsduell des Jean de Carrouges gegen Jacques Le Gris von 1386, in: Agon und Distinktion. Soziale Räume des Zweikampfs

zwischen Mittelalter und Neuzeit, ed. by U. ISRAEL and C. JASER, Berlin 2016, pp. 23-84.

RÜHL JOACHIM K., Regulations for the Joust in Fifteenth-Century Europe: Francesco Sforza Visconti (1465) and John Tiptoft (1466), in: The International Journal of the History of Sport 18/2 (2001), pp. 193-208.

RUSSELL MICHAEL J, The champion's master in trial by battle: a note, in: Journal of Legal History 5/1 (1984), pp. 76-78.

RUSSELL MICHAEL J, Accoutrements of Battle, in: Law Quarterly Review, 99/3 (1983), pp. 432-442.

STANGIER, THOMAS, "Ich hab herz als ein leb..." Zweikampfrealität und Tugendideal in den Fechtbüchern Hans Talhoffers und Paulus Kals, in: Ritterwelten im Spätmittelalter (Schriften aus den Museen der Stadt Landshut 29), ed. by FRANZ NIEHOFF, Landshut 2009 pp. 79-93.

TELLIEZ, ROMAIN, Preuves et épreuves à la fin du Moyen Âge. Remarques sur le duel judiciaire à la lumière des actes du Parlement 1254-1350, in: Hommes, cultures et sociétés à la fin du Moyen Âge: Liber discipulorum en l'honneur de Philippe Contamine (Cultures et civilisations médiévales 57), ed. by PATRICK GILLI/JACQUES PAVIOT, Paris 2012, pp. 107-121.

VONES LUDWIG, Un mode de résolution des conflits au bas Moyen Age: le duel des princes, in: La Guerre, la violence et les gens au Moyen Age, I: Guerre et violence, ed. by PHILIPPE CONTAMINE/ OLIVIER GUYOJEANNIN, Paris 1996, pp. 321-332.

WELLE RAINER, "...und wisse das alle höbischeit kompt von deme ringen" der Ringkampf als adelige Kunst im 15. und 16. Jahrhundert: eine sozialhistorische und Bewegungsbiographische Interpretation aufgrund der handschriftlichen und gedruckten Ringlehren des Spätmittelalters (Forum Sozialgeschichte 4), Pfaffenweiler 1993.

ZABINSKI, GRZEGORZ, The Longsword Teachings of Master Liechtenauer: The Early Sixteenth Century Swordsmanship Comments in the "Goliath" Manuscript, Torun 2010.

Appendix 1. Edition of sources

(For references and transcription norms, see "Acknowledgment" at the end of the Appendix)

A. About the kampf

Hans Talhoffer, "Von dem kempfen", in Hans Talhoffer compendium (*Alte Armatur und Ringkunst*), 1459. Kobenhavn, Det Kongelige Bibliotek, Thott 290 2°, ff. 8r-10v.

A1. [8r] hie vint man geschriben von dem kempfen
Item wie daz nun sy daz die die decretaleß kempf verbieten, So hat doch die gewonhait herbracht von kaisern und kŭnigen fürsten und hern noch gestatten und kempfen laussen, und darzu glichen schierm gebent, und besunder und umb ettliche sachen und artikeln, alß her nach geschriben staht. Item zu dem ersten maul daz Im nymant gern sin Eer laut abschniden[a] mit wortten ainem der sin genoß ist Er wolte Er hebat mit im kempfen wie wol er doch nit recht wol von Im kem ob er wŏlte und darumb so ist kåmpfen ain mŭtwill
A2. Item der sachen und ardickelen sind siben Darumb man noch pfligt zu kempfen:
Item daz erst ist mortt
Daz ander verråtterniß
Das dritt ketzerÿ
Daz vierd wŏhher an sinem herrn trulos wirt
Daz fŭnfft umb fanknuß in striten oder sunßt
Daz sechst umb valsch
Daz sibent da ainer junckfrowen oder frowen benotzogt
A3. Item spricht ain man den andern kempflich an, der sol komen fŭr gericht und sol durch sinen fürsprechen sin sach für legen, darumb er in denn an kagt und sol den man nennen mit dem touff namen und zŭ namen. So ist recht, daz er in für gericht lad und in dry stund beclag uff dryen gerichten nach ain ander kumpt er denn nit und veranttwurt sich nach nymant von sinen wegen, so mag er sich fŭrbaß nit mer veranttwurten, [8v] er bewyse dann Ehafte nott als recht sy, so sol man in verurtailen alß fer in daz sin bott innerhalb landes begriffen hant. Je dar nach, alß die ansprach ist gegangen, darnach sol daz urtail ouch gan.

A4. Item der da kempflich angesprochen wirt uff den dryen gerichten und er ainost zů der antwort kumpt und legnot darumb man in an gesprochen hat und spricht er sy des also unschuldig und der sag uff in daz nit war sy und daz wöll er widerumb mit kempfen beherten und uff in daz wysen alß denn recht sy un dem land darinn eß sy und forttert dar über mit urtail seinen lertag, so werdent im sechß wochen ertailt zu sinem lertag und vier tag von dem gericht werdent im auch ertailt, daruff sie kempfen sůllent alß in dem land gewonhait und recht ist. Item versprechent sich zwen man willkürlich gen einander ain kampfez vor gericht, den git an auch sechs wochen lertag und sol in frid bannen baiden, und wolcher under den den frid brech, uber den richtet man on den kampf alß recht ist.

A5. wie ainer dem anderen mit recht uß(b) gan mag

Item ist daz ein man kempflich angesprochen wiert von aim der nit alß gůt ist alß er, dem mag er mit recht uß gan ob er wil oder ob ain man echtloß gesagt wůrde oder worden wer, dem mag man ouch des kampfes absin. Item spricht aber der edler den mindern an zu kempfen, so mag der den minderen nit wol absin.

A6. [9r] Item wie aber zwen mann nit mit ainander mügent kempfen und wolcher wil under den zwayen dem andern wol uß gan mag

Item wenn zween mann gesinnt sind biß uff die fünffte sipp oder näher die mügent durch recht nit mit ein ander kempfen und des müssen siben mann schwern die vatter und můtter halb mäge sind.

A7. Item wie aber ainer dem anderen kampfes absin mag mit solichem gelimpf alß hie geschriben ståt

Item ob ain lamer man oder einer der böse ougen hett und kampfes an gesprochen wirt der mag sich der auch wol behellffen und dem gesunden ußgan, eß sy denn daz wyse lůt daz gelich nach der person machen und daz müssent wyß lůt uff ir eid tun und daz also glich machen. Es mag auch der lam oder mit den bosen ougen wol ainen an ir statt gewinnen der für iro ainen kempfe.

A8. Item wenn also die sechß wochen uß sind und der letst tag komen ist den in der richter beschaiden haut daruff kempfen sullen, so sullen sie beide für den richter komen mit solichem ertzögen und in solich acht alß die gewonhait und das recht lert in dem lande dar inn sie kempfen sullen oder nach dem alß sie mit ainander gewillkůrt habent. Item etc.

A9. Item so soll da der cleger schweren daz er der sach darumb er dem ainen man zugesprochen haut schuldig sy und denn so sol man in ainen ring machen und grieß wartten und urttail geben [9v] nach wyser luta raut und nach des landeß gewonhait. Und wer uff den tag in den ring nit kumpt den urttailt man sigeloß in irre denn Ehafte nott die sol er bewysen alß recht ist –

A10. Hie staut wie man sich halten sol wenn die kempfer in dem ring komen sind uff die stund und uff die zit so man pheindiglich kempfen sol WEnn die kempfer also in den ring komen sind So sol der richter von stund an alle stůr und ler vestecklich verbieten by lyb und gůt und sol nicht gestatten daz man einem für den andern nicht zulege und sel inß beiden machen so er imer gelichest mag ungenerde.

A11. Das ist was recht wer ob der kempfer ainer uss dem ring fluch oder getriben wurd
Item wolcher kempfer uss dem ring kumpt Ee denn der kampf ain ende haut Er werde daruß geschlagen von dem andern oder fluche daruß oder wie er daruß kåme oder aber ob er der sache vergicht darumb man in denn mit recht an gesprochen haut, den sol man sigeloß urttailen. Oder wolcher den andern erschlecht und ertötett der haut gesiget. Dem sol man aber richten alß des landes gewonhait und recht ist darumb sie dem mit ainander gekemppffet hand.

A12. [10r] Nun merck uff dissen punten der ist notturfftlich zů uerstend
Item des ersten so soltu den maister wol erkennen der dich lerren wil dz sin kunst recht und gewer sy und dz er frum sy und dich nit veruntruwe und dich nit verkůrtz in der lerr und wiß die gwer zů zerbraitten da mit er kempfen wil. Och sol er den maister nit uff nemen er schwer im dann sin frumen zwerbent und sin schaden zwendent deß glich sol er dem maister wider umb sweren sin kunst nit witter zleren.

A13. Hie merck uff den maister
Item der maister der ain understat zu leren, der sol wißen daß er den man wol erken, den er lerren wil, ob er sie schwach oder starck, und ob er gåch zornig sÿ oder senftmůttig, och ob er gůtten auttem hab oder nit, och ob er arbaitten můg in die in die harr; und wenn du inn wol erkunet haust in der lerr, un wz arbait er uermag dar nach můstu in lerren dz im nůtz ist gen sinnen vind. Och sol der kempffer und der maister sich hůtten dz sie niemand zu sehen laussend und in sunder sie gwer da mit

sy arbaittent und sich baid hůtten vor vil geselschafft und von dem vechten wenig sagen dz kain abmercken da von kom.

A14. von kuntschafft

wie der kempffer und der maister kuntschafft mŏchte hon zu rem widertail, wz sin wesen wer, ob er sy strarck oder swach, ob er och sy gechzornig oder nit, und wie sin touff nam hieß, ob man wŏlt dar uß bracticiern oder rechnen. Es ist och nottůrfftig zu wissen wz maister in lerr dz man sich darnach můg richten.

A15. wenn er nun gelert ist und in den schrancken sol gon

So sol er zu dem ersten bichten, dar nach sol im ain priester ain meß lesen von unßer frowen und von sant Jŏrgen, und der priester sol im segnen sant Johanns myne und dem kempfer geben. Dar nach sol der maister in ernstlich versůchen [10v] und inn under richten dar uff er bliben sol, und sol in uff kein ding haissen acht hon dann uff sin vind, und den ernstlich an schowen.

A16. Merck uff dz infůren

Item wenn der man kompt in den schrancken so sol er machen mit dem rechten fůß ain krůtz und mit der hand ains an die brust und sol fůrsich gon im namen des vatters und suns und des hailigen gaists. Dann sind in die grießwartten nemen und sind inn fůrren gegen der sunnen umbhe. So sol dann der kempfer die fůrsten und herren bitten und die⁽ᶜ⁾ umb den kraiß stand dz sy im wŏlle helffen got bitten dz er Im sig wŏlle geben gegen sinem vind und alz er war und recht hab.

A17. Dar nach sol man in setzen in den sessel

Wenn er nun gesessen ist so soll man im fůrspannen ain tůch und sin bar hinder im an den schrancken und sine gwer sind wol gehenckt sin und gericht nach nottůrfft

A18. Die grieß wartten oder tǎpffer

Der maister und die grieß wartten sŏllend mercken uff den richter oder uff den, der den kampff an lauffen wirt. Wann der růfft zu dem ersten mal, so sol er den man haisen uff ston un dz tůch von im ziehen, und wann man růfft zů dem dritten mǎl so sol er in haissen hin gon und in got enpfelhen.

A19. Von dem nach richter

Item der kempffer sel wartten das im nůtzit an dem lib über den ring oder schrancken uß gang dann wz dar über kem: so stat der nach richter an dem schrancken der hott imß ab mit recht ob er angerůft wirt.

a. ab added in superscript. - b. corrected in superscript above a non legible word. - c. inserted in superscript

B. Prologue to the Königsegg treatise
Hans Talhoffer, Prologue, in [Königsegg treatise], 1446-1459. Königseggwald, Gräfliches Schloss, Hs. XIX 17-3, fol. 1r.

B1. [1r] Item Es ist zů wissent des ersten wen ain bÿder man zeschaffen haut das Im geschriben wůrt zů dem ernst oder er aim schribt so sol er gedencken das er stelle nach aim maister der in zů dem kampff versorge<u>n</u> kend^(a) vnd sol Im den maister haissen geloben das er Im trẅlich sein kunst mittaill Vnd sein haimlichait nit sag vnd auch nit wider in sÿ das er die kunst niemat wissen lauß die er In ler<u>en</u>

B2. Item Es sol auch der Junckher sich hůtten das er nit vill gehaimß mit den lůtten hab das sein haimlichait niemen erfar vnd das im nit werd v<u>e</u>rgeben vnd besunder so sol er alltag frů vff stån vnd hören ain meß vnd dar nach hain gån vnd sol essen ain schnÿtte santj Johans brott vnd sich arbaitten zwů stund in der ler vnd nit vil faists dings essen Vnd nach mittag aber zwů stund Vnd zenacht so er schlauffen wil så sol er essen ain Ruggj schnÿtte brot vß ainem kaltten wasser das macht Im gůtten autem vnd wit vmb das hertz

B3. It<u>em</u> wer den das der sôlte fůr sich gån So sol erschriben In ai<u>n</u> stat die Im den dar zů gefelt vmb in lauß vnd vmb glichen schirm vnd wen Im das zů geseÿt wůrt so sol er begern das man Im ain frÿeß gelaitt geb fůr sich selb vnd alle dÿ die mit Im dar koment

B4. It<u>em</u> Es sol auch der schirm maister den Junckher niemen der da kempffen will vnd sol In fůren ain haimlich stat als in ain kůrchen vnd sol in haissen nyder [knien]^(b) vnd got bitten das er Im v<u>e</u>rlich ain gluckhafft stund vnd^(c) Im v<u>e</u>rlich sůg das er seinem feind angesůg

B5. [Vnd ain gut herez vnd starck fewst hab das ist auch fast gut dar zu]^(d)

a. i corrected with e. - b. barely legible because of a fold in the parchment. - c. barely legible because of a fold in the parchment. - d. variant in the later copies Wien, Kunsthistorisches Museum, KK5342, fol. 1r and Augsburg, Universitätsbibliothek, Cod.I.6.2°.1, fol. 2r.

**C. Advices for the master accompanying his client to the *kampf*.
Anonymous, s.t., in Paulus Kal compendium (*Allerley Kempf zur Rosz vnd Fuesz jn vnnd on harnisch*), ca. 1480. Wien, Kunsthistorisches Museum, KK5126, ff. 128v-129r.**

C1. [128v] Tout zw dem erstn sol im sein fursprech wandel dingenn vnd alle recht die ein chempfer von rechtz wegenn habenn sol es sey warner lůsner grieswartl vnd was ein chempfer habenn sol.

C2. Jtem wenn er sein warn benennt so sol er fragenn wie er warnenn sol das er recht thu vnnd nicht vnrecht.

C3. Jtem er sol auch fragenn ob er vnd der warner wol zw dem chempfer gen můge dy weyl er an seiner rue siczt vnnd mit in ir notturfft redenn.

C4. Jtem er sol aber fragenn ob er ein sig gewinne oder verlornn ob er vnnd sein warner wol zw im gen můgen vnd ir noturfft wol mit ym redenn also so er wider an sein rue chumbt ym chrais.

C5. Jtem wenn er denn grieswertel oder lusner genannt so sol er in fragenn wie er lůsen Sol das er recht thue vnnd nicht vnrecht.

C6. Jtem er sol auch fragenn wie er mit der stångenn thun sol das er recht thue.

C7. Jtem er sol auch fragenn ob ir ainer der stangenn begert wie er die vntterstossenn sol das er recht thue vnnd nicht vnrecht.

C8. Jtem er sol auch fragenn was die grieswertel oder lusner hornn oder sehenn wie sy das furbringen das sy recht thunn vnnd nicht vnrecht.

C9. Jtem er sol auch fragenn was die grieswårtl ein můtiglich sagenn als die das gesehenn oder gehort habenn ob es icht billichenn do bey beleyb.

C10. Jtem er sol auch fragenn ob die griswertel mit ein ander nicht stóssig sein vnd nit vber ains mochten wern zw sagenn was dann dy vrtailer gesehenn oder gehort hiettenn ob es nit billichenn do peleybe das weybe leyb vnd das die auch dar vmb sagenn sůllenn.

C11. Er sol auch fragenn es sey griswertl oder vrtailer wie sy darvmben sagenn sullenn das sy recht thunn das man das ausfunndig[a] mach.

C12. Es sol auch denn chempfer fragen wellicher ein anchlager sey ob er icht billichen die wal vnnd die vorfart hab zu dem chrais zw siczenn mit seinem stull wo er wil.

C13. Er so auch denn chempfer fragenn wie manigen cholben er habenn sul vnd was er habenn sol zw dem champf.

C14. Er sol auch fragenn ob er ein cholbenn verwůrff der aus dem chrais chemb was recht werr.

C15. Er sol auch fragenn ob er ein cholbenn verwůrff der im chrais be lib ob im der nicht, billichenn zw staten wider chem ob er sein begert.

C16. Jtem er sol fragenn ob sein grieswårtl ycht billichenn ein cholbenn bey im habenn sull oder eins begert das er im denn mocht zw pringenn das das [sic] er Recht dar ann tat vnnd nicht vnnrecht.

C17. Er sol fragn was aus dem chrais chem es wer an hennden am leyb an ann [sic] fuessenn ain schilt ann cholbenn was darvmb Recht sey.

C18. Er sol fragenn wie manige stanngenn er begerenn sul vnd wie offt er den Sig domit verlorn hab[b].

C19. [129r] Er sol fragenn ob man sy nicht billichen beschauenn sul ob sy nichtz vngleichs oder vnpillichs bey in hettenn.

C20. Er sol auch fragen ob man die schilt vnnd anndern Zeug nicht billichenn beschauen sull[c].

C21. Er sol fragn wie offt er sein zue habm sull vnnd wie lanng.

C22. Er sol fragenn wie er auf stenn sull zw dem champf.

C23. Er sol fragenn ob icht pillichenn beleyb panalenn puntten vnd artikelen als die vor mit recht ertaylt sein wordenn vnd in dem puech geschribenn stenn.

C24. Er sol fragen welcher des chambs der nyderlig wie man zw dem selbm richten sol er sol fragenn wer richtenn sull.

C25. Er sol fragn ob yemand steurt oder lernnit mit wortten oder mit werckenn was darvmb recht sey vnnd ob man das icht billichenn verpiett vnd wie man das verpietenn sull.

C26. Ob auf lauff hinder dem ring geschehe ob das denn chempfernn kain schadn pringen sold[d].

a. "i" with two points above. - b. Four last words reported below the line on the right hand side. - c. Last word reported below the line on the right hand side. - d. Last word reported below the line on the right hand side.

Acknowledgement and transcription norms

The transcriptions are based on the following works: A) BACHMANN, s.d., online; B) SCHULZE, 2010, p. 22; C) LORBEER/LORBEER/MEIER, 2006, pp. 91-92. All transcriptions in this appendix have been revised by the author and the following norms have been applied: Resolution of the abbreviation by underscoring; <u> and <v> / <i> and <j> / <ß> were reproduced as in the original; the diphtongs /uo/, /ue/, /ae/, /oe/, were marked superscript vowels with the special characters <u̥>, <ů>, <o̊>, <å>; the uppercase and lowercase were respected.

Six Weeks to Prepare for Combat

Appendix 2. Pictorial representation of the training days

Iconographical cycle of the training days, in Hans Talhoffer, compendium, 1448. Gotha, Forschungsbibliothek, Hs Chart. A558.

163

The Body of the *Condottiero*
A Link Between Physical Pain and Military Virtue as it was Interpreted in Renaissance Italy

GIULIA MOROSINI

Within the context of this conference about the body in the Middle Ages, I would like to analyse the symbolic function of the body, and in particular wounds and mutilations, had for the Italian military class in the Renaissance. Therefore, I asked myself the following questions: Did wounds and scars have a specific meaning in the military mentality of the Renaissance? If the answer is yes, with what connotation? Did they rely on a moral system which identified the positive and negative characteristics of the military action? In the space of this article I shall attempt to answer to these questions, well aware of the fact that this subject needs, due to its extent, a wider documentary spectrum. This article aims only to be a preliminary and exploratory work, with the intent to offer some starting points for a consequent reflection. Within the tight space allowed, it is not possible to deeply investigate the mass of more and less famous *condottieri* who populated Italy during the XV century. Therefore, I preferred to focus my attention on four characters, who cover a time frame from the beginning of the XV century until the first years of the XVI century, namely Braccio da Montone, Sigismondo Malatesta,

Federico di Montefeltro and Giovanni de' Medici.[1] Although they differ extremely with respect to temperament and personal and political history, these characters represented the excellence of the contemporary military class of Italian *condottieri*. For each of these captains I refer in particular to the *commentarii* of their lives, to personal letters, to Renaissance literature and to coeval chronicles.[2] If the subject is considered from a factual angle, the document's selection, and the exclusion of political and government sources, may seems a little incomplete to meticulously retrace events, battles and military strategies. The selected sources, instead, can be enlightening if they are considered not for the accurate narration of the events, but for the stylistic elements which were used to consecrate the *condottiero* to posterity. Through the identification of recurrent themes within the *condottieri*'s eulogies it is possible to reconstruct the cornerstones around which were developed the fundamental ideas of the Renaissance military mentality. In other words, it is possible to identify some exemplary virtues and behaviours ascribable to the perfect *condottiero* or to the perfect soldier, and the symbols that embodied these virtues. Then, the spectrum of investigation may be expanded by the comparison between these sources and the military and moral treatises of the Renaissance; thus, the extent at which the measure of the idealization of the behaviours present in the treatises has permeated the everyday life of the soldier can be observed.

For Braccio da Montone, I refer to the chronicle of his life written by Giovanni Antonio Campano around 1458, and the following vulgarisation made by Pompeo Pellini at the end of XVI century. Campano dedicated his work to Braccio's son, Carlo Fortebracci, and collected the information about Braccio's life and deeds through the testimonies of Braccio's veterans, the *bracceschi*. Campano's chronicle shows an effort of symbolic sublimation of the main character, which becomes the

---

1   On Braccio see: *Braccio da Montone e i Fortebracci. Le compagnie di ventura nell'Italia del XV secolo*, Narni, 1993; On Sigismondo see: TABANELLI, 1977; FALCIONI, 2006; ZAMA, 1965, pp. 131-193; FRANCESCHINI, 1973, pp. 311-388; YRIARTE, 1882. On Federico see: FRANCESCHINI, 1961 and 1970, pp. 431-544; TOMMASOLI, 1978; DE LA SIZERANNE, 1972. On Giovanni see: CARDINI, 2001a, pp. 148-179; SCALINI, 2001b, pp. 180-201.
2   About the humanistic historiography see: DI STEFANO, 1992. About the genre of *commentarii* see: IANZITI, 1992, pp. 1029-1063.

representative of the virtue par excellence, the military virtue, "a new virtue which can be identified with the *military art*. From here, the encounter between this biography and the genre of the *de arte militari* treatises can be noticed through an accurate reading."[3] The most interesting chronicle about Sigismondo is the one written by Gaspare Broglio Tartaglia da Lavello; son of the famous *condottiero* Tartaglia da Lavello and educated to the profession of arms, Gaspare served Sigismondo as ambassador, captain and political advisor since 1443 until the death of Sigismondo (1468), and was eyewitness of most of the narrated event.[4] For Federico di Montefeltro the more detailed biography is the one composed by Pierantonio Paltroni after 1470. Instructed to write the captain's biography, Paltroni has followed Federico in every military campaign since 1439; he was therefore present at the narrated events and recounts them with a not overstated partisan spirit.[5] In the end, about Giovanni de' Medici the most interesting source are the letters written by Pietro Aretino,[6] who followed Giovanni since 1525 and was a witness of his last days. Furthermore, the biographies written in the XVI century by Giovan Battista Tedaldi (1495-1575) have to be taken into account, who personally served Giovanni, and by Gian Girolamo Rossi (1505-1564), bishop of Pavia.[7] These biographies and chronicles must be amended by various quotations taken from contemporary authors and chronicles.

In conclusion, in the space of this article it is not possible to analyse, not even with a summary, the army's structure or the Renaissance Italian warfare, for which I refer to the studies in the footnote.[8]

---

3   TATEO, 1990, p. 114. On this subject see also: FINZI, 1993, pp. 37-59, and the introduction by Valentini in CAMPANO, 1929.
4   The *Cronaca Malatestiana* is extracted from the unpublished *Cronica Universale*. See the item BROGLIO, Gaspare, in: Dizionario Biografico degli Italiani, Treccani.
5   About the life of Paltroni see the introduction to the publication of his *commentarii* written by Walter Tommasoli: PALTRONI, 1966, pp. 9-28.
6   About Pietro Aretino see: LARIVAILLE, 1980.
7   TEDALDI, 1833, pp. 11-18; ROSSI, 1833.
8   DEL TREPPO, 1973, pp. 253-275 and 2001, pp. 417-452; PIERI, 1952 and 1966, pp. 99-119; ANCONA, 1973, pp. 643-665; STORTI, 1997, pp. 257-271; MALLETT, 1974, 1988, pp. 257-271, and 2007; DEL NEGRO, 2001; CONTAMINE, 1986; WALEY, 1993, pp. 111-128; CARDINI, 2001b, pp. 8-41; ARFAIOLI, 2005, pp. 1-27.

The virtue of *Fortitudo*

Necessarily, the analysis of the soldier's body and its risks is interlaced with the XIV and XV century moral and military literature, and therefore with the moral virtues that are submitted to the ideal military action. Contamine, in his *La guerre au Moyen Âge*, has sketched a preliminary history of the courage, analysing its description in some treatises and identifying the concept of courage with the virtue of *fortitude*.[9] *Fortitudo* is one of the four cardinal virtues, according to the system invented by Plato, in which the fortitude, often combined with the courage, is the one that grants resoluteness and tenacity in difficulties. Tommaso d'Aquino pinpointed fortitude as the strength in the line of duty that is the virtue which makes the man intrepid in front of any danger. In the laical context, fortitude is the typical characteristic of the strong man who does not hesitate in front of enemies or obstacles, and is therefore often associated to the military world. In the military context, *fortitudo* have to deal, at the same time, with the fear of death and with bravery and for this reason, both boldness and military skills derive from fortitude.[10] A suitable example is offered by the *Tractatus de bello, de represaliis et de duello* written around 1360 by Giovanni da Legnano, an Italian jurist and canon lawyer at the University of Bologna, who was read and printed during the XV century. The professor asserts that war is composed of three elements: brawn, fortitude and weapons. For the author, *fortitudo* is the most important, since it gives the strength both to assault and to wait the enemies' assault and, therefore, it's a virtue sided between courage and fear.[11] Military and moral literature played a central role in the definition of the war's virtues and the composition of the perfect soldier's code of conduct. "Many of the legal and military treatises which constituted the framework of a sort of international code of arms in the fifteenth century were Italian. Giovanni da Legnano, Egidio Colonna, and Bartolomeo da Saliceto were amongst the most influential writers and codifiers in the

---

9 CONTAMINE, 1986, pp. 339-351.
10 *Fortitudo* consists of seven different components: magnanimity, trust, self-confidence, munificence, tenacity, tolerance (also called patience or resoluteness) and perseverance.
11 See: ERMINI, 1923; *DA LEGNANO, Giovanni* in Dizionario Biografico degli Italiani, Treccani.

fourteenth century", even though the XV century produced more practical than theoretical treatises. In the everyday life of the army probably were active conventions formed as "a combination of standard legal codes and long-standing military and chivalric custom"[12], which relied largely on the captains' model and the competition between soldiers.[13]

In summary, the virtue of *fortitudo* was rooted within the military culture of the Italian Renaissance, and represented both the courage to resist to the fear and to not give in to the enemy's provocations, and both the courage to rush into the battle without fearing pain, wounds and death. It symbolised the virtue of the soldier who is able to attack but also to wait and to endure deprivations and suffering, without falling prey to the instinct but applying an essentially human rationality. Braccio insisted on this quality of the Italian soldiers during a dispute with Alfonso V d'Aragona in 1423[14] about the differences between Italians soldiers and the foreigner ones:

"I primarily think that the wars do not consist of the number of the soldiers, but of the virtue [...] and this virtue is not ascribed to the sturdiness of the body, but to the spirit's prudence. You [...], like wild beasts, start running into enemies' arms, and you die mostly because of your disorderly fury than because of the virtue of others, and you think that your recklessness has to be celebrated as virtue."[15]

---

12 MALLETT, 1974, pp. 205f.
13 About the factors of cohesion within the Italian army see: ZUG TUCCI, 1993, pp. 157-177.
14 On the army of Alfonso d'Aragona, and his dispute with Braccio see the chapter *Alfonso V d'Aragona e le armi italiane*, in: PIERI, 1966, pp. 91-97. For the entire narration of the fact see: CAMPANO, 1929, pp. 165-168; PELLINI, 1572, pp. 111-114.
15 PELLINI, 1572, p. 111: "Io primieramente sono d'oppenione, che le guerre non consistano nel numero de' soldati, ma nel valore, [...] et che questo valore non s'habbia tanto da attribuire alla gagliardezza del corpo, quanto alla prudenza dell'animo. Voi [...] vi date à guisa di fiere precipitosamente correndo nell'armi de' nemici, et morite piu tosto per cagion della vostra disordinata furia, che per prodezza altrui, et giudicate, che s'habbia à celebrare per virtù la vostra temerità". See: FINZI, 1993, pp. 45-50.

Hence, to possess the virtue of the soldier means to be aware of when it is advantageous to attack and when, instead, it is necessary to wait and placate the instinct and the battle's adrenaline. Again, Braccio makes this idea explicit when he affirmed: "I'm aware that these Germans madly run not just toward the battle, but toward the death, which happens when someone is totally ignorant of the military art, and allow itself to be ruled by its idiotic ferocity."[16] This double connotation of *fortitudo* as firmness and courage takes largely account of the impulsiveness and instinct; this virtue of the sensitivity's control in the crucial moment of the fought war is part of the soldier's training, and is underlined for example, in the fencing manuals of the XV century.[17] In fact, it is present in the most famous Italian fencing manual, the *Floss Duellatorum* by Fiore dei Liberi of Cividale. The treatise, dedicated to Niccolò III d'Este, was written between 1400 and 1409, and includes the sword in one and two hands, in armor, daga, spear etc. In every surviving manuscript, there is an image, called the *segno di scherma*, or "the seven swords", which presents the seven basic strokes of the sword and the four basic virtues of the fencer.[18]

---

16 IBID., pp. 113f.: "Io intendo, che cotesti Tedeschi, che voi dite, vanno pazzamente correndo non dirò alla battaglia, ma alla morte, il che è forza, che si faccia quando altri è del tutto ignorante dell'arte della guerra, et si lascia governare dalla sua stolta ferocità".

17 In the space of this article it is not possible to investigate the different perception of the body within the development of the fencing treatises through the XV and XVI century. I would like only to underline that if in the first part of the XV century, following the example of Fiore de' Liberi, the body which applies the sword and military techniques is performing an art, since the end of the century, with the work of Filippo Vadi (1483-87), the body and the swordsmanship are compared to a science associated to music and to geometry: "La geometria e musica comparte/ le loro virtù scientifiche in la spada/ per adornare el gran lume de Marte", RUBBOLI/ CESARI, 2005, pp. 36f.. This interpretation of the body is well integrated in an arc of development which increasingly understands the body as a machine, starting with the anatomy treatises of the XVI and XVII century. The idea of the swordsmanship as a perfect and calculated science will have its full exemplification in fencing manuals such as the *Trattato di Scientia d'Arme* by Camillo Agrippa, and the *Gran simulacro dell'arte e dell'uso della scherma* by Ridolfo Capoferro.

18 Until now were found four different manuscripts: the Getty manuscript, Ludwig XV 13, J.Paul Getty Museum, Los Angeles, California, published in a critical edition by MALIPIERO, 2006; the Morgan manuscript, Morgan MS. M. 383, Morgan Library & Museum, New York City; the *Florius de*

These virtues are embodied by four different animals [19] : *forteza* (*fortitudo*) represented by the elephant, *presteza* (*celeritas*) represented by the tiger, *ardimento* (*audatia*) embodied by the lion and, in the end, *avisamento* (*prudentia*) embodied by the lynx. The gloss of fortitude says: "I am the elephant and I have a castle as cargo, and I do not kneel or lose my place."[20] The fencer (and the soldier) must share the qualities that the elephant symbolised during the Middle Ages, namely justice, patience, obedience and both physical and moral strength. Drawn positioned under the feet of the *magister*, fortitude is the first and basic virtue a fencer must learn during its education. This iconography of the elephant as representative of fortitude had a wide diffusion. For example, it fulfills a double symbolic function in the medals by Matteo de' Pasti and some anonymous of Rimini made for Sigismondo Malatesta on the occasion of the inauguration of the Malatestian Temple. On the downside of these medals, dated 1446 and 1447, the personification of *fortitudo* sustained by two elephants is represented, which were both the heraldic animals of the Malatesta family and both the animal representation of fortitude.[21]

---

arte luctandi Miss. Latin 11269, Bibliothèque nationale de France, Parigi; the Pisani-Dossi manuscript, *Floss Duellatorum in armis, sine armis, equester et pedester*, now in a private collection, published in a critical edition by RAPISARDI, 2008. In this article I refer to the Getty manuscript.

19 The comparison to the animal world, and to the different qualities and virtues attributed to them, was very frequent. For example, in the *Arte Gladiatoria dimicandi* by Filippo Vadi (although written on the basis of the Floss) the virtues of the fencer are embodied by other animals, namely the bear, the ram, the snake and the greyhound. See: RUBBOLI/CESARI, 2005, pp. 61f.. On the interpretation of the animals see: PASTOUREAU, 2012.

20 "Ellefante son e un castello porto per chargo / e non mi inzinochio ne perdo vargo", Ludwig XV 13, f. 32r, J.Paul Getty Museum, Los Angeles, California.

21 Reproductions n. 5-6-7-8 in: CALABI/CORNAGGIA, 1927, pp. 38f.. See also the marble medallion representing *fortitudo* with the same characteristics inside the Malatestian Temple in Rimini, probably made by Antonio di Duccio, in: IBID., n. 3, p. 47. The concept of *fortitudo* was dear to the cultural framework of Sigismondo, as he wrote in one of his sonnets: "La lima rode el ferro, l'acqua i marmi/ Per lo spesso cader de l'alto tecto,/ el continuo bussar spezza omne muro./ Non debb'io adonca al tucto abandonarmi,/ Ma porger sempre prieghi al duro pecto,/ Sperano che fia umìle ben che sia duro.", TURCHINI, 1985, p. 12.

Hence, *fortitudo* is the virtue of resisting and enduring, but it is also the virtue of the courage to attack and to hold the enemy's stare and going into battle.[22] When debating military practice, the central role played by ferocity and by violence cannot be forgotten.[23] In this context the virtue represented by the lion in the *Floss Duellatorum* comes into play: "Nobody has a more brave heart than me lion, and I invite everybody to battle."[24] If the *condottieri* have to embody to their soldiers all the virtues that they require, courage and ferocity have to be released at the appropriate time. "All the Princes are creatures of violence, and without it the soldier's ferocity becomes the tameness of a monk. No virtue is looked with more regard by the troops", Pietro Aretino affirmed, "because when it matures the furies which are moving it, it is converted into glory."[25] In conclusion, the central issue concerning the possession of the virtue of fortitude is not to erase anger and ferocity, but to apply them with rationality, distancing them from an instinctive and beastly attitude, as narrated by Giangirolamo Rossi about a conversation between Giovanni de' Medici and one of his soldiers: "Some were saying to one of his soldiers 'You go bravely that you are right'; and then [Giovanni] said to him 'Do not rely on this, but on your heart, and on your hands, otherwise you will appear like a beast.'"[26]

---

22 The subject of the ferocious gaze is recurrent, but it cannot be analyzed in this article. For example, Braccio says about the opponent soldiers: "They are not men capable of hold for a long time the gaze of our furious eyes", PELLINI, 1572, p. 65. "Non sono però huomini da sostenere lungamente lo sguardo de gli occhi nostri adirati".
23 About violence in the late Middle Ages see: HALE, 1972, pp. 19-37.
24 "Più de mi leone non porta core ardito, pero di bataglia fazo azaschun invito", f. 32r, Ludwig XV 13, J.Paul Getty Museum, Los Angeles, California.
25 "Tutti i Principi son creature della violenza, e senza essa la ferocità del soldato diventa mansuetudine fratesca. Niuna vertù ha in sé la milizia di più riguardo [...] per ciò ch'ella nel maturare i furori che la movano, si converte in gloria". Letter of Pietro Aretino to the captain Vincenzo Bovetto, November 25, 1537, in: ARETINO, 1997, t. I, book I, pp. 349f..
26 ROSSI, 1833, p. 171: "Dicendo alcuni ad un suo soldato che andava a combattere: 'va' arditamente, che hai ragione'; egli gli disse: 'non ti confidare in questo, ma nel quore, e nelle mani, altrimenti parrai una bestia'".

Deprivations, pain and scars: the interpretation of the soldier's body

Apart from the ideal virtue, in the everyday practice of warfare and in the soldier's life, fortitude coincided with the endurance of the pain, with the ability to suffer the training in arms and the war's deprivations. In particular the deprivations of the body were a badge of honour for soldiers and their *condottieri*, since the good training of the soldier corresponded to his ability to endure pain and strain. Jean de Bueil, in *Le Jouvencel* (about 1466), interpreted war as a school of asceticism, fit for the purpose to get the body used to deprivations, which requires "pain and struggle" and the ability to bear "suffering, dangers, poverty and famines."[27] For this reason, it is easy to notice many references both to their ability to endure, and to the deprivations that they shared with their soldiers in XV century's chronicles and treatises about the good qualities of the *condottieri*. The exemplary nature of the *condottieri*'s action for their soldiers will be analysed later in this article. For now, it can be noticed how the same themes are proposed in many descriptions and eulogies. The conduct of Sigismondo Malatesta, for example, during the 1448 siege of Piombino, is described by Roberto Valturio in these terms:

> "The military seriousness of Sigismondo excelled; in the resistance of the difficulties of the wakefulness, the thirst, the starvation and of every hardship [...]. He was happy to break the mouldy and black bread with his soldiers that otherwise would have been thrown to the dogs [...] He was not nauseate to drink the muddy and sulphate waters; on the contrary he savoured them so playfully that, by seeing him, the soldiers did not mind the deprivations of wines and clean waters."[28]

The same was written about Sigismondo's greater enemy, Federico di Montefeltro, who was described as "patient about cold and heat, starvation, thirst, sleepiness and difficulties as much as he wanted, without one could presume that any of these things gave him stress or

---

27 Quoted in: CONTAMINE, 1986, pp. 343f..
28 The passage, quoted in TABANELLI, 1977, p. 75, is taken from *De Re Militari*, written by Roberto Valturio, book VII, chapter 17.

bother."[29] Similar terms are used by Braccio da Montone during the dispute with Alfonso V d'Aragona. Braccio, as reported by Giovanni Campano, describes the soldiers as:

"those who had hardened the body by heat, and cold, those who from childhood are used to sleep in stables, and have learned to suffer dust, wind, hunger, thirst, sleepiness, and others great difficulties, without any pleasure and, raised between enemy's arms, have learned to disregard the wounds, to throw and parry the blows."[30]

The bond between the *condottiero* and his soldiers, characterised by respect and imitation, is created therefore through the suffering of the body. In fact, of Braccio is said that

"he did not send his soldiers within troubles, but he went with them in person, and, just like them, he submitted himself in difficulties, starvation, and wakefulness, he gave all the spoils to his own, wanted for himself just glories and the command. Therefore the love, that the army had for him, was born, and the goodwill of the soldiers."[31]

---

29 PALTRONI, 1966, pp. 53f.: "patientissimo de freddo et de caldo, de fame, de sete, de sonno et de fadica quanto a lui piacea, senza che si potesse presumere che alcuna de queste cose gli desse afanno o molestia".
30 PELLINI, 1572, p. 112: "Quelli, che hanno indurati, et incalliti i corpi dal caldo, et dal freddo, i quali infin dalla fanciullezza si sono avezzi à dormire nelle stalle, et hanno imparato à sopportare la polvere, il vento, la fame, la sete, il sonno, et altre fatiche grandissime, senz'alcun piacere, et allevatisi infra l'armi de' nemici, hanno imparato a disprezzare le ferite, à menare, et à riparare i colpi".
31 PELLINI, 1572, p. 20: "Egli non mandava i soldati ne' pericoli, ma v'andava con esso loro in persona, et non meno di loro si sottometteva alle fatiche, alla fame, et alle vigilie, dava tutta la preda à suoi, solo per sé voleva la glorie, et l'imperio. quindi poi nacque quell'amore, che gli portava l'essercito, et la gran benevolenza de' soldati".
The subject of the difference between glory and spoils, between the motivation of the *condottiero* and of the soldiers, although of a great interest, is too extended to be analyzed in this article.

As the final recipient of the war's dangers and pain, the body becomes the cornerstone of the life of the armies, where deprivations, wounds and mutilations were certainties of the profession.

Even though very different from the kind of war that was fought beyond the Alps, "Italian Renaissance warfare was far from bloodless but rarely unnecessarily brutal."[32] The wounds, especially those originated from the new firearms, were common between mercenaries and professional soldiers, therefore more wounds and scars decorated the body of the veteran. This characteristic of the Italian armies is well illustrated by Braccio in the aforementioned dispute with Alfonso, while explaining the peculiarity, or the supposed superiority, of the Italian soldiers. The Italian warfare is more technical, more professional and involves a smaller number of soldiers more expert in the profession of arms, well trained at the military life. "Better is to use a small number of well-trained soldiers, than a malpractice multitude"[33], Braccio affirmed, criticising the Spanish "bad war", which "represented a concept of total war, a determination to ensure that the enemy did not fight again, which was largely alien to contemporary Italian attitudes to war."[34] In fact, it was common in the XV century for the Italian *condotte* to make an explicit request of soldiers "good, apt, experts, and adequate to the profession of arms."[35]

In this framework of interpretation, the good care of the body, and its training, assumes a key role, due to its double function; on one hand, a fragile body which needed to be protected by an increasingly sophisticated armor[36] and, on the other, a strong body reinforced by

---

32 MALLETT, 1974, p. 200.
33 PELLINI, 1572, p. 112: "Meglio è però di servirsi d'un picciol numero bene amaestrato, che d'una mal prattica moltitudine". This idea was already present in Vegezio, when he affirmed that "In every conflict the number is not as useful as the courage", quoted in: CONTAMINE, 1986, p. 341.
34 MALLETT, 1974, p. 200.
35 "Buoni, apti, experti et idonei nel mestiero delle armi", 1478, September 10th, Conventions for the *condotta* of Ercole d'Este, Duke of Ferrara, as general captain of the League between Venice, Milan, Florence and Ferrara. Document written out in full in: CANESTRINI, 2007, doc. n. XXVII, pp. 156-164.
36 Putting the life in danger did not correspond to the sacrifice or an absolute devotion, which were concepts aliens to the XV century's military mentality. Therefore the armor's development both for men and horses is originated

deprivations and battles, which bears the signs of the scars as a testimony of the soldier's value and courage.[37] Particularly wounds, scars and calluses are fundamental themes in the construction of the fictional speeches of the *condottieri* to their soldiers, as narrated in the chronicles, at a time when they had to instil courage and pride in his troops. For example, Braccio said to his soldiers before the battle of Sant'Egidio, in the 1416: "[the enemies], accustomed to idleness, will never be able to stand in front of you, who are full of scars and calluses on your faces and on your hands."[38] Similar words were spoken by the opponent captain, Carlo Malatesta, while was appealing to his soldiers' bravery: "Who turns his back gives to the enemy the chance to strike him without fail. And there are no more dishonoured wounds than those in the back and, on the contrary, none is more honoured than those in the chest and in the face."[39] It can be noticed how scars were a defined symbol within the military world, which represented virtue, courage and dedication to the profession of arms. One may therefore think that to be injured during the battle was a source of pride among the soldiers. Giovanni Antonio Campano, while composing his biography of Braccio da Montone, relied on the tales and the memories of the *condottiero*'s veterans, the

---

from this idea, CONTAMINE, 1986, p. 346. About armors and warfare during the Italian wars see: SCALINI, 2001a, pp. 102-147.

37 In the same dispute Braccio affirms: "It also happens, that very few die for our way to battle, therefore, we Italians are all covered in iron, and rarely happens that the blows penetrate at the flesh, or are deadly". PELLINI, 1572, p. 112: "aviene anco, che ne muoiono pochi dal nostro modo d'armare, conciosiacosa, che noi Italiani andiamo tutti coperti di ferro, et rare volte incontra, che i colpi penetrino al vivo, ò siano mortali".

38 PELLINI, 1572, pp. 65f.: "[i nemici], assuefatti ad un lungo otio, non potranno mai stare à fronte con esso voi, pieni di cicatrici, et di calli il volto, et le mani"; CAMPANO, 1929, pp. 97f.: "Veterani si qui 'sunt hostium milites, quos ille per oppida disiectos uxoribus enervandos exhauriendosque dispersarat, desueta iam bello sunt et longo otio soluta corpora, nequicquam nostris cicatricibus et duratis callo lacertis congressura". The battle took place on July 12th 1416.

39 IBID., pp. 67f.: "chi volta le spalle, da occasione al nemico di poterlo offendere à man salva. ne ci sono feirte più disonorate di quelle di dietro, e per lo contrario, niuna più honorata di quelle del petto, et del viso"; CAMPANO, 1929, p. 99: "Sed qui terga vertit hosti, feriendum se impune offert, nec ulla tam foeda vulnera, quam quae tergo excipiuntur: contra nulla honestior quam adverso in pectore fronteque cicatrix".

bracceschi; and, it is no accident that, in the narration of the winning battle of Rocca Contrada of 1407, he underlined how two of the most trusted soldiers of Braccio, Spinta and Guglielmo Mecca, received (they and their horses) respectively 105 and 72 wounds, "an event worth of memory for all the people who will come."[40] *Fortitudo*, in this case, is the virtue that allows soldiers to endure the enemy's attack, and the pain of the injuries.

This interpretation of scars, endurance and training of the body, and its symbolic meaning, was well known within the Italian military system and played a role even in the selection of the soldiers. In the following extract from the biography of Braccio, Campano (during the narration of the intense military campaign of the 1412-1413) compares the *bracceschi* to the enemies, praises the veterans' qualities and summarises all the different aspects of the interpretation of the body:

"Most of the enemies were new soldiers, and the *bracceschi* were all veterans [...]. Those were effeminate due to the home's pleasures, they did not dare to see the people in battle, and these, having the bodies hardened by the sun, and the wind, and accustomed to the wounds, did not fear even the blows of the swords. [...] They were more eager for the glory of their captain than of their own profit; and it is sure that he used a wonderful diligence in the selection of soldiers, and he did not want them big and large, so that the horses (as he used to say) would not have been weakened by the heavy weight, but small, and less than of a medium stature, as long as they were strong and violent, and had a soldier's inclination and, above all, he liked the most those who were respectable for the signs of the wounds in the face and who had the other limbs torn by blows."[41]

---

40 IBID., p. 15: "Un certo Spinta, ch'era stato in fin da fanciullo suo soldato [di Braccio] hebbe trà lui, e'l cavallo, 105 ferite, et guglielmo Mecca 72. Cosa veramente degna di memoria à tutte le genti che verranno". CAMPANO, 1929, pp. 28-29: "Omnes vulnerati, inter quos Spinta quidam, qui sub Braccio iam inde a puero militaverat, una cum equo centum et quinque confossus vulneribus, Gulielmus Mecha duobus et septuaginta. Res omni posteritate memorabilis".
41 IBID., p. 44: "i nemici erano la maggior parte soldati nuovi, et i bracceschi veterani tutti [...]. Quelli finalmente essendo effeminati nelle delitie di casa, non ardivano di veder le genti in battaglia, et questi havendo i corpi indurati

The visible scars in the face are, therefore, a material demonstration of the soldier's virtue, as an ability to suffer and endure blows and wounds. In other words, they display the awareness of the human body's fragility but, at the same time, also the capacity to endure pain, to tackle and to overcome it, regenerating the spirit in the same way the skin does with the scars. "The skin, 'the man's shell', is a particularly rich field; place of exchange between the body's inside and outside, organ of touch, it constantly reveals its vulnerability, its receptivity to blows and cuts, but also its formidable regeneration skill: the skin is a permanent source of life."[42] The skin, hence, the face's skin in particular, becomes an identification sign, a canvas on which are incised the soldier's characteristics, a means to the revelation of someone's virtues. "Therefore, the skin it's a piece that worth for the whole. Surely is the casing, the sack in which the body mass resides, namely the bone structure, the flesh and the blood; but it is also fundamentally what characterises and identifies."[43] The scars in the face, in fact, were one of the recommended aspects useful to the identification and registration of the foot soldier, in the first years of the XVI century, as we can read in

---

dal sole, et dal vento, et assuefatti alle ferite, non temevano pure i colpi delle spade. [...] Erano più desiderosi della gloria del lor capitano che del lor proprio guadagno; et certa cosa è, ch'egli usava una maravigliosa diligenza nella elettion de' soldati, ne gli voleva grandi, et grossi, affine che i cavalli (come egli solea dire) dal troppo gran peso non s'indebolissero, ma piccioli, et meno che di mediocre statura, purche fossero robusti et gagliardi, et che havessero buona presenza di soldato, et gli piacevano sopra tutti gli altri coloro, che fossero stati riguardevoli per li segni delle ferite del volto, et che dalle percosse havessero lacerate l'altre membra del corpo."; CAMPANO, 1929, pp. 70f.: "Hostium plerique tirones, Bracciani veterani omnes [...]. Denique illis emolliti domesticis deliciis animi ferri aciem expavescebant; Braccianis durata sole ventoque et plena vulneribus corpora ne ictus quidem gladiorum formidabant [...]. Nam illud quoque constat, in militibus deligendis singulari usum diligentia; nec magnos aut procer, ne, quod dicere solebat, equos nimio fatigarent pondere, sed breves et infra mediocres, robustos tamen ac 'bonae habitudinis conducere libentius consuesse; maxime omnium quos adversa fronte cicatrices et deformata plagis ac vulneribus membra, insignia bellicae virtutis, notarent".
42 GÉLIS, 2000, p. 103.
43 IBID., pp. 110f..

the *Avvertenze ai Dieci di Balìa*.[44] So, as can be noticed, this framework of interpretation of the suffering of the body, and in particular of scars and wounds, was well established within the Renaissance military mentality, as stated by Pietro Aretino, while was comforting Giovanni de' Medici on his deathbed, reminding him that "The wounds and the loss of limbs are the necklaces and the medals of the family members of Mars."[45]

"Non feci mai cose indegne di me"[46]
The condottiero and his example through suffering, death and the body.

The just described cultural frame of mind was valid both for the soldiers and the captains; *condottieri* had to lead and command the soldiers through respect, fear and example, showing their acknowledgment of the displaying of the soldiers' virtues and, at the same time, had to provide prove that they embodied all the qualities requested from the troops. It has already been noticed, with the previous examples, how the *condottiero* submitted himself to the deprivations of war, together with his soldiers. Now it is interesting to highlight how this just described cultural approach implicated the need of a continuous manifestation of bravery by the *condottieri*; furthermore how, in the *a posteriori* tale of their deeds, these men are transformed into exemplary soldiers, thanks to a narrative process in which the body keeps to play a key role.

The captain was a role model for his soldiers and, to ensure that the troops would have followed him into battle, he had to become an example

---

44 Around 1500, *Avvertenze ai Dieci di Balìa per la condotta dei Conestabili al tempo della guerra di Pisa*. About the way to register the foot soldiers is written: "I would like that, as first thing, it will be written the name of that particular soldier, and the name of his father, and his place; and then the time that he has; what weapons he carries; and then his height, and it will be written as many signs as he has on the face". Document written out in full in: CANESTRINI, 2007, doc. n. LXI, pp. 258-268.
45 "Le ferite e la perdita dei membri, sono le collane e le medaglie de i famigliari di Marte". Letter from Pietro Aretino to Francesco de gli Albizzi, December 10th 1526, in: ARETINO, 1997, t. I, book I, p. 55.
46 See note n. 74.

of bravery and be at the head of his troops, thus demonstrating his boldness and the absence of fear of pain and wounds. Since the bravery of an isolated man is insufficient to achieve victory, the *condottiero* must draw, through the example, the moltitudine into battle; therefore, the individual's courage becomes everyone's courage.

> "If the soldiers see the captain hesitant, irresolute, and distrustful of his own strength, they cannot, under any circumstances, keep themselves for fleeing, but if they see him full of ardour, and of hope, cheerfully approaching the army, urging the soldiers to fight, they do not have any fear, even if they would find themselves in great and evident danger."[47]

From these words, attributed to Angelo della Pergola, it can be noticed that the *condottiero* must have been not only fearless but, to be able to lead the soldiers, he had also to desire the battle and to show his urge to fight. This scenario happened during the battle of Monteluro, fought on December 8, 1443 [48], when Sigismondo Malatesta (at the time *condottiero* of the general captain Francesco Sforza), led his soldiers against the troops of Niccolò Piccinino, although Sforza did not want to engage:

> "[Sigismondo] trembled in his mind because he wanted to engage battle [with a captain of Niccolò Piccinino], and sent the trumpeters to his camp so that every man would have get on his horse. [...] Sigismondo, passionate and eager for going against the aforementioned captain, had this thought, and then put it in place, and mounted on the horse with his helmet in his head, with some of his men, ferociously went to find the captain of Niccolò Piccinino [...]. And [Francesco Sforza] went to

---

47 PELLINI, 1572, p. 13: "Il capitano, il quale, se i soldati veggono esser timido, irresoluto, et diffidente delle sue forze, non possono per niuna diligenza del mondo ritenersi dalla fuga, ma se all'incontro lo veggono tutto pieno d'ardire, et di speranza, andare allegramente intorno all'essercito, essortando i soldati à combattere, non hanno alcun timore, etiandio se in grave et manifesto pericolo si vedessero."

48 For a report of the battle in the contemporary chronicles see: PALTRONI, 1966, pp. 63-65; SIMONETTA, 1934, pp. 132-134; ANONIMO RIMINESE, 1922, p. 95; GIOVANNI PEDRINO, 1986, p. 207.

separate them and he could not do it, because Sigismondo was impetuous due to his ardour."[49]

Sigismondo and his troops achieved a great victory, thanks to the quick attack, "and first for Sigismondo's virtue; but not that his lordship was not wounded."[50] So it is during this fearless ride into the battle, when the *condottiero* shows his disregard for pain and wounds that the bond between the captain and the soldiers grow stronger. "What captured the heart of his troops, was that, in troubles, he was saying 'Follow me' and not 'Go in front of me'",[51] told Pietro Aretino about Giovanni de' Medici and the Black Bands. This attitude had the power, as outlined in Angelo della Pergola's speech, to instill courage and bravery into the soldiers, creating a spirit of excitement and restlessness, well described in the verses of the XV century anonymous poem about the battle of Aquila: "They heard the captain's speech/ Who is coward becomes paladin./ They all shouted: 'we are already come to blows by now,/ And we will see who is not violent.'"[52] Hence, the virtues are manifested, obviously, through the actions, but also through the signs these actions leave on the soldier's body. Therefore, more scars testify greater virtue and courage and, for this reason, the *condottieri* are expected to be more decorated

---

49 BROGLIO, 1982, pp. 107f.: "Nella sua mente [Sigismondo] tucto fremiva de volerse atacare co' lui [un capitano di Niccolò Piccinino], e mandò al suo canpo i suoi trombetti che ogni homo montasse a cavallo. [...] inanimito lo illustrissimo signore miser Sigismondo e aceso di volontade d'andare a trovare el prefato capitano, e facto dicto pensiero, lo mise assequitione, e montato a cavallo col suo elmetto in testa, con alquanti di suoi andò ferocemente a trovare lo prefato capitano di Niccolò Piccinino [...]. e andò la signoria sua per distacarlo e non podè, per che lo illustrissimo signore miser Sigismondo inanimato più e'l acendiva".
50 IBID.: "Prima per la vertù hoperata per lo prefato signore miser Sigismondo di Malatesti; non però che sua signoria non fosse ferita".
51 "E quel che tirava a sé il core de le genti sue, era il dire ne i pericoli 'Venitimi dietro', e non 'Andatimi innanzi'". Letter from Pietro Aretino to Francesco de gli Albizzi, December 10th 1526, in: ARETINO, 1997, t. I, book I, p. 58.
52 ANONIMO, 1935, p. 143: "Odenno lo parlar dello capetano/ Deventa paladinu chi è codardu./ Grydano tucty: 'Omay sciamo alle mano,/ Et vederasse chi non è galliardo'". The oratory talent of the *condottieri* is another subject dear to humanism, but it cannot be analyzed here.

with scars and wounds. One more time, Braccio's words during his dispute with Alfonso make explicit this framework of interpretation:

> "Those, who exceed all the others for virtue, courage and faith and are followed by soldiers, captains and colonels, are our Generals and captains of the Italian armies. And there is nothing, which they are feeling more proud of, than to show a great quantity of wounds in the chest, and the body all lacerated by scars."[53]

So, through *condottieri*'s body images and quality descriptions, this consideration for the scars within the military mentality, also as a valid symbol in the development of the relationship between the captain and his troops, can be realised one more time. Again, it is said of Giovanni de' Medici that "He testified his love for the army, embellishing his legs, limb and the chest with the signs printed by arms."[54] As a summary of this two aspects of the captain's courage, namely to lead by example and to endure pain and wounds, stands Federico di Montefeltro's actions during the battle of San Fabiano, fought on July 22 1460.[55] Two days earlier, Federico suffered a sprain to the loins during a skirmish and "nowise he could move or go, but he was like dead and had such pain and passion that it was a marvel."[56] Then, the command passed to

---

53 PELLINI, 1572, pp. 113f.: "Quelli, che avanzano tutti gli altri di virtù, di valore, et di fede, sono seguiti dà soldati, dà capitani et dà Colonnelli, et questi sono i nostri Generali, et capitani de gli esserciti Italiani. Ne cosa alcuna è, di che essi più honorati si tengano, che del mostrare una gran quantità di ferite nel petto, et il corpo tutto lacerato dalle cicatrici"; CAMPANO, 1929, p. 168: "Hi sunt imperatores nostri: haec italica imperia. Nullum preclarius insigne quam vulnerum adverso pectore moltitudo et deformata cicatricibus corpora".
54 "Era il testimonio de l'amore che portava a la milizia, ricamandosi le gambe, le braccia e il busto con i segni che stampavano l'armi". Letter from Pietro Aretino to Francesco de gli Albizzi, December 10th 1526, in: ARETINO, 1997, t. I, book I, p. 58. See also the aspect's description of Braccio in: PELLINI, 1572, pp. 93f.; CAMPANO, 1929, pp. 142f..
55 See the report of the battle written by the chancellor of Alessandro Sforza in: ANONIMO VERONESE, 1915, pp. 140f..
56 PALTRONI, 1966, p. 149: "In su'l mover del cavallo, che se mosse disconcio, el conte Federico prese una storta et una doglia alli lumbi, che *vulgariter* se chiama el mal del dilombato, che per niuno modo si potea moviere né

Alessandro Sforza who, on July 22, was attracted into battle by the opponent captain Jacopo Piccinino. Federico's troops were finding themselves on a disadvantageous field of battle and started to retreat. Federico "was feeling so much pain that he had no spirit to climb on his horse; nonetheless he had himself mounted on the horse in the best way possible and in a great pain", and with four squires he arrived at the field. "And due to his arrival the troops found spirit, solace and big hope [...] not without enormous danger for his person because, without wearing his armour, he struggled where the soldiers were not safe, and his horse was wounded and damaged, and he was alive thanks to a miracle."[57]

In conclusion, on the subject of the exemplar captain, it is interesting to linger on the deaths of Braccio da Montone and Giovanni de' Medici. Without probing the extended and complicated interpretation of Renaissance funeral rituality[58], it is useful to underline the role played by the condottieri's manifestation of wounds and mutilations, and the effect this display had on the contemporaries and in the later literary transpositions. In the battle of Aquila, fought on June 2 1424, Braccio was mortally wounded in the neck by an anonymous soldier, carried to the enemy camp where he remained for three days inside of the opponent captain's pavilion, Jacopo Caldora[59], where he was visited by captains, doctors and soldiers. He spent his last days refusing any doctors'

---

andare, se non como quasi fusse morto et stava cum tanta doglia et passione che era una maraviglia".
57 IBID., pp. 153-155: "La doglia lo apresava per modo che non li bastava l'animo a montare a cavallo; pure si fece mectere a cavallo el meglio possette et cum grandissima doglia"; "Et per la venuta sua li suoi ne presero animo, conforto et speranza grandissima [...], non senza grandissimo pericolo de la sua persona perché, senza arme indosso, se adoperò dove li armati non istavano securi, et fo ferito et guasto el cavallo che havia sotto, et fu miraculo che lui non fusse morto". The battle of San Fabiano is narrated in SER GUERRIERO DA GUBBIO, 1902, pp. 70f.: "El signore conte era in lo alogiamento amalato; el quale sentendo li soi havere el peggio et quasi messi in volta, così amalato se fecie porre a cavallo". See also: PICCOLOMINI, 1984, pp. 747-749. See also: TOMMASOLI, 1978, p. 137.
58 On this subject see: ARIÉS, 1980; SALVESTRINI/VARANINI/ZANGARINI, 2007; ZUG TUCCI, 2007, pp. 243-274.
59 For a description of the battle in the contemporaries sources see: BROGLIO, 1982, p. 40; ANONIMO RIMINESE, 1922, pp. 57-58; PELLINI, 1572, pp. 139-142; CAMPANO, 1929, pp. 203-205; SIMONETTA, 1934, pp. 17-20; ANONIMO, 1935, pp. 187-227.

remedies, food or drink, without speaking to anybody; he remained silent in the display of his mortal wounds to anybody who wanted to admire them, "as if he did not want the enemies to have of himself more than a silent body."[60] Braccio died at the age of 56, in a way that drove his biographer to wonder the reasons of his silence: "But either he did not hear, or he faked not to hear, he never answered to him [Jacopo] nor to others with a single word, either because his deep and mortal lesions took out his spirit, or because, although the fate had given his almost lost body in the enemies' will, nonetheless he felt undefeated in his soul."[61] Wether the silence was caused by the wounds or by Braccio's stubbornness in demonstrating his virtue to the victorious enemy, his death struck the soldiers and the contemporaries deeply. The soldiers' attachment to their captain is well illustrated in the circumstances of his last days, when:

> "A lot of his soldiers [...] (while he was still alive) went to visit him and comfort him, but they never got him to speak or eat something"; "These discontent and quite soldiers, during the night, were seen to go in the enemy pavilion, and during the day (since it was permitted to them) they surrounded Braccio's bed touching him, gazing at him, and sighing; and

---

60 PELLINI, 1572, p. 139: "Et havendo già passato tre giorni interi senza mangiare et senza bere et senza pur mai dire una parola, quasi non volendo che i nemici havessero di se in poter loro altro, che un corpo mutolo". An excellent and in-depth analysis of Braccio's death, of the different causes of his silence and of the meanings of the death in battle can be found in: ZUG TUCCI, 2001, pp. 143-163.
61 PELLINI, 1572, p. 140: "Ma egli o che non udisse, ò che fingesse di non udire, non rispose mai, nè a lui, ne ad altri pur una minima parola, ò perché le mortali et profonde piaghe gli havesero tolto il sentimento, o perché quantunque la fortuna havesse dato in poter de' nemici il suo già quasi perduto corpo, egli nondimeno ritenesse ancora seco l'animo invitto"; CAMPANO, 1929, pp. 203f.: "Exemptum equo et intra tabernaculum subductum, benigne aut non audientem aut audire nolentem est affatus. Sed ne unum quidem elicere quisquam potuit verbum, vel quod alte descendentes mortiferae plagae vim omnem sensumque exhauserant, vel ut, quoniam fortuna victum corpus in potestatem hosti tradidisset, animum sibi invictum ipse retineret. [...] Sed destinatus ad mortem animus omnem medicamentorum opem respuebat. Quippe totum 'triduum sine cibo, sine potu, mutus cum egisset, incertum vulneribus an inedia, est extinctus, anno aetatis sexto et quinquagesimo".

when they came out from the pavilion, they covered their heads and cried, and made the enemies cry as well."[62]

And when he finally died, *"Illo mortuo, totis castris secutum silentium."*[63] His silence became everyone's silence and through his body Braccio became a representation of virtue, acknowledged both by his soldiers and by the enemies; his wounds were the tangible sign of military attitude, a mentality based on courage, example and control over the body and the pain, which permeated his army and his military school and was handed down through the following generations of soldiers and *condottieri*. The new techniques that Braccio introduced within the military practice (based on a smaller number of well-trained soldiers, on quick attacks and the continuous use of reserves) described by Giovanni Antonio Campano, contain all the four virtues of the fencer mentioned above about the *Floss Duellatorum*. A military strategy which relies on the war skills of the soldiers, who have to be carefully recruited and continuously trained by (and through) the war's deprivations, in which we can spot *fortitudo*; a strategy based on the *condottiero*'s virtue, his promptness (*celeritas*) and his courage to lead the troops into battle (*audatia*); finally, a technique which makes extensive use of *prudentia*,

---

62 IBID. pp. 139f.: "Molti de' suoi soldati [...] andarono (mentre egli ancora spirava) à visitarlo, et confortarlo, ne mai poterono ottener da lui, ch'egli parlasse, ò che si ricreasse almeno alquanto col cibo"; "Questi, venuta la notte, tutti malcontenti et queti, si vedevano andare intorno al padiglione nemico, et il giorno (poi ch'era loro permesso di farlo) gli circondavano il letto, toccandolo, rimirandolo, et sospirandogli intorno et quando uscivano dal padiglione, copertisi il capo, et piangendo, facevano uscir le lacrime dagli occhi etiandio a' nemici".

63 CAMPANO, 1929, p. 205: "Illo mortuo, totis castris secutum silentium, quasi plus esset in amisso doloris, quam laetitiae in capto. Eius milites, qui aut proelio superfuerant aut ab hostibus erant dimissi, plerique, facta potestate, spirantem adhuc consolandi gratia adierunt, remotisque arbitris, 'ut vocem tolleret utque cibum sumeret hortati, nihil profecerunt. Nec ullum in ducem tantus militum amor. Illi tabernaculum hostis noctu maesti ac taciti perlustrare, illi interdiu, facta quotiens vellent potestate, frequentes ad lectum perstare, tangere, intueri, suspirare cernebantur, et ubi tabernaculo excessissent, obvoluto capite plorantes, nulli non hostium lacrimas excutiebant".

in order to avoid the unforeseen and to risk as few lives as possible, distrusting the empty and ferocious temerity.

Like Braccio, Giovanni of the Black Bands found his death due to a wound in battle. He was the general captain of the papal army during the war of the League of Cognac that lasted from 1526 to 1530. In a battle with the landsknechts leaded by Georg von Frundsberg[64], Giovanni was hit by a shot of falconet in the right leg. The battle took place in Governolo, near Mantua, on November 25, 1526.[65] Giovanni was transported to Mantua, to the palace of Aloioso Gonzaga (lord of Castel Goffredo), and there medicated by Doctor Abramo Ariè (the personal doctor of Federico II Gonzaga, duke of Mantua). After a couple of days the doctor decided to amputate the wounded leg. Despite that, Giovanni died on the night of November 30 at the age of 28. The news of his death echoed throughout all of Italy, and everyone that reported the fact underlined Giovanni's conduct during his last days.[66] In particular, the fact that he did not want to be held by anyone during the leg amputation and his ability to endure such pain and torment. The most reliable sources are the letters of Pietro Aretino, who eye-witnessed the event: "The doctors send to find eight or ten men to hold Giovanni steady while they were violently sawing, 'Not even twenty (Giovanni said smiling) could hold me'. He went there with determined look, and he took a candle in his hand, so he could make light onto himself, and I ran away."[67] All the contemporary chronicles agree on Giovanni's endurance of the pain, like in Rossi's biography, where it is written that "While they were sawing,

---

64 About the landsknechts see: BAUMANN, 1996.
65 About the Italian war in the first years of the XVI century see: PIERI, 1952, pp. 536-593.
66 About the last days of Giovanni and his funeral: CISERI, 2001, pp. 202-221. See also: SCALINI, 2001c, pp. 222-229.
67 "Dissero si trovassero otto o dieci persone che lo tenessero mentre la violenza del segare durava. 'Né anco XX (disse egli sorridendo) mi terrebbero'. Recatosi là con fermissimo volto, presa la candela in mano, nel far lume a se medesimo, io me ne fuggì": letter from Pietro Aretino to Francesco de gli Albizzi, December 10th 1526, in: ARETINO, 1997, t. I, book I, pp. 55f..

he did not want to be tied up nor held steady by anyone, enduring that torture with great tenacity"[68], or in Tedaldi's:

"The doctors at last decided to saw off his leg, and he suffered with great tenacity without being held by anyone, and then he wanted to see the amputated leg, that was carried to him in a silver bucket, he stared at it saying 'I, for this and other things, utterly thanks God [...] and if I will not be able to carry out the profession of arms by feet, I will carry it out on the horse.'"[69]

Giovanni personifies the perfect *condottiero* who patiently suffers huge pain, so much so that, to prove his courage, Aretino said that he "laughed while cutting the nerve."[70] The biographies, though, are not unanimous about what Giovanni has done with the amputated leg: if Tedaldi said that he wanted to see it, Rossi affirms that "he set it on fire and he wanted it in his hand"[71]; Marin Sanudo recounts "messer Zanin de' Medici had sawed off his leg, and he picked it up in the hands swearing vengeance."[72] I believe that Giovanni's reaction to the amputation, and how it was perceived by his contemporaries, provides a good example of how wounds and pain could be symbolised and become an expression of military virtue. Giovanni's sawed-off leg is a concrete symbol that conveys his bravery and *fortitudo*, his predisposition to command and the deserved loyalty of his soldiers. From this perspective, the fact that "he wanted to have his foot with the piece of his leg fetched to himself, laughing on us, because we could not stand to see what he had

---

68 Rossi, 1833, p. 172: "Mentre gliela segavano non volse esser legato, né tenuto da alcuno, sopportando tal martorio costantissimamente".
69 Tedaldi, 1833, p. 98: "I medici per ultimo si risolverno a segargli la gamba, la qual senza voler esser tenuto, sopportò con animo costante, e volse dipoi vederla segata, la quale portatagli in un bacino d'argento, fissamente riguardò dicendo: 'Io dì questa cosa, et d'ogni altra cosa ringratio sommamente quel vero Dio [...] et se io non potrò fare il mestiere delle armi a piedi, lo farò a cavallo'".
70 "Rise nel tagliarsi il nerbo": letter from Pietro Aretino to Francesco de gli Albizzi, December 10th 1526, in: Aretino, 1997, t. I, book I, p. 56.
71 Rossi, 1833, p. 172: "Datogli fuoco la volle in mano".
72 Sanudo, 1969-1979, vol. XLIII, col. 348: "*Di Mantoa, fo lettere del Marchese, di 28, al suo orator.* Come al signor Zanin di Medici era stà taià la gamba, la qual tolse in man zurando vendetta".

suffered"[73], becomes an additional demonstration of virtue that the *condottiero* reveals through his relationship with the body, the scars and the pain.

Giovanni, a young and ambitious captain deeply connected to his Black Bands, until the last moments of his life claimed his own personal research of the perfect military virtue; in fact, in front of the confessor who was arrived to his sickbed, Giovanni said: "Father, because I am a professor of arms I lived according to the soldier's custom, but I would have lived like the religious, if I had worn the clothes that you wear. And were it not that it is not legit, I would confess in front of each, because I never did things unbecoming of me."[74] For Giovanni the virtue resides "in the honourable fulfilment, and above all technically irreproachable, of the chosen profession. We are in the presence of a real moral of the action". If the Aretino's words are "expression of the moral of a group rather than of an individual moral"[75], they are therefore expression of the military mentality that I tried here to preliminarily investigate; a mentality which makes a key point of the devotion to the profession and of the sacrifice of the body to the honour of the soldier and of the visible scars the materialisation of the so praised military action. Until the last moment, he was faithful to his soldier's nature and wanted to die in a camp bed; he died as an example of the soldier whose virtue can do nothing against the "cowardice" of the fire arms, of the *abominioso ordigno*[76]; his tormented body as symbol of the implacable changes of the practice of war.

---

73 "Si faceva portare oltra il piede con il pezzo de la gamba, ridendosi di noi, che non potevamo sofferire di vedere quello che egli aveva patito": letter from Pietro Aretino to Francesco de gli Albizzi, December 10th 1526, in: ARETINO, 1997, t. I, book I, p. 56.
74 IBID.: "Padre, per esser io professor d'armi son visso secondo il costume de i soldati, come anco sarei vivuto come quello de i religiosi, se io avessi vestito l'abito che vestite voi. E se non che non è lecito, mi confessarei in presenza di ciascuno, perché non feci mai cose indegne di me".
75 Quotations taken from: LARIVAILLE, 1980, p. 85.
76 In Ludovico Ariosto's *Orlando Furioso* (canto IX, octaves 90-91) Orlando throws the arquebus in the sea, deploring the advantage that it grants against the enemy, addressing it with these words: "Acciò più non istea/ mai cavallier per te d'esser ardito,/ né quanto il buono val, mai più si vanti/ il rio per te valer, qui giù rimanti./ O maladetto, o abominoso ordigno,/ che

Finally, I would like to briefly touch upon the rivalry between Sigismondo Malatesta and Federico di Montefeltro and mention how, during one of the many moments in which they confronted each other, the corporeity and the symbolism of pain operated as clear provocations, according to the military framework of interpretation illustrated above. It is impossible here to retrace the landmarks, which have constellated a rivalry and an hatred that lasted a lifetime.[77] Simplified: throughout their entire lives, they were sworn enemies, due to be lords of adjacent territorial states, always commanding opposite armies which were used to steal castles and lands to one another. In the spring of 1457, Borso d'Este, duke of Modena, had promoted a meeting between the two lords with the purpose of reconciliation, in order to stop a feud that could have damaged the recently achieved peace of Lodi of 1454. The meeting, which took place in the castle of Belfiore on May 6 and 7[78], is narrated in the *commentarii* of Pierantonio Paltroni. The author insists that Sigismondo's complaining about leg pain caused by a fall from his horse, underlined his unwillingness to make peace with Federico, and understands it as a provocation to the Duke of Urbino. In fact, he affirms: "Sigismondo did not ride [towards Federico at his arrival in Belfiore] because he had a little leg pain; which was not true, but Sigismondo faked it, and he had no pain at all."[79] Due to Sigismondo's inability, the Duke

---

fabricato nel tartareo fondo/ fosti per man di Belzebù maligno/ che ruinar per te disegnò il mondo,/ all'inferno, onde uscisti, ti rasigno".

77 About this subject see: a letter from Federico to Francesco Sforza of November 5 1451 in FRANCESCHINI, 1961, pp. 92-94; an insulting letter of Sigismondo against Federico in FRANCESCHINI, 1970, pp. 445f.; the letter from Federico in reply of the insult in FRANCESCHINI, 1956, pp. 46-49; a letter from Sigismondo to Giovanni de' Medici of December 24 1451, in YRIARTE, 1882, pp. 425f.. See also: PALTRONI, 1966, p. 51; DE LA SIZERANNE, 1972, pp. 45-120.

78 About the meeting of Belfiore in the contemporary sources see: GIOVANNI DI M. PEDRINO, 1986, p. 310; ANONIMO VERONESE, 1915, p. 91; BALDI, 1824, vol. 1, pp. 179-183 and vol. 2, pp. 8-29; SER GUERRIERO DA GUBBIO, 1902, pp. 66-67. See also the letter from Borso d'Este to his ambassador in Milan, Ugolotto Facino, of May 1457, written out in full in: SORANZO, 1911, pp. 466f..

79 This and all the following quotations are taken from the complete narration of the event in: PALTRONI, 1966, pp. 113-124. "Sigismondo non era

of Modena asked to Federico to accompany him to Sigismondo's chamber. "Then together went to Sigismondo's chamber, but he did not wait for them to go up to his room and, well showing that he had leg pain, helping himself with a stick, he went down to a loggia, and there he met the Duke of Modena and Federico."[80] Often in the past, Sigismondo had accused Federico of cowardice and of avoiding direct conflicts and duels, although Federico was wounded and lost an eye during a joust in 1450[81] (which weakened his military performances). Again on this occasion, Sigismondo was exploiting the leg pain as a demonstration of painful valour (as much as Federico and his scars in the face) on one hand, and on the other hand was mocking the Duke of Urbino by implying his lack of commitment in the frontline.

The subtle provocation of Sigismondo was abundantly noticed by the participating and exacerbated even more, if possible, the attitudes. The reconciliation started with Sigismondo and his *famigli,* who arrived "with weapons at side, like those who deliberated to do everything but words [...] or frighten others."[82] After a long discussion constellated by reciprocal teasing, Sigismondo provoked Federico, implying his cowardice and Federico answered sarcastically; then the meeting ended up in a disaster, with swords drawn and reciprocal insults: "Rising up with hands on his weapon, Sigismondo said 'For the body of God, I'll remove your guts from your body'. The Count, rising up *similiter* 'And I

---

cavalcato perché havea un poco male a una gamba: la qual cosa non era vera, ma finse el signore Sigissmondo havere male, ma non havea male niuno".
80 IBID.: "De compagnia se ne andarno inverso la camera del signore Sigissmondo, el quale non aspectò però che andassero su a la camera ma, mostrando pure che la gamba li dolesse, apogiandose ad un bastone, venne giù a una loggia che ce era, et illi incontrò el signore Duca de Modena et el conte Federico".
81 About the injuring of Federico see: BALDI, 1824, vol. 1, p.198; FRANCESCHINI, 1970, pp. 462-464. About the duels between Sigismondo and Federico see the letter from Sigismondo of February 21 1445 written out in full in TABANELLI, 1977, pp. 50-52, and Federico's answer in OSIO, 1970, vol. 3, part II, n. 317, pp. 363-365. About the honor of the duel see: CAVINA, 2005.
82 PALTRONI, IBID.: "Haveano a lato le arme assai giuste, como quilli che haveano deliberato fare altro che parole [...] o mictere paura da altri".

will take away your innards.'" [83] After the considerations made throughout this article, it is easier to understand how the pain showed by Sigismondo was seen such an annoying provocation to Federico. In their personal, military and political rivalry, Sigismondo leads also the conflict on a symbolic level, in which he tried to embody a moral and military superiority through the show of the leg pain (fake or not), knowing that his provocation would have been acknowledged by Federico, who shared with him the same military mentality.

Conclusions

In a world that strives to remove the pain from the body, to protect the soul's sack which accompanies the man throughout his journey on earth, to proudly show the suffering of the body becomes a tangible demonstration, almost ascetic, of their own moral qualities. In the everyday normality of the bodies marked by diseases and, therefore, by weakness, the signs of the wounds and of the battle become a manifestation of moral and physical strength. The system of values in force within the Renaissance military life identified in the wounds the strength, the courage to face the pain and to overcome it; the same courage that was needed to face the battle and the war's deprivations, namely that *fortitudo* which was so dear to the military and moral treatises.

On the pain, the wounds, the resistance and the deprivations, the training and the suffering, as well as on the joys, is developed and strengthened the relationship between the *condottiero* and the soldiers; the awareness to each possess a sensitive body, which dies and suffers in the same way, puts in contact and unites. Through the body, its dangers and its pleasures, through a sensitive, material and visible experience, through the memento of their own deeds incised on the skin, is formed the special relationship between the *condottiero* and his veterans.

On the contrary, on the instinct's rationalization and on the discipline of the body, as well as on the manifestation of a superior ability to endure

---

83 IBID.: "El signor Sigissmondo alora, levandose su cum le mane in su l'arme, disse: 'Per lo corpo de Dio, io te cavarò le budelle dal corpo'. Et el Conte disse, levandose *similiter*: 'Et io te cavarò la corada a te'".

pain and a minor fear to feel it, is formed the reputation and the virtue of the *condottiero*. Between the basic requirements useful to command the troops, pain, courage, rationality and generosity are parts of a cultural framework, which places the materiality of the body and its sensitive perception at the center of a theoretical system of virtues. A body which has to be showed to others, which, since childhood, has to be educated to patience and strength, which has to suffer and to overcome suffering so it can become a symbol of the perfect military virtue; a virtue that can grant by itself the unique desire of the *condottieri*, that is to earn a name that will be consecrated to posterity.

Bibliography

Sources

ANONIMO, Cantari sulla guerra aquilana di Braccio, ed. by ROBERTO VALENTINI, Roma 1935.

ANONIMO RIMINESE, Cronache Malatestiane del secolo XIV e XV, ed. by ALDO FRANCESCO MASSERA, in: Rerum Italicarum Scriptores, volume XV, part II, Bologna 1922.

ANONIMO VERONESE, Cronica, ed. by GIOVANNI SORANZO, Deputazione veneta di storia patria, Venezia 1915.

ARETINO, PIETRO, Lettere, ed. by PAOLO PROCACCIOLI, volume I, book I, Roma 1997.

BALDI, BERNARDINO, Vita e fatti di Federigo di Montefeltro duca di Urbino Istoria, vol. 1-2-3, Roma 1824.

BROGLIO TARTAGLIA, GASPARE, Cronaca Malatestiana del secolo XV (dalla Cronaca Universale), ed. by ANTONIO LUCIANI, Rimini 1982.

CAMPANO, GIOVANNI ANTONIO, Bracci Perusini vita et gesta ab anno 1368 usque ad 1424, ed. by ROBERTO VALENTINI, in: Rerum Italicarum Scriptores, volume XIX, part IV, Bologna 1929.

CANESTRINI, GIUSEPPE, Documenti per servire alla storia della milizia italiana dal XIII secolo al XVI, raccolti negli archivj della Toscana e preceduti da un discorso di Giuseppe Canestrini, Ruggello 2007.

FIORE DE' LIBERI, Floss Duellatorum in armis, sine armis, equester et pedester, ed. by GIOVANNI RAPISARDI, Torino 2008.

GIOVANNI DI M. PEDRINO, Cronica del suo tempo, ed. by GINO BORGHEZIO/MARCO VATTASSO, volume II, Roma 1986.

MALIPERIO, MASSIMO, Il Fior di Battaglia di Fiore dei Liberi da Cividale (Il Codice Ludwig XV 13 del J. Paul Getty Museum), Udine 2006.

OSIO, LUIGI (ed.), Documenti diplomatici tratti dagli archivj milanesi e coordinati per cura di Luigi Osio, Milano 1970.

PALTRONI, PIERANTONIO, Commentari della vita et gesti dell'illustrissimo Federico Duca d'Urbino, ed. by WALTER TOMMASOLI, Urbino 1966.

PELLINI, POMPEO, L'Historie et Vite di Braccio Fortebracci detto da Montone, et di Nicolo Piccinino perugini, Venezia 1572.

PICCOLOMINI, ENEA SILVIO or PIO II, I Commentarii, ed. by LUIGI TOTARO, Milano 1984.

ROSSI, GIANGIROLAMO, Vita di Giovanni de' Medici celebre capitano delle bande nere, in: Notizie dei secoli XV e XVI sull'Italia, Polonia e Russia, raccolte e pubblicate da Sebastiano Ciampi colle vite di Bona Sforza de' duchi di Milano regina di Polonia e Giovanni de' Medici detto delle Bande Nere, Firenze 1833, pp. 135-180.

SANUDO, MARIN, I Diarii, Bologna 1969-1979.

SER GUERRIERO DA GUBBIO, Cronaca dall'anno 1350 all'anno 1472, ed. by GIUSEPPE MAZZATINTI, in: Rerum Italicarum Scriptores, volume XXI, part IV, Città di Castello 1902.

SIMONETTA, GIOVANNI, Rerum Gestarum Francisci Sfortiae Commentarii, ed. by GIOVANNI SORANZO, in: Rerum Italicarum Scriptores, volume XXI, part III, Bologna 1932-34.

TEDALDI, GIOVAN BATTISTA, Discorso sulla nobiltà e virtù di Giovanni de' Medici, in: Notizie dei secoli XV e XVI sull'Italia, Polonia e Russia, raccolte e pubblicate da Sebastiano Ciampi colle vite di Bona Sforza de' duchi di Milano regina di Polonia e Giovanni de' Medici detto delle Bande Nere, Firenze 1833, pp. 89-101.

TURCHINI, ANGELO (ed.), Isotta bella sola ai nostri giorni, sonetti d'amore di Sigismondo Pandolfo Malatesta, Rimini 1985.

VADI, FILIPPO, L'Arte Cavalleresca del Combattimento, ed. by MARCO RUBBOLI/LUCA CESARI, Rimini 2005.

Literature

ANCONA, CLEMENTE, Milizie e condottieri, in: Storia d'Italia, vol. 5, Torino 1973, pp. 643-665.

ARFAIOLI, MAURIZIO, The Black Bands of Giovanni. Infantry and Diplomacy during the Italian Wars (1526-1528), Pisa 2005.

ARIÉS, PHILIPPE, L'uomo e la Morte dal medioevo a oggi, Roma-Bari 1980.

BAUMANN, REINHARD, I Lanzichenecchi: la loro storia e cultura dal tardo Medioevo alla guerra dei Trent'anni, Torino 1996.1

CALABI, AUGUSTO/CORNAGGIA, GIANLUIGI, Matteo dei Pasti. La sua opera medaglistica distinta da quella degli anonimi riminesi del XV secolo in relazione ai medaglioni malatestiani aggiunte le falsificazioni, Milano 1927.

CARDINI, FRANCO, Giovanni gentiluomo, in: Giovanni delle Bande Nere, ed. by MARIO SCALINI, Firenze 2001a, pp. 148-179.

ID., La crisi militare e la politica italiana fra Quattrocento e Cinquecento, in: Giovanni delle Bande Nere, ed. by MARIO SCALINI, Firenze 2001b, pp. 8-41.

CAVINA, MARCO, Il sangue dell'onore: storia del duello, Roma, 2005.

CISERI, ILARIA, Gli ultimi giorni di Giovanni delle Bande Nere, le esequie e il ritorno del suo sepolcro a Firenze, in: Giovanni delle Bande Nere, ed. by MARIO SCALINI, Firenze 2001, pp. 202-221.

CONTAMINE, PHILIPPE, La guerra nel Medioevo, Bologna, 1986.

DE LA SIZERANNE, ROBERT, Federico di Montefeltro: capitano, principe, mecenate (1422-1482), Urbino 1972.

DEL NEGRO, PIERO, Guerra ed eserciti da Machiavelli a Napoleone, Roma 2001.

DEL TREPPO, MARIO, Gli aspetti organizzativi, economici e sociali di una compagnia di ventura italiana, in: Rivista Storica Italiana, fasc. 3, Napoli 1973, pp. 253-275.

ID., Sulla struttura della compagnia o condotta militare, in: Condottieri e uomini d'arme nell'Italia del Rinascimento, ed. by MARIO DEL TREPPO, Napoli 2001, pp. 417-452.

ID. (ed.), Condottieri e uomini d'arme nell'Italia del Rinascimento, Napoli 2001.

DI STEFANO, ANITA et al. (ed.), La storiografia umanistica, convegno internazionale di studi, Messina 22-25 ottobre 1987, Messina 1992.

ERMINI, GIUSEPPE, I trattati della guerra e della pace di Giovanni da Legnano, Imola 1923.

FALCIONI, ANNA (ed.), La signoria di Sigismondo Pandolfo Malatesti: la politica e le imprese militari, vol. 2, Rimini 2006.

FINZI, CLAUDIO, Una "vita" di Braccio di Giannantonio Campano, in: Braccio da Montone e i Fortebracci. Le compagnie di ventura nell'Italia del XV secolo, Atti del convegno internazionale di studi, Montone 23-25 marzo 1990, Narni 1993, pp. 37-59.

FRANCESCHINI, GINO, I Malatesta, Varese 1973.

ID., I Montefeltro, Varese 1970.

ID., Federico di Montefeltro. Dalla concessione del vicariato apostolico alla pace di Lodi 1447-1454, Sansepolcro 1961.

ID., La prima giovinezza di Federico di Montefeltro ed una sua lettera ingiuriosa contro Sigismondo Pandolfo Malatesta, in: Atti e Memorie della Deputazione di storia patria per le Marche, 11, Ancona 1956, pp. 27-75.

GÉLIS, JACQUES, La spoglia dell'uomo. Contributo all'immaginario della pelle, in: Corpi. Storia, metafore, rappresentazioni tra Medioevo ed età contemporanea, ed. by CLAUDIO PANCINO, Venezia 2000, pp. 102-120.

HALE, JOHN RIGBY, Violence in the late Middle Ages. A background, in: Violence and civil disorders in Italian cities, 1200-1500, ed. by LAURO MARTINES, Berkley et al. 1972, pp. 19-37.

IANZITI, GARY, I "Commentarii": appunti per la storia di un genere storiografico, in: Archivio Storico Italiano, CL, disp. IV, Firenze 1992, pp. 1029-1063.

LARIVAILLE, PAUL, Pietro Aretino fra Rinascimento e manierismo, Roma 1980.

MALLETT, MICHAEL, L'organizzazione militare di Venezia nel '400, Roma 2007.

ID., Il condottiero, in: L'uomo del Rinascimento, ed. by EUGENIO GARIN, Roma-Bari 1988, pp. 43-72.

ID., Mercenaries and their Masters. Warfare in Renaissance Italy, London 1974.

PASTOUREAU, MICHEL, Bestiari del Medioevo, Torino 2012.

PIERI, PIERO, Scritti vari, Torino 1966.
ID., La scienza militare italiana del Rinascimento, in: Scritti vari, Torino 1966, pp. 99-119.
ID., Il Rinascimento e la crisi militare italiana, Torino 1952.
SALVESTRINI, FRANCESCO et al. (eds.), La morte e i suoi riti in Italia tra Medioevo e prima età Moderna, Firenze 2007.
SCALINI, MARIO, Tecniche e tecnologia nelle guerre d'Italia, in: Giovanni delle Bande Nere, ed. by MARIO SCALINI, Firenze 2001a, pp. 102-147.
ID., Condottiero, cavaliere o soldato?, in: Giovanni delle Bande Nere, ed. by MARIO SCALINI, Firenze 2001b, pp. 180-201.
ID., I resti dell'armatura funebre di Giovanni delle Bande Nere e alcuni oggetti a lui legati, in: Giovanni delle Bande Nere, ed. by MARIO SCALINI, Firenze 2001c, pp. 222-229.
SORANZO, GIOVANNI, Pio II e la politica italiana nella lotta contro i Malatesti. 1457-1463, Padova 1911.
STORTI, FRANCESCO, Istituzioni militari in Italia tra Medioevo ed età Moderna, in: Studi Storici, XXXVIII/1, Roma 1997, pp. 257-271.
TABANELLI, MARIO, Sigismondo Pandolfo Malatesta. Signore del Medioevo e del Rinascimento, Faenza 1977.
TATEO FRANCESCO, Storia esemplare di un condottiero: la "Vita di Braccio" di Giovanni Antonio Campano, in: ID., I miti della storiografia umanistica, Roma, 1990, pp. 99-120.
TOMMASOLI, WALTER, La vita di Federico da Montefeltro. 1422/1482, Urbino 1978.
WALEY, DANIEL, I mercenari e la guerra nell'età di Braccio da Montone, in: Braccio da Montone e i Fortebracci. Le compagnie di ventura nell'Italia del XV secolo, Atti del convegno internazionale di studi, Montone 23-25 marzo 1990, Narni 1993, pp. 111-128.
YRIARTE, CHARLES, Un condottiere au XV siecle. Rimini; études sur les lettres et les arts à la cour des Malatesta, d'après les papiers d'État des archives d'Italie. Avec 200 dessins d'après les monuments du temps, Paris 1882.
ZAMA, PIERO, I Malatesti, Faenza 1965.
ZUG TUCCI, HANNELORE, Morte e funerale del condottiero, in: La morte e i suoi rituali in Italia tra Medioevo e prima età moderna, ed. by FRANCESCO SALVESTRINI et al., Firenze 2007, pp. 243-274.

ID., La morte del condottiero: Braccio, i Bracceschi e altri, in: Condottieri e uomini d'arme nell'Italia del Rinascimento, ed. by MARIO DEL TREPPO, Napoli 2001, pp. 143-163.

ID., Fattori di coesione dell'esercito tra Medioevo ed età Moderna, in: Braccio da Montone e i Fortebracci. Le compagnie di ventura nell'Italia del XV secolo, Atti del convegno internazionale di studi, Montone 23-25 marzo 1990, Narni 1993, pp. 157-177.

Two Kinds of War?
Brutality and Atrocity in Later Medieval Scotland

ALASTAIR J. MACDONALD

Introduction: Approaches to Brutality in Anglo-Scottish Conflict

Later medieval Scotland was profoundly shaped by war. Following the invasion and conquest of the kingdom by Edward I, king of England, in 1296 there was swift rebellion; Anglo-Scottish warfare continued for centuries thereafter. The most intensive conflict was in two periods usually labelled as the first (1296-1328) and second (1332-1357) wars of independence. There were, though, frequent and sometimes lengthy recurrences of Anglo-Scottish hostilities later in the fourteenth century, at intervals in the fifteenth century and with renewed intensity in the sixteenth century.[1] The role played by war in the political development of the later medieval Scottish kingdom is enormous and has received deservedly detailed scholarly attention.[2] These conflicts were also fundamental in shaping the self-perception of the Scots as a warrior people whose identity was located in unwavering commitment to a communal struggle for freedom against external domination.[3]

---

1 From 1357 I estimate there was open Anglo-Scottish warfare in roughly one in three of the next 150 years.
2 War and politics were absolutely intertwined as the title *The Wars of Scotland* for a general history of this era would suggest: BROWN, 2004.
3 See, for instance, COWAN, 2003.

With frequent warfare so firmly at the heart of fundamental historical developments like these it is no surprise that there has been much academic examination of the topic, albeit mostly not until the last couple of decades.[4] Despite such attention many aspects of war, especially within wider cultural and social rather than purely military contexts, remain somewhat neglected. A case in point is the specific subject of the present article, which aims to investigate the level of brutality and atrocity in later medieval Anglo-Scottish conflict, and to suggest appropriate strategies for understanding such manifestations. By far the most detailed engagement with conduct in these wars has been offered by Matthew Strickland.[5] He gives close attention to the period up to 1307, but not beyond. The present article considers evidence from later years and is also written partly as an attempt to engage with some of the approaches and interpretations offered in Strickland's work. Other than this, coverage of military behaviour is much patchier. Iain MacInnes deals with aspects of the topic for the second wars of independence period; and the present author touches on some themes in various articles.[6] There is good coverage of specific aspects of martial behaviour, such as treatment of prisoners and ransoms.[7] Chivalry, of course, has been covered in a Scottish context, although overwhelmingly in terms of its political importance and its presentation in the late fourteenth-century romance by John Barbour, *The Bruce*, rather than in how a chivalric ethos might have influenced military practice in reality.[8] Impacts of war have been widely studied, but the conduct of warriors and soldiers, although these themes may emerge implicitly, are rarely the focus of attention.[9]

---

4   The welcome arrival of the *Military History of Scotland* came only in 2012 (SPIERS et al., 2012). See also: DUNCAN, 1992; MCNAMEE, 1997; MACDONALD, 2000; CORNELL, 2009; KING/SIMPKIN, 2012.
5   STRICKLAND, 2000, 2008a.
6   MACINNES, 2008; MACDONALD, 2012a, pp. 167f.; MACDONALD, 2013b, pp. 332f..
7   KING, 2002. See also the consideration of military ethics in: KING, 2008.
8   Engagements with Scottish chivalry and/or the works of Barbour include: KLIMAN, 1973; CAMERON, 1998; STEVENSON, 2006; FORAN, 2010; BOARDMAN/FORAN, 2015.
9   Studies discussing the impacts of war on particular regions and groups include: SCAMMELL, 1958; BARROW, 1962, 1992; NEVILLE, 1993.

Despite a lack of detailed scholarly attention to the conduct of war there is still an impression in mainstream Scottish historiography that, in the 1296-1328 period at any rate, war was indeed marked by particular brutality.[10] This is because there is broad acceptance that the Scots pursued guerrilla war in this period, a mode of combat operation taken by its nature to entail a pronounced level of viciousness. One of the main intentions of this paper is to offer a critique of the use of guerrilla war as a concept in the extant historiography in relation to the themes of atrocity and brutality. The widely accepted story goes like this. The Scots started off fighting a conventional war in 1296 adhering to accepted standards of aristocratic-led martial conduct common in western Christendom, with disastrous results. They offered honourable, open battle to Edward I's powerful host at Dunbar and were routed. Resistance was broken, and the conquest of Scotland followed swiftly.[11] Then, first under William Wallace from 1297 and later Robert I from 1307, the Scots adopted guerrilla war – a form of combat alien to the knightly forces of their English enemies that ultimately brought military success and hard-won independence to the Scots. It is an image of there being a binary divide in the types of war practised in the later middle ages, a clear demarcation between 'accepted conventions' and 'guerrilla tactics'.[12] The binary paradigm is most starkly represented in Geoffrey Barrow's hugely influential *Robert Bruce and the Community of the Realm of Scotland*, where chapter 5 is entitled 'Two Kinds of War', and in which the alleged transition from one to the other is described.[13]

A second concept which has been deployed to explore levels of barbarousness in Anglo-Scottish conflict is also examined here. This draws on the typologies discussed in *Transcultural Wars*, edited by Hans-Henning Kortüm.[14] The scheme laid out there posits an initial divide between 'intracultural' and 'transcultural'. Intracultural war is

---

10 This being so my focus will mainly be on this period, although there is a perception that long afterwards Anglo-Scottish warfare was still more brutal than that practised in other zones: GRUMMITT, 2011, p. 194.
11 PRESTWICH, 1997, pp. 470-4; BARROW, 2005, pp. 91-9.
12 CAMERON, 1998, p. 15. See also: ALLMAND, 2000, p. 21; MCNAMEE, 2006, pp. 127f., 288. There is a fuller discussion of Guerrilla warfare in MACDONALD, 2016.
13 BARROW, 2005, ch. 5.
14 KORTÜM, 2006.

fought within a culture, in which the clash occurs between societies sharing fundamental values and outlook and in which ethics and conventions guiding military activity are shared by the combatants. In transcultural conflict there is no such agreement and the differences tend towards enhanced levels of atrocity. Transcultural conflict has in turn been split into two categories,[15] both of which have been applied to Anglo-Scottish warfare. The sub-divisions are 'intercultural' wars, which feature a clash between fundamentally different ethnic and cultural groups with divergent understandings of accepted martial behaviour, and 'subcultural' wars. This last categorisation is taken to occur where there are many shared cultural factors (a shared 'big culture') between enemies at war, but there are crucial divergences that lead to a high level of intensity as the combatants fight for ownership of the larger culture which they share. A suggested exemplification is conflict between heretics and doctrinally conventional Catholics, for instance as seen in the thirteenth-century Albigensian Crusades.[16] There were numerous cultural similarities between the combatants but the differences were of such importance that the scale of violence in the conflict was very extreme.

There have been attempts to apply the intercultural typology to Anglo-Scottish conflict. This has overlapping aspects with the paradigm of 'two types of war' but is not precisely identical. It is widely accepted that from the eleventh century military encounters between the English and their Welsh and Irish neighbours were of notable brutality. 'Celtic' practice in war was unrestrained by the chivalric conventions which normally moulded post-Conquest English military behaviour. Faced with enemies who could be depicted as both brutal in war and barbarous by nature the English in turn abandoned the normal constraints in their military activity and engaged in a heightened level of atrocity.[17] It has been recognised that a similar intensification was one part of warfare between England and Scotland at the same time: the

---

15 IBID., pp. 23-6; MORILLO, 2006, pp. 29f. Confusingly, the terms 'transcultural' and 'intercultural' are also used in the volume as oppositional terms rather than one being a sub-category of the other as in Kortüm's scheme (STRICKLAND, 2006).
16 MORILLO, 2006, pp. 36-41.
17 GILLINGHAM, 1992a, 1992b; STRICKLAND, 2000, pp. 49, 52f.; STRICKLAND, 2008b, pp. 306-10.

armed forces of Scottish kings drew heavily on manpower from a Gaelic linguistic and cultural background, although it has been recognised that much of the aristocratic military leadership was aligned perfectly well with an Anglo-Norman cultural milieu.[18] For the wars from 1296 it has similarly been suggested that an intensifying factor lay in the Gaelic ethnicity and martial culture of some of the Scottish forces and English reactions to these circumstances.[19] While this 'Celtic'/ Anglo-Norman opposition is how the intercultural approach to war has been applied in an Anglo-Scottish context the subcultural categorisation actually seems more promising as an approach to explaining levels of brutality, so it will also be given consideration here.

In the attempt to scrutinize brutality in Anglo-Scottish conflict in the light of the approaches mentioned above three categories of behaviour in war are examined. These are extreme behaviour towards non-combatants, towards combatants, and deployment of violence with symbolic intent. By reference to these themes the question of whether Scotland was an especially brutal war zone will be addressed. The two major models already outlined (a binary divide in war; and the transcultural typologies) will also be discussed to seek to assess how useful these approaches are in practice.

Non-Combatants

It is very difficult to assess whether especially brutal treatment was inflicted on non-combatants in specific war-zones at particular times. This is because medieval warfare by its intrinsic nature was targeted at ordinary communities, and devastating impacts on civilians was the normal currency of war, as has been demonstrated abundantly in many scholarly investigations.[20] The typical mode of war was to raid enemy

---

18 For discussion of the 'markedly hybrid' Scottish forces in the twelfth century see STRICKLAND, 1992, pp. 221-5.
19 STRICKLAND, 2000, pp. 39-55.
20 A considered discussion of the wide acceptance of doleful impacts of war on non-combatants is in DE MARCO, 2000, pp. 29-35. For the brutal nature of medieval warfare more broadly see: WRIGHT, 1998; ALLMAND, 1999; ROGERS, 2002. For the tricky issue of defining non-combatants see STRICKLAND, 2006, pp. 109-17.

territory with a view to damaging economic capacity and undermining the morale of the targeted communities. This might have the intention of forcing a ruler whose territories were attacked to offer battle, or it might be intended to terrorize non-combatants into changing allegiance, if unprotected by their overlord.[21] Both of these goals were regularly at play in the waging of Anglo-Scottish war. Destruction of the fabric of societies was the intention of warfare, not a by-product. The infliction of suffering on ordinary people was normal and accepted and we must embrace this before even beginning to investigate the extremes of atrocity and brutality that are the subject of this article.

To identify what was regarded as extreme the best place to start is with contemporary chronicle accounts, specifically the allegations raised against enemies forces. As is often stated, chroniclers tended not to have military experience, and there are limits to how far we can suppose their vision of unacceptable behaviour in war accords with the ethics of combatants.[22] Nevertheless, soldiers did also write chronicles; and historical writing was increasingly aimed at secular audiences and must be accepted as reflecting wider than purely clerical opinion.[23] The consistency of the communal evidence of chronicle writing is strongly suggestive of firm and widely held attitudes towards what was regarded as extreme behaviour in war. It was thought despicable to kill certain categories of people: children, especially infants; women, notably those who were virgins, pregnant or nursing, or elderly; and clerics. Sexual molestation of women was condemned, with violation of virgins seen as especially reprehensible. Spoliation of churches, and church property, was also widely condemned. Finally, the infliction of deliberate or ostentatious cruelty, not just towards the groups already mentioned, might attract the opprobrium of chroniclers.[24]

If these categorisations form a basic guide to what was regarded as extreme behaviour in relation to non-combatants in war, the chroniclers

---

21 The latter has been covered in a Scottish context in MACINNES, 2007.
22 GIVEN-WILSON, 2004, pp. 99-111.
23 LE BEL, 2011; GRAY, 2005; TAYLOR, 2009.
24 Other categories of evidence are tracts discussing military ethics and regulatory ordinances for armies. They suggest similar taboos in relation to women, clerics and ecclesiastical property: BOUVET, 1949; CURRY, 2011. It has recently been argued that such stipulations had very limited practical effect: COX, 2013. See also, in general: KEEN, 1965.

remain frustratingly poor guides as to when these taboos were actually broken on a significant scale. For the very reason that chroniclers convince us that they demarcate what are regarded as outrages – their consistent listings of the same categories of transgression in war – there is a strongly formulaic feel to chronicle reportage of military action. All chroniclers, on all sides, bemoan the same sorts of abuses among soldiers – ravaging of virgins, massacres of women and children and so on, so that it becomes very hard to take these as real descriptions rather than renderings of a grizzly template aimed at disparaging an enemy.

We sometimes get more circumstantial details. But that does not necessarily make war descriptions any easier to deal with. The St Albans chronicler Thomas Walsingham writes with great specificity about a Scottish raid on northern England in 1379, during which the invaders, 'enemies of the human race', decapitated local men and played football with the severed heads.[25] Is this garish tale true? The chronicler is highly prejudiced towards the Scots and was certainly prone to embellishment and fabrication when it suited his purposes. On the other hand, Walsingham was a strictly contemporary writer, had excellent sources of information, and was often accurate regarding Anglo-Scottish border affairs.[26] Maybe the Scots did kick severed heads around in 1379; but even if so it is hard to generalise about conduct in war from such cases.

A further concrete example from the same era is instructive. Another contemporary chronicler with good sources of information on northern English affairs, Henry Knighton, provides a different specific example of a Scottish atrocity enacted against non-combatants. In 1389, he records, the Scots invaded, killing and burning. They assailed members of society usually mentioned in such accounts: nursing infants, women pregnant and in childbirth, and helpless old men. The additional circumstantial detail is that the attackers are stated to have shut two hundred of their victims in their houses, fastened the doors and set the dwellings on fire.[27] What to make of this? We must certainly be cautious: the very wording used by Knighton echoes an atrocity allegation from almost one hundred years before. In 1296 the Anglo-

---

25 WALSINGHAM, 2003, pp. 306f.
26 GOODMAN, 1992, pp. 5f.
27 KNIGHTON, 1995, pp. 526f.

Scottish war commenced with a Scottish raid into northern England. This was described in graphic terms in the *Lanercost Chronicle*, the product of a local priory of Augustinian Canons, and then reproduced in English royal propaganda, reaching its final form in a letter to Pope Boniface VIII in 1301. The Scots, in their attack, are depicted enacting great devastation, including burning of churches. More specifically, they are described as:

> "slaying children in the cradle and women lying in childbed with brutal and inhuman savagery and, terrible as it is to hear, vilely cutting off the breasts of women. Small school-children of tender years learning their first letters and grammar, they burned, in the school where they were, to the number of about two hundred, by blocking the doors of the school and setting it on fire."[28]

Clearly Knighton has picked up on the earlier report, changing some detail but sticking with the unlikely two hundred fatalities. This does not mean that we need absolutely to reject the account given by the later chronicler. People may well have been burned alive in 1389, and Knighton's adaptation of previous propaganda does not rule this out. But the plagiarism of an earlier account adapted to a new setting does force us to question whether this sort of specific detail is ultimately very helpful in identifying patterns of particular brutality towards non-combatants.

The alleged atrocities of 1296, in particular, also raise immediate questions about the utility of the two models mentioned at the beginning of this article. If there was particular Scottish savagery in this year's invasion it certainly cannot be placed in a straightforwardly intercultural context. There will have been Gaelic-speaking forces among the invading Scots, but English-speakers will have outnumbered them, given the linguistic balance in southern Scotland.[29] The noble leaders, meanwhile, were culturally similar to their English counterparts – there was clearly no great ethnic or cultural divide between the

---

28 STONES, 1970, p. 107.
29 Geoffrey Barrow long since dispelled the notion that 'English' Scots were uncommitted to the independence struggle: BARROW, 1976.

Scottish and English aristocracies.³⁰ Clearly, also, the usefulness of a binary divide between conventional, chivalric war and a nastier guerrilla alternative is also brought under immediate question. The 1296 Scottish raid is described as featuring atrocities rendered in as lurid a fashion as anything that would follow – yet by the traditional conception in the historiography the Scots at this stage were fighting conventional war, having not yet learned that a guerrilla strategy would be essential for success against the might of England. Leaving the alleged extremes to one side, there was nothing remotely unusual or unchivalric about burning and devastating the lands of one's enemies, and this is exactly what the Sots were doing in 1296.

One period when we might imagine particularly brutal policies towards non-combatants were pursued is between 1307 and 1314. In these years Robert I, having seized the throne, was seeking to establish his authority as an independent king of Scots in the face of English garrisons and domestic Scottish opponents. The means of enforcing his rule on recalcitrant communities was by terrorising them into changing allegiance. This was no doubt a vicious process, although specific evidence of its operation is normally lacking. One well known moment in the process of marking out the king's regional authority, taken to be of particular brutality, was the 'Herschip', or harrying, of Buchan, a district in northern Scotland, in 1308.³¹ We actually have very little concrete detail, the notoriety of this episode resting instead on a brief account in Barbour's *Bruce*. Whatever one makes of the level of atrocity inflicted in this process, it again does not fit well with the models at issue. The systematic devastation of Buchan was not guerrilla activity, but represented, as we have seen, a widely practised and thus 'conventional' form of conflict. Nor are there clear-cut ethnic or linguistic fault lines that might allow a neat intercultural model to be applied: in 1308 Robert I's forces were no doubt largely Gaelic-speaking in his operations in northern Scotland – but the people of Buchan they preyed on were mainly Gaelic speakers as well.³²

---

30   STRINGER, 1995, pp. 87f.
31   BARBOUR, 1997, pp. 332-5.
32   HORSBURGH, 1994, pp. 15f. It is argued here that the Herschip of Buchan itself was an important engine of linguistic change in the region, encouraging the move from Gaelic to English. That seems questionable, though, given that the ejected magnate family (the Comyns) was not

That there was no simple divide in these years between guerrilla and conventional war can perhaps be shown best in another part of Scotland, the south. Up to 1314 there were many strongholds in southern Scotland in English hands, notably Stirling, Roxburgh, Edinburgh and Berwick, as well as many Scottish communities continuing to withhold their allegiance from Robert I. The king's forces assailed recalcitrant Scots in these areas until they changed allegiance, just as in northern Scotland. And they also fought against English forces in a manner that might fit with depictions of guerrilla warfare as usually understood: swift movements, avoidance of major battles, surprise attacks. But at precisely the same time English forces known as 'schavaldours' were coming to prominence.[33] These were garrison soldiers, irregularly paid and provisioned, who engaged in essentially unregulated military activity. They lived off the communities, both in northern England and Scotland, which surrounded their strongholds. This was criminality, banditry, irregular warfare; and it was practiced by forces notionally under the control of the English crown. There is, in this theatre of conflict, emphatically no divide between a supposed Scottish guerrilla war and a conventional form of military behaviour pursued by their English enemies.

From 1311, and especially from 1314, there was regular raiding of northern England as Robert I's position became more secure in Scotland.[34] The rationale of such attacks was often to extort money from the target communities. This was carried out with great success by the Scots and helped provide the financial basis allowing for a generally better resourced military establishment, and more ambitious activities, notably major campaigns in Ireland between 1315 and 1318. This extraction of resources was brutal, no doubt, but its intention was not to kill non-combatants, nor to ruin completely economic productivity.[35] As such, it is hard to see that in these particular episodes of Anglo-Scottish conflict there was unusually severe atrocity directed at non-combatants. There was great suffering of non-combatants in these wars.

Gaelic-speaking and that many of the lesser aristocratic kindreds were not displaced: YOUNG, 1993, pp. 193, 199.
33 KING, 2003.
34 MCNAMEE, 1997, pp. 72-115.
35 A punitive, rather than extractive, intention did mark Scottish raiding from 1318, however: DUNCAN, 1992, pp. 147f.

But the periods and places where this was most acute are not explained by the models being considered, and specific circumstances beyond the typologies at issue seem more promising as a strategy of explanation.

Combatants

Atrocities inflicted on combatants will be taken to be the massacre or mistreatment of captives. Such instances can certainly be found in Anglo-Scottish warfare. One famous atrocity occurred after the capture of Douglas Castle in 1308 by one of Robert I's foremost commanders, Sir James Douglas. He beheaded the prisoners taken and threw the bodies into the castle cellar before setting them alight.[36] Less well known, but attested in both English and Scottish sources is the execution by the English king Edward III of prisoners after his victory at the battle of Halidon Hill in 1333.[37] Such events are not, however, attested with frequency. Both sides might threaten the execution of combatants, but shirk from following through with such actions. The English earl of Salisbury, besieging Dunbar Castle in 1338, threatened, if the fortress was not surrendered, to execute the captive earl of Moray, whose sister, Agnes, countess of Dunbar, was leading the defence.[38] In a similar incident later in the same year the Scots sought to enforce the surrender of Edinburgh Castle's English garrison by indicating that a prisoner in their hands, Sir John Stirling, would otherwise be executed.[39] In neither case were the threats carried out.

Such restraint, and the limited evidence of other executions, suggests that conventions of captivity and ransom widespread in war elsewhere in western Christendom were usually observed in Anglo-Scottish conflict as well.[40] There is in fact only one phase of the Anglo-Scottish wars, in 1306-7, when we have evidence of systematic flouting of accepted practices in relation to captured enemies.[41] This is dealt

---

36 BARBOUR, 1997, pp. 202-11. It should be noted that some doubt has been cast on whether this event actually occurred: CAMERON, 1999, p. 73.
37 NICHOLSON, 1965, p. 138.
38 STEVENSON, 1839, pp. 296f.
39 CORNELL, 2008, pp. 114f.
40 KING, 2002.
41 BARROW, 2005, pp. 209f.; STRICKLAND, 2008a.

with in more detail below, but the bald circumstance in itself again challenges both of our models: that Anglo-Scottish war can be fitted into a simple pattern of ethnically-based intercultural conflict; and that there was a clash of clearly distinct types of war, guerrilla and conventional, with attendant erosion of mitigating conventions. Put simply, the contention that the Anglo-Scottish war-zone was a particularly vicious one has not actually been established by any detailed survey of evidence.

A lack of regular massacres of combatants in Anglo-Scottish war might seem especially surprising given another feature that offers prospects for lower levels of restraint in such conflict: the Scots' forces were from a wider social spread in society than their English enemies. This is clearly accepted as being true by most authorities, but has received little detailed academic scrutiny, referred to, if at all, usually in passing.[42] It was essential that the Scots drew on a broad spectrum of society to oppose the far larger and more wealthy kingdom of England that they faced in war from 1296. Soldiers were frequently unpaid, allowing a wide spread of the peasantry to be mustered in arms in performance of obligatory military service. Barbour's writing, for instance, makes the peasant basis of Scottish armed forces in the reign of Robert I clear and the same pattern persisted throughout the later middle ages, evident for instance in the *mediocres* of the region capturing Jedburgh Castle from its English garrison on their own initiative in 1409.[43]

Given the truism that the lower orders were not included in chivalric convention, and so not protected by it, alongside the related idea that they were more likely to massacre aristocratic opponents in response, the paucity of evidence of atrocities enacted on captured enemies in Anglo-Scottish warfare seems strange. The cross-social element of conflict would seem to invite, among our typologies, a categorisation of subcultural struggle, with attendant expectation of heightened levels of

---

42   It is argued that the social make-up of Scottish forces had significant effects on how the Scots represented themselves in war in MACDONALD, 2013b, pp. 328-32. Caldwell deals with the social class issue in a military context: CALDWELL, 2012, pp. 286-8. For the social spread of Scots involved in war see also: DUNCAN, 1992, pp. 138-46; MACDONALD, 2012b, pp. 276f.

43   BARBOUR, 1997, pp. 706-9; BOWER. 1987, p. 72.

brutality.⁴⁴ Again, that this expectation is not matched by the evidence raises questions about the usefulness of such typologies: yes, Scottish forces featured a greater proportion of the lower orders than English ones, as well as a deeper penetration down the social scale in recruitment. But in all western war in the Middle Ages there were commoners on the battlefield – it is problematic indeed to try to define the point at which this trait assumes a weight sufficient to dictate our categorisation of the whole conflict.

This is not to deny that the presence in greater numbers of soldiers drawn from the lower orders led to higher mortality in later medieval warfare.⁴⁵ The battlefield in particular became a more dangerous place, partly because commoners fought in large units and their spear-bearing ranks or missile troops of necessity killed with limited discrimination. Such developments made aristocrats more liable to be killed, but lower order troops were clearly even more vulnerable. They were less well protected by armour than their social superiors, and there was less incentive in fiscal terms for enemy combatants to capture them. Commoners died in awful numbers in some of the great Scottish battlefield defeats in this period. There is strong evidence that many thousands of infantry were killed in the major defeat of the Scots at Dunbar at the outset of the wars with England, in 1296.⁴⁶ The last great battle of the Anglo-Scottish wars was at Pinkie Cleuch in 1547, and the story was the same: in the encounter, and especially in the vigorous pursuit of the fleeing footsoldiers, thousands of Scottish commoners were cut down.⁴⁷ But the evidence that the lower orders were habitually excluded from mercy when captured (or indeed less likely to show mercy to aristocrats) is not strong, in the Anglo-Scottish setting anyway.

Turing to the phase of war when there is clear evidence of systematic brutality towards captives is illuminating in this context. In

---

44 That other authorities (such as MORILLO, 2006, pp. 52f.) can see this social opposition as having intercultural rather than subcultural resonances shows how ultimately subjective the various typological categorisations are (in this case, it has been decided that different classes from similar societies do not share the same 'big culture', but why?).
45 ROGERS, 1995, pp. 62f.
46 MACDONALD, 2013a, p. 203; CALDWELL, 2012, p. 270.
47 CALDWELL, 1991, pp. 85-7.

1306 when Robert I rose up to seize the Scottish throne and make his bid for independence, Edward I of England, who after a decade of labours thought he had finally pacified Scotland, was enraged. From the English king's perspective the crimes Robert I was guilty of could not be forgiven. He embarked on his bid for power by killing his chief domestic political rival, John Comyn of Badenoch, in a church. Thus guilty of sacrilege and murder, by having himself crowned king of Scots Robert was also a usurper and a traitor. There could be no mercy now for this miscreant, whose previous transgressions (in Edward's view) had already been treated with considerable leniency.[48] The prominent male secular figures who fell into English hands as Robert I's rising met with initial failure were invariably executed. This was a transgression of normal ethical boundaries in the treatment of captives, starkly shown by the execution even of a cleric, Hugh the Chaplain, taken at the battle of Methven in 1306.[49] Aristocratic women were not killed, but might be imprisoned in ostentatiously punitive fashion.[50] But Edward I's quarrel was with those who possessed political agency; there was no particular animus against ordinary soldiers, merely serving in war at the behest of their social betters. Orders were issued by the English crown that, despite the febrile atmosphere of rage and revenge, ordinary commons should have their lives spared.[51]

The circumstances of the years 1306-7 were unusual, but the fact of lower order survival after capture was not. One example occurred at the battle of Culblean in 1335. In this encounter supporters of David II (Robert I's son) defeated David of Strathbogie, earl of Atholl, a key supporter of the rival, and English-backed, claimant to the Scottish crown, Edward Balliol. Strathbogie was killed in battle, but his captured soldiers were allowed to go free.[52] Another case is the great Scottish battlefield defeat at Neville's Cross, near Durham, in 1346. One of the deponents in a legal case that took place in York in 1364 was a low status Scot (a skinner from Peebles) who had been captured in the battle. Despite being part of a force that had plundered its way through a swathe of northern England, he had clearly been spared after capture;

---
48 STRICKLAND, 2008a.
49 LUARD, 1890, pp. 132f.
50 See below, p. 211.
51 BAIN, 1884, no. 1755; PALGRAVE, 1837, pp. 361-3; BLACK, 1898, p. 509.
52 BOWER, 1996, pp. 116f.

and his fate had been sufficiently comfortable for him to settle among his erstwhile enemies.[53] These examples are anecdotal, but they could be added to. They quite clearly show, in any case, that commoners might be shown mercy in war, contrary to the frequent assumption that they were excluded from such chivalric niceties. The topic requires more work, but the completeness of the exclusion of the lower orders from martial codes has surely been overstated.[54] To this extent, chivalry was for warriors, and not just aristocratic ones.

Symbolic Violence

One of the most fruitful contexts in which to examine brutality and atrocity in Anglo-Scottish warfare is where there is a symbolic quality to actions in which a message, often in visual form, is presented to a viewing 'audience'. Going to the trouble of such symbolic communication is suggestive of a high level of engagement by the perpetrators of violence: they have a statement to make and want it to be seen. Edward I's actions in 1306-7 are collectively a good case in point. The English king's furious response to those rising against him, whom he felt guilty of the grossest crimes and betrayals, was to enact highly visual torments on those he regarded as traitors.[55] Appeals for mercy for the earl of Atholl, in recognition of his kinship to Edward I were met with a further visual statement: his elevated status, a status that he had disgraced, was recognised to the extent that he was hanged on a gallows higher than other miscreants dealt with at the same time.[56] Much notice has been taken of Edward's treatment of two captured Scottish noblewomen, Mary Bruce, Robert I's sister, and Isabella, countess of Buchan, the latter having assisted at his inauguration. They were imprisoned in cages in public view at Roxburgh and Berwick respectively.[57] The English king did not feel able to execute aristocratic

---

53 OWEN, 1978, pp. 332, 343f. Another deponent was an English cook who had been held captive by the Scots in seemingly benign conditions.
54 KEEN, 1984; ABELS, 2008.
55 STRICKLAND, 2008a.
56 BARROW, 2005, p. 209.
57 NEVILLE, 1993, pp. 124-6; SEABOURNE, 2011, pp. 74-9.

females, but in stark visual display their disgrace was made clear nonetheless.

The attempt to view Edward I's brutality within an intercultural typology cannot succeed, at least not in terms of seeing heightened ethnic hostilities pitting Gaelic Scots against English.[58] Edward I's fury was not that Robert I and his fellow rebels were culturally or ethnically different. It is the opposite: he was enraged that Robert and others had broken their faith to him as true knights. Their behaviour was unpardonable precisely because people like the earl of Atholl (and even more Sir Simon Fraser, who had been a household knight) lived in a shared cultural world with Edward I.[59] Grotesque humiliation at best, or the full horrors of exemplary execution, was the lot of such people. Edward I in 1306-7 exhibited a strongly-felt response to particular intensifying circumstances located in the precise politics of the time; his behaviour is not easily accounted for in the current typologies on offer to us to aid our understanding of heightened atrocity in war.

Symbolic violence enacted by the Scots is equally telling. One of the early acts in the rising of William Wallace in 1297 was his killing of the English sheriff of Lanark, William Heselrig. There is evidence that he was dispatched with furious violence, literally hacked to pieces.[60] This savagery was expressive of deep hatred, made visible by the manner of killing. Something similar was enacted on the remains of Hugh Cressingham, Edward I's treasurer in occupied Scotland, killed at the battle of Stirling Bridge later in the same year. The hated representative of Edward I's rule in Scotland, he was flayed and his skin put to disparaging use by the Scots, either by being cut into tokens and circulated among the Scottish host as macabre momentos of victory, or by being made into a sword-belt for Wallace himself (both could have happened, of course).[61] Finally, a hated enemy of the Scots, Elias the Clerk, was displayed in death with his severed head protruding

---

58 Prestwich sees the incidents of 1306-7 as amenable to an intercultural reading: PRESTWICH, 2006, p. 48.
59 Fraser was subjected to mockery and humiliation before his execution: LUARD, 1890, pp. 319f.; STRICKLAND, 2008a, pp. 97, 108f.
60 DUNCAN, 2007, pp. 58f.
61 GUISBOROUGH, 1957, p. 303; STEVENSON, 1839, p. 190.

from his anus in 1317, a grizzly statement of disparagement and contempt originating with Sir James Douglas.[62]

There was a highly charged backdrop to all of these incidents in the intensive conflict being waged at the time, a conflict which was of an existential nature in regard to the continuance of an autonomous Scottish kingdom. But each of these cases suggests something beyond this. Personal animus of one kind or another was the intensifying factor leading to these prominent displays of brutality. In the case of Heselrig there is a later tradition stating that he murdered Wallace's lover and that the latter acted in a spirit of revenge.[63] Absence of sources means that we cannot be sure, but the suggestion of a particular hostility being acted out against Heselrig is persuasive. Cressingham's rapacity and viciousness, meanwhile, is well attested in a variety of sources, including English authorities.[64] It is not surprising that the Scots would want to make an emphatic statement of revenge on their chief oppressor. We do not know what particular intensifying factors caused the hatred which Sir James Douglas expressed for Elias the Clerk in the display of his corpse. In the circumstances of continuous frontier war there were abundant prospects for the formation of deep enmities. Elias was one of the schavaldours, the English garrison forces making a living in the troubled badlands of the early fourteenth-century Anglo-Scottish border. He had plenty of chance to come to blows with, and for grievances to form in relation to, the most unflinching of the border warriors among the Scots, Sir James Douglas.

A final example of visual and symbolic brutality again relates to Douglas. There is good evidence from different source witnesses that at least some captured English archers in the early fourteenth century were subjected to hand amputations before being released.[65] Again, this does not fit comfortably with the typologies under discussion. The atrocity cannot be seen as being caused by an intercultural clash featuring divergent elements of language or ethnicity or mode of fighting. Sir James Douglas was not a savage Gaelic-speaking warlord, but an

---

62 GALBRAITH, 1928, p. 208. The likely veracity of this story is considered in MACDONALD, 2013b, pp. 332f.
63 HARY, 2003, pp. 114-18.
64 GUISBOROUGH, 1957, pp. 298-303.
65 STEVENSON, 1893, p. 192; KNIGHTON, 1889, p. 460. The mutilations are discussed in MACDONALD, 2013a, p. 199.

English-speaking aristocrat. Similarly, while he was an expert at small-scale warfare which might be defined as 'guerrilla' in nature, this did not require him to operate beyond the bounds of accepted chivalric norms. He was quite explicitly lauded as a flower of chivalry in Scottish sources, but also further afield.[66] Chivalry related to warriors – and war, as they all knew, but modern commentators can seem to forget, was a very nasty business. The context for understanding the hand amputations practiced by Sir James Douglas is a specific one. From the Scottish viewpoint archers were a dangerous aspect of the English military set-up. He thus sought to convey a stark message of the ruthless treatment such soldiers might receive if they dared to operate against the Scots. The mutilated archers returned home; they became walking propaganda illustrating Douglas's point in England. Anglo-Scottish war had raged, without much interruption, for two decades when the amputations were carried out. It was an existential war, in which hostility was based on the desperate nature of the struggle and the intertwined imperatives of increasingly national conflict alongside the quest for personal and familial political power.[67] Particular circumstances produced specific instances of ostentatious, symbolic brutality, instances that are not easily accounted for in the extant typological categorisations.

Conclusion

I suggest a rejection of the typological models mentioned at the start of this paper and the embrace instead of more complex patterns of shifting circumstances to account for brutality and atrocity in Anglo-Scottish war. It is easy, in my estimation, to reject a straightforward binary divide between guerrilla war and conventional war in the Anglo-Scottish sphere, and indeed in medieval conflict more broadly. In warfare in this era most soldiers were not full-time professionals and standing armies had not developed in either England or Scotland. Uniforms were not routinely worn.[68] All armies had common people

---

66 CAMERON, 2000, pp. 111-15.
67 The latter theme is explored in detail in: BROWN, 1998.
68 JONES, 2010, pp. 57-67.

among their forces – determining regular and irregular troops, a key aspect of a guerrilla war identification, is thus an impossible task. Raiding of enemy territory remained the ubiquitous military strategy of the time, by no means the preserve of notional guerrillas. Small unit operations, trickery and surprise: these, again, were characteristics rooted in conventional military activity.[69]

We can also reject a simple intercultural model, certainly in the way it is usually applied to Scotland. In the wars with England from 1296 the equation of Scotland with other 'Celtic' zones is deeply problematic. Anglo-Scottish war was not fundamentally a clash of alien cultures, one Gaelic and one Anglo-French. There were certainly Gaelic-speakers in Scottish forces.[70] But there were many English-speakers also; and there were many 'Celtic' warriors, Welsh and Irish, among 'English' forces ranged against the Scots. Edward I employed thousands of such troops, often many more than there were Gaels in Scottish forces.[71] Aristocratic leaders on both sides, meanwhile, were culturally of precisely the same stock and the pre-war linkages between a vibrant cross-border society have long since been outlined in detail.[72] There are other problems with seeing Anglo-Scottish war as influenced by an intercultural opposition of Gaelic against English ethnic groups. One plank of the case is the suggestion of continuity between English perceptions of the Scots at war in the twelfth century, who were indeed stigmatised as akin to the allegedly barbarous Welsh and Irish, with the situation in 1296 and beyond.[73] This suggestion of continuity ignores the fact that Scotland had been subject to many Anglicising influences in the intervening period: it had become a very different polity and society on the cusp of the fourteenth century. By 1296 there had been two centuries of acculturation and accommodation between various ethnic groups, including an influential Anglo-French aristocratic elite and long-established, including Gaelic-speaking, populations. In the

---

69 MACDONALD, 2013b; HARARI, 2007.
70 BOARDMAN, 2012.
71 For Irish forces in Edward I's armies see LYDON, 1954-6, 1961-2a, 1961-2b, 2008. The Welsh infantry contingent of nearly 11,000 men at Falkirk in 1298 was more numerous in itself than all but the greatest of medieval Scottish hosts. PRESTWICH, 1997, p. 479.
72 BARROW, 1966; STRINGER, 1995, pp. 87f.
73 STRICKLAND, 2000, pp. 39-52.

context of war in royal service the evidence is of a wide degree of homogeneity emerging from the ethnic mix.[74] The Scots were indeed castigated in English chronicles for their military outrages after 1296, and sometimes there are suggestive inferences that Gaelic-speakers are to blame.[75] But more commonly there is no sense at all of this angle: the Scots are vilified as national enemies, but not ones that emerge from a notably alien cultural or linguistic background.[76]

A final problematic feature of positing a more brutal, Gaelic way of war which impacted on the wider Anglo-Scottish conflict is the question of whether there was indeed a significantly more ruthless military culture within Gaelic Scotland. There has been a considerable body of recent work exploring attitudes within mainstream Scottish political society to the kingdom's Gaels. Hostility, in various manifestations, was expressed to them, both before and during the later middle ages.[77] Military issues feature in these negative stereotypings: the Gaels are warlike by nature, and they are also lawless, at times expressed in a militarised context. But nowhere in the later medieval characterisations is there the suggestion that they are especially *vicious* in war. There are clear signs of this perception, of barbarian brutality, being linked to Gaelic-speaking Scots in the twelfth century and (decreasingly) the thirteenth, but this motif has much less force and

---

74 In Barbour's writing (from the 1370s referring to the early fourteenth century) there is a depiction of Gaelic forces functioning harmoniously alongside other Scottish soldiers: BROUN, 2009, pp. 56-8. See also: BOARDMAN, 2012; MACGREGOR, 2012. Barrow depicts a thirteenth-century army in which there are divergent service obligations and legal mechanisms, but this relates to social class and conditions of tenure rather than language and ethnicity: BARROW, 1990.

75 The Scots shown enacting atrocities in the margins of the early fourteenth-century Luttrell Psalter were perhaps intended to be barbaric Gaelic-speakers. Atrocities in William Wallace's 1297 invasion of England were attributed to Gaelic-speaking natives of Galloway. CAMILLE, 1998, pp. 284-91; STRICKLAND, 2000, pp. 45f.; MCNAMEE, 1990.

76 In Laurence Minot's highly anti-Scottish poetry of the mid fourteenth century, for instance, 'wild' (Gaelic-speaking) and 'tame' Scots are equally castigated: MINOT, 1887, p. 3.

77 MACGREGOR, 2009; BROUN, 2009. Broun has shown that a hostile attitude to the Gaels was not first formulated in Scottish historiography in the late fourteenth-century chronicle previously attributed to John of Fordun, as traditionally thought.

explicitness by the time of the wars from 1296. One of the traits singled out for condemnation in the twelfth century, for instance, was the enslavement of captives in war. This practice had died out among Scottish forces by the thirteenth century.[78] The attempt to suggest that a culture of more than normal brutality in war persisted in the Scottish *Gàidhealtachd* right through the medieval period has leaned heavily on the poetry composed for Archibald, earl of Argyll prior to his involvement in war with England in 1513. The poem exhorts him to enact graphic cruelties on the English, including the burning of women and children.[79] Yet this isolated evidence has surely been read too literally as a guide to actual military practice. The genre of Gaelic praise poetry is consciously hyperbolic and bombastic: Argyll is being represented as a great chief because of how terrible he can be in war, but to this reader it seems an almost playfully overblown image rather than a description of real military ethics.[80]

If it is accepted that viewing Anglo-Scottish conflict through the lens of a Gaelic/English intercultural typology is unsuitable, there remains a more suitable angle. This is to deploy a conception based on social class. As we have seen, Scottish forces were drawn from a wider social spectrum than was the case for England. While this has been noted by a number of historians, discussions of the ramifications of this circumstance have been very limited.[81] Hostility based on social class can certainly be seen on both sides: one core depiction of Scottish forces by English witnesses is as uncouth brigands, of low status and manners, and there is a mirroring Scottish motif of lampooning perceived English elitism and bombast.[82] There seems more promise in

---

78 STRICKLAND, 2012, p. 117.
79 WATSON, 1937, pp. 158-164; STRICKLAND, 2000, p. 49; STRICKLAND, 2006, p. 122; STRICKLAND, 2008b, p. 117.
80 It is worth noting in this context that the *The Vows of the Heron*, a poem concerned with the outbreak of the Hundred Years War, also contains bombastic statements, in this case of the brutality to be visited on French non-combatants (DE MARCO, 2000). The Anglo-French cultural environment of this poem is of course located far from the allegedly rougher world of Gaelic Scotland.
81 See above, note 42.
82 For English accounts of Wallace as of lowly stock, leading a vicious army of brigands see FRASER, 2002, pp. 5-15, 19f.. For Scottish mockery of English social pretensions see MACDONALD, 2013b, pp. 327-32.

seeking to locate intensification of Anglo-Scottish hostilities in social make-up rather than ethnicity. But in any case, our questioning of whether Scottish Gaelic warfare was especially vicious raises the same issue in relation to Anglo-Scottish warfare more broadly. Were the wars from 1296 actually especially brutal? In their impact they undoubtedly were devastating for the communities exposed to regular war.[83] But the evidence is far less persuasive that this was because normal constraints were routinely flouted. There are few studies on this topic, but for the Anglo-Scottish wars after 1328, at any rate, there do not seem to have been engrained patterns of particular brutality.[84]

The prospect of social class operating as a better category for approaching the theme of atrocity than Gaelic-English ethnic hostility suggests a subcultural rather than intercultural typology. Scotland and England shared a larger 'big culture' with many commonalities of society and politics. But they had divergences, as we have seen, in the social make-up of armies and in the national aspirations of the Scots, the legitimacy of which was denied by their enemies. These factors may have led to intensified conflict, and demonization of the enemy, as combatants expressed their deep differences. This does not escape, though, from fundamental problems that seem to bedevil all of the available typologies – intercultural, subcultural and intracultural – questioning their general utility.[85] The categorisations are in this author's opinion too subjective and shifting to provide meaningful, overarching explanatory frameworks for medieval warfare. This is because all of these things could be argued to exist simultaneously, and it is a highly subjective decision to decide which military characteristics should be privileged as the ones that best define and shape the conflict.[86]

---

83 BARROW, 1992.
84 MACINNES, 2008, pp. 239-46; MACDONALD, 2000; KING, 2002.
85 A different approach, advancing the concept of 'assymetry' as a tool to understand conduct in war is suggested in COX, 2012.
86 For example, one of Kortüm's diagrams (KORTÜM, 2006, p. 26) categorises the Franco-Prussian war as intracultural and the American Civil War as subcultural. Presumably a silently subjective process has allowed combatants who shared a language and nationality (Americans) to be regarded as more alien to each other in conflict than those who did not (Germans and French).

Anglo-Scottish war could be intercultural: it *did* feature troops of different languages and ethnicities clashing. But it could, at precisely the same time, also be subcultural, as essentially similar societies fought a war charged by social class and contested national aspirations. And it could also be intracultural: Anglo-Scottish war could and often was combat within a culture where shared conventions applied and where respect and even friendship might develop.[87] There has been little examination of that side of things in this paper, but one excellent example is the case of Sir Thomas Gray. Captured by the Scots on the border in 1355 he was held captive in Edinburgh Castle. In what must have been a benign enough confinement he was given access to the writing and research materials to enable him to embark on his chronicle, the *Scalacronica*.[88] It is a work not marked by any great animus towards England's regular foes for the last half century, the Scots.[89]

With intracultural, subcultural and intercultural typologies all being visible at the same time I would argue that these categorisations are not very useful in offering general frameworks for understanding Anglo-Scottish war. In my opinion we will have better success with a more common-sense approach, taking account of specific circumstances that might have a moderating or exacerbating effect on the levels and nature of violence. One final example might prove to be useful. At the start of the wars, in 1296, English forces stormed and sacked Berwick, a process in which all the sources agree there was considerable loss of life among non-combatants.[90] Scottish historians have tended to view this as a particularly appalling atrocity.[91] It is, naturally, hard to divine much meaning in this event viewing it from the available standpoint of guerrilla vs conventional war (the Sots are not taken to have started guerrilla war yet), nor an intercultural clash of English vs Gaelic (there were Flemings among the victims at Berwick but it must be doubted if Gaels were). So what accounts for the sack of Berwick? One explanation is that a loss of leadership control led to the ferocity of the attack. That may be the case, or it may have been an exacerbating factor

---

87   GOODMAN, 2007; KING, 2007.
88   GRAY, 2005, pp. xvii-xviii, xl-xli.
89   KING, 2000.
90   There is a full account in STRICKLAND, 2000, pp. 64-7.
91   BARROW, 2005, pp. 92f.; GRANT, 1998, p. 20.

in the nature of the resulting rampage.[92] But there are ample reasons why Edward I would have wanted to sack Berwick. For one thing, it was quite within his rights to do so: it was widely accepted that a strongpoint taken by storm might be subjected to pillage.[93] The Scots also deserved to be punished: they had invaded Edward's realm, they were defying their rightful overlord, and the people of Berwick had been given and had refused the opportunity to submit. But more than this, there was a perfectly understandable and practical policy reason for the sack of Berwick: a salutary lesson could be given to the Scots about the consequences of resisting the English king. It was a lesson that bore fruit for Edward in the ensuing rapid conquest of the kingdom. Specific circumstances, rather than typological models account for the sack of Berwick. The key factors that explain abnormal atrocity and brutality in Anglo-Scottish war are specific ones: the level of desperation of the struggle at any given time; issues of personality, class, ethnicity and religion; particular policy aims (as at Berwick). All might, and did, profoundly shape the way that war was waged.

Bibliography

Sources

BAIN, JOSEPH (ed.), Calendar of Documents relating to Scotland, Volume 2, Edinburgh 1884.
BARBOUR, JOHN, The Bruce, ed. by A. A. M. DUNCAN, Edinburgh 1997.
BLACK, J. G. (Ed.), Calendar of Patent Rolls, 1301-7, London 1898.
BOUVET, HONORÉ, The Tree of Battles of Honoré Bonet, ed. by G. W. COOPLAND, Liverpool 1949.
BOWER, WALTER, Scotichronicon, Volume 7, ed. by D. E. R. WATT, Aberdeen 1996.
ID., Scotichronicon, Volume 8, ed. by D. E. R. WATT, Aberdeen 1987.

---

92 STRICKLAND, 2000, pp. 65f.
93 STRICKLAND, 2006, p.113.

GALBRAITH, V. H. (ed.), Extracts from the Historia Aurea and a French "Brut" (1317-47), in: English Historical Review 43 (1928), pp. 2013-17.
GRAY, THOMAS, Sir Thomas Gray, Scalacronica, 1272-1363 (Surtees Society 209), ed. by ANDY KING, Woodbridge 2005.
GUISBOROUGH, WALTER OF, The Chronicle of Walter of Guisborough, ed. by HARRY ROTHWELL (Camden Society, Series 3, 89), London 1957.
HARY, Blind Harry, The Wallace, ed. by ANNE MCKIM, Edinburgh 2003.
KNIGHTON, HENRY, Knighton's Chronicle 1337-1396, ed. by G. H. MARTIN, Oxford 1995.
ID., Chronicon Henrici Knighton, Volume 1 (Rolls Series 92), ed. by J. R. LUMBY, London 1889.
LE BEL, JEAN, The True Chronicles of Jean le Bel 1290-1360, ed. by NIGEL BRYANT, Woodbridge 2011.
LUARD H. R. (ed.), Flores Historiarum, Volume 3 (Rolls Series 95), London 1890.
MINOT, LAURENCE, The Poems of Laurence Minot, ed. by JOSEPH HALL, Oxford 1887.
PALGRAVE, FRANCIS (ed.), Documents and Records Illustrating the History of Scotland, Preserved in the Treasury, London 1837.
STEVENSON, J. (ed.), Chronicon de Lanercost (Bannatyne Club 65), Edinburgh 1839.
STEVENSON, W. H. (ed.), Calendar of Close Rolls, 1313-18, London 1893.
STONES, E. L. G. (ed.), Anglo-Scottish Relations 1174-1328: Some Select Documents, Oxford 1970.
WALSINGHAM, THOMAS, The St Albans Chronicle: The Chronica Majora of Thomas Walsingham, I 1376-1394, ed. by J. TAYLOR et al., Oxford 2003.
WATSON, WILLIAM J. (ed.), Scottish Verse from the Book of the Dean of Lismore, Edinburgh 1937.

Literature

ABELS, RICHARD, Cultural Representations and the Practice of War in the Middle Ages, in: Journal of Medieval Military History 6 (2008), pp. 1-31.
ALLMAND, CHRISTOPHER, The Reporting of War in the Middle Ages, in: War and Society in Medieval and Early Modern Britain, ed. by DIANA DUNN, Liverpool 2000, pp. 17-33.
ID., War and the Non-Combatant in the Middle Ages, in: Medieval Warfare. A History, ed. by MAURICE KEEN, Oxford 1999, pp. 253-72.
BARROW, G. W. S., Robert Bruce and the Community of the Realm of Scotland, 4th ed., Edinburgh 2005.
ID., The Aftermath of War, in: Scotland and its Neighbours in the Middle Ages, London 1992, pp. 177-200.
ID., The Army of Alexander III's Scotland, in: Scotland in the Reign of Alexander III, 1249-1286, ed. by NORMAN H. REID, Edinburgh 1990, pp. 132-47.
ID., Lothian in the First War of Independence, 1296-1328, in: Scottish Historical Review 55 (1976), pp. 151-71.
ID., The Anglo-Scottish Border, in: Northern History 1 (1966), pp. 21-42.
ID., The Scottish Clergy in the War of Independence, in: Scottish Historical Review 41 (1962), pp. 1-22.
BOARDMAN, STEPHEN I./FORAN, SUSAN (Eds.), Barbour's Bruce and its Cultural Contexts. Politics, Chivalry and Literature in Late Medieval Scotland, Cambridge 2015.
BOARDMAN, STEVE, Highland Scots and Anglo-Scottish Warfare, c.1300-1513, in: England and Scotland at War, c.1296-c.1513, ed. by ANDY KING/DAVID SIMPKIN, Leiden 2012, pp. 231-53.
BROUN, DAUVIT, Attitudes of Gall to Gaedhel in Scotland before John of Fordun, in: Mìorun Mòr nan Gall, "The Great Ill-Will of the Lowlander"? Lowland Perceptions of the Highlands, Medieval and Modern, ed. by DAUVIT BROUN/MARTIN MACGREGOR, Chippenham 2009, pp. 49-82.
BROWN, MICHAEL, The Wars of Scotland 1214-1371, Edinburgh 2004.
ID., The Black Douglases, East Linton 1998.

CALDWELL, DAVID H., Scottish Spearmen, 1298-1314. An Answer to Cavalry, in: War in History 19 (2012), pp. 267-89.
ID., The Battle of Pinkie, in: Scotland and War, AD 79-1918, ed. by NORMAN MACDOUGALL, Edinburgh 1991, pp. 61-94.
CAMERON, SONJA, Sir James Douglas, Spain, and the Holy Land, in: Freedom and Authority. Historical and Historiographical Essays presented to Grant G. Simpson, ed. by TERRY BROTHERSTONE/ DAVID DITCHBURN, East Linton 2000, pp. 108-17.
ID., Keeping the Customer Satisfied: Barbour's Bruce and a phantom division at Bannockburn, in: The Polar Twins, ed. by EDWARD J. COWAN/DOUGLAS GIFFORD, Edinburgh 1999, pp. 61-74.
ID., Chivalry and Warfare in Barbour's Bruce, in: Armies, Chivalry and Warfare in Medieval Britain and France, ed. by MATTHEW STRICKLAND, Stamford 1998, pp. 13-29.
CAMILLE, MICHAEL, Mirror in Parchment. The Luttrell Psalter and the Making of Medieval England, London 1998.
CORNELL, DAVID, Bannockburn. The Triumph of Robert the Bruce, New Haven CT 2009.
ID., Sir John Stirling. Edward III's Scottish Captain, in: Northern History 45 (2008), pp. 111-23.
COWAN, EDWARD J., "For Freedom Alone". The Declaration of Arbroath, 1320, East Linton 2003.
COX, RORY, A Law of War? English protection and destruction of ecclesiastical property during the fourteenth century, in: English Historical Review 128 (2013), pp. 1381-1417.
ID., Asymmetric Warfare and Military Conduct in the Middle Ages, in: Journal of Medieval History, 38 (2012), pp. 100-25.
CURRY, ANNE, Disciplinary Ordinances for English and Franco-Scottish Armies in 1385. An international code?, in: Journal of Medieval History 37 (2011), pp. 269-94.
DE MARCO, PATRICIA, Inscribing the Body with Meaning. Chivalric culture and the norms of violence in The Vows of the Heron, in: Inscribing the Hundred Years War in French and English Cultures, ed. by DENISE N. BAKER, Albany NY 2000, pp. 27-54.
DUNCAN, A. A. M., William, Son of Alan Wallace. The Documents, in: The Wallace Book, ed. by E. J. COWAN, Edinburgh 2007, pp. 42-63.

ID., The War of the Scots 1306-23, in: Transactions of the Royal Historical Society, Series 6, 2 (1992), pp. 125-51.

FORAN, SUSAN, A Great Romance. Chivalry and War in Barbour's Bruce, in: Fourteenth-Century England VI, ed. by C. GIVEN-WILSON, Woodbridge 2010, pp. 1-25.

GILLINGHAM, JOHN, Conquering the Barbarians: War and chivalry in twelfth-century Britain and Ireland, in: The Haskins Society Journal 4 (1992a), pp. 67-84.

ID., The Beginnings of English Imperialism, Journal of Historical Sociology 5 (1992b), pp. 392-409.

GIVEN-WILSON, CHRIS, Chronicles. The Writing of History in Medieval England, London 2004.

GOODMAN, ANTHONY, Anglo-Scottish Relations in the Later Fourteenth Century. Alienation or acculturation?, in: England and Scotland in the Fourteenth Century. New Perspectives, ed. by: ANDY KING/M. A. PENMAN, Woodbridge 2007, pp. 236-53.

ID., Introduction, in: ANTHONY GOODMAN/ANTHONY TUCK (eds.), War and Border Societies in the Middle Ages, London 1992.

GRANT, ALEXANDER, Disaster at Neville's Cross: The Scottish Point of View, in: The Battle of Neville's Cross 1346, ed. by DAVID ROLLASON/MICHAEL PRESTWICH, Stamford 1998, pp. 15-35.

GRUMMITT, DAVID, Changing Perceptions of the Soldier in Late Medieval England, in: Parliament, Personalities and Power. Papers presented to Linda S. Clark (The Fifteenth Century 10), ed. by HANNES KLEINEKE, Woodbridge 2011, pp. 189-202.

HARARI, Y. N., Special Operations in the Age of Chivalry, 1100-1500, Woodbridge 2007.

HORSBURGH, DAVIE, Gaelic and Scots in Grampian. An outline history, Aberdeen 1994.

JONES, ROBERT W., Bloodied Banners. Martial Display on the Medieval Battlefield, Woodbridge 2010.

KEEN, M. H., Chivalry, New Haven CT 1984.

ID., The Laws of War in the Late Middle Ages, London 1965.

KING, ANDY, War and Peace. A Knight's Tale. The Ethics of War in Sir Thomas Gray's Scalacronica, in: War, Government and Aristocracy in the British Isles c.1150-1500. Essays in Honour of Michael

Prestwich, ed. by CHRIS GIVEN-WILSON et al., Woodbridge 2008, pp. 148-62.
ID., Best of Enemies. Were the fourteenth-century Anglo-Scottish Marches a 'Frontier Society'?, in: England and Scotland in the Fourteenth Century. New Perspectives, ed. by ANDY KING/M. A. PENMAN, Woodbridge 2007, pp. 116-35.
ID., Bandits, Robbers and Schavaldours. War and disorder in Northumberland in the reign of Edward II', in: Thirteenth Century England IX, ed. by MICHAEL PRESTWICH et al., Woodbridge 2003, pp. 115-29.
ID., "According to the Custom used in French and Scottish Wars". Prisoners and casualties on the Scottish marches in the fourteenth century, in: Journal of Medieval History 28 (2002), pp. 263-90.
ID., Englishmen, Scots and Marchers. National and local identities in Thomas Gray's Scalacronica, in: Northern History 36 (2000), pp. 217-31.
KING, ANDY/SIMPKIN DAVID (eds.), England and Scotland at War, c.1296-c.1513 (History of Warfare 78), Leiden 2012.
KLIMAN, BERNICE W., The Idea of Chivalry in John Barbour's Bruce, in: Mediaeval Studies 35 (1973), pp. 477-508.
KORTÜM, HANS-HENNING, Clash of Typologies – the naming of wars and the invention of typologies, in: Transcultural Wars from the Middle Ages to the 21st Century, ed. by HANS-HENNING KORTÜM, Berlin 2006, pp. 11-26.
LYDON, J. F., Edward I, Ireland and the war in Scotland, 1303-1304, in: Government, War and Society in Medieval Ireland, ed. by PETER CROOKS, Dublin 2008, pp. 200-15.
ID., An Irish Army in Scotland, 1296, in: Irish Sword 5 (1961-2a), pp. 184-9.
ID., Irish Levies in the Scottish Wars, 1296-1302, in: Irish Sword 5 (1961-2b), pp. 207-17.
ID., The Hobelar. An Irish contribution to medieval warfare, in: Irish Sword 2 (1954-6), pp. 12-16.
MACDONALD, ALASTAIR J., Good King Robert's Testament? Guerrilla Warfare in Later Medieval Scotland, in: Unconventional Warfare. Guerrillas and Counterinsurgency in History, ed. by Brian Hughes/Fergus Robson, Basingstoke 2016, [forthcoming].

ID., Courage, Fear and the Experience of the Later Medieval Scottish Soldier, in: Scottish Historical Review 92 (2013a), pp. 179-206.

ID., Trickery, Mockery and the Scottish Way of War, in: Proceedings of the Society of Antiquaries of Scotland 143 (2013b), pp. 319-37.

ID., The Kingdom of Scotland at War, 1332-1488, in: A Military History of Scotland, ed. by EDWARD M. SPIERS et al., Edinburgh 2012a, pp. 179-206.

ID., Triumph and Disaster. Scottish military leadership in the later middle ages, in: England and Scotland at War, c.1296-c.1513 (History of Warfare 78), ed. by ANDY KING/DAVID SIMPKIN, Leiden 2012b, pp. 255-82.

ID., Border Bloodshed. Scotland and England at War, 1369-1403, East Linton 2000.

MACGREGOR, MARTIN, Warfare in Gaelic Scotland in the Later Middle Ages, in: A Military History of Scotland, ed. by EDWARD M. SPIERS et al., Edinburgh 2012, pp. 209-31.

ID., Gaelic Barbarity and Scottish Identity in the Later Middle Ages, in: Mìorun Mòr nan Gall, "The Great Ill-Will of the Lowlander"? Lowland Perceptions of the Highlands, Medieval and Modern, ed. by DAUVIT BROUN/MARTIN MACGREGOR, Chippenham 2009, pp. 7-48.

MACINNES, IAIN A., Scotland at War. Its conduct and the behaviour of Scottish soldiers, 1332-1357 (unpublished PhD thesis), University of Aberdeen 2008.

ID., "Shock and Awe": The use of terror as a psychological weapon during the Bruce-Balliol Civil War, 1332-1338, in: England and Scotland in the Fourteenth Century. New Perspectives, ed. by ANDY KING/MICHAEL A. PENMAN, Woodbridge 2007, pp. 40-59.

MCNAMEE, C. J., Robert the Bruce. Our Most Valiant Prince, King and Lord, Edinburgh 2006.

ID., The Wars of the Bruces. Scotland, England and Ireland, 1306-1328, East Linton 1997.

ID., William Wallace's Invasion of Northern England in 1297, in: Northern History 26 (1990), pp. 40-58.

MORILLO, STEPHEN, A General Typology of Transcultural Wars – the early middle ages and beyond, in: Transcultural Wars from the

Middle Ages to the 21st Century, ed. by HANS-HENNING KORTÜM, Berlin 2006, pp. 29-42.
NEVILLE, CYNTHIA J., Widows of War. Edward I and the women of Scotland during the War of Independence, in: Wife and Widow in Medieval England, ed. by SUE SHERIDAN WALKER, Ann Arbor MI 1993, pp. 109-39.
NICHOLSON, RANALD, Edward III and the Scots. The Formative Years of a Military Career 1327-1335, Oxford 1965.
OWEN, DOROTHY M., White Annays and Others, in: Medieval Women, ed. by DEREK BAKER, Oxford 1978, pp. 331-46.
PRESTWICH, MICHAEL, Transcultural Warfare – the later middle ages, in: Transcultural Wars from the Middle Ages to the 21st Century, ed. by HANS-HENNING KORTÜM, Berlin 2006, pp. 43-56.
ID., Edward I, new ed., London 1997.
ROGERS, CLIFFORD J., By Fire and Sword: Bellum Hostile and "Civilians" in the Hundred Years War, in: Civilians in the Path of War, ed. by MARK GRIMSLEY/CLIFFORD J. ROGERS, Lincoln NE 2002, pp. 33-78.
ID., The Military Revolutions of the Hundred Years War, in: The Military Revolution Debate, ed. by CLIFFORD J. ROGERS, Boulder CO 1995, pp. 55-93.
SCAMMEL, JEAN, Robert I and the North of England, in: English Historical Review 73 (1958), pp. 385-403.
SEABOURNE, GWEN, Imprisoning Medieval Women. The Non-Judicial Confinement and Abduction of Women in England, c.1170-1509, Farnham 2011.
SPIERS, EDWARD M. et al. (eds.), A Military History of Scotland, Edinburgh 2012.
STEVENSON, KATIE, Chivalry and Knighthood in Scotland, 1424-1513, Woodbridge 2006.
STRICKLAND, MATTHEW, The Kings of Scots at War, c.1093-1286, in: A Military History of Scotland, ed. by EDWARD M. SPIERS et al., Edinburgh 2012, pp. 94-132.
ID., Treason, Feud and the Growth of State Violence. Edward I and the "War of the Earl of Carrick", 1306-7, in: War, Government and Aristocracy in the British Isles c.1150-1500. Essays in Honour of

Michael Prestwich, ed. by CHRIS GIVEN-WILSON et al., Woodbridge 2008a, pp. 84-113.
ID., War and Chivalry. The Conduct and Perception of War in England and Normandy, 1066-1217, Cambridge 2008b.
ID., Rules of War or War without Rules? – Some reflections on conduct and the treatment of non-combatants in medieval transcultural wars, in: Transcultural Wars from the Middle Ages to the 21st Century, ed. by HANS-HENNING KORTÜM, Berlin 2006, pp. 107-40.
ID., A Law of Arms or a Law of Treason? Conduct in war in Edward I's campaigns in Scotland, 1296-1307, in: Violence in Medieval Society, ed. by RICHARD W. KAEUPER, Woodbridge 2000, pp. 39-77.
ID., Securing the North. Invasion and the strategy of defence in twelfth-century Anglo-Scottish warfare, in: Anglo-Norman Warfare, ed. by MATTHEW STRICKLAND, Woodbridge 1992, pp. 208-29.
STRINGER, KEITH, Scottish Foundations. Thirteenth-century perspectives, in: Uniting the Kingdom? The Making of British History, ed. by ALEXANDER GRANT/KEITH STRINGER, London 1995, pp. 85-96.
TAYLOR, CRAIG, English writings on chivalry and warfare during the Hundred Years War, in: Soldiers, Nobles and Gentlemen. Essays in Honour of Maurice Keen, ed. by PETER COSS/CHRISTOPHER TYERMAN, Woodbridge 2009, pp. 64-84.
WRIGHT, NICHOLAS, Knights and Peasants. The Hundred Years War in the French Countryside, Woodbridge 1998.
YOUNG, ALAN, The Earls and Earldom of Buchan in the Thirteenth Century, in: Medieval Scotland. Crown, Lordship and Community. Essays presented to G. W. S. Barrow, ed. by ALEXANDER GRANT/KEITH J. STRINGER, Edinburgh 1993, pp. 174-202.

Logistics and Food Supply in the *Crònica* of Ramon Muntaner

JUDITH MENGLER

Ramon Muntaner and the Expedition to the East

"In the midst of such hearty feasting, while everyone was celebrating, Friar Roger was deep in thought; but even this seemed stubborn of him, nobody in the world had greater foresight than he. And his thoughts were these: 'You have lost this lord, as have, likewise, those Catalan and Aragonese men who have served him, for he is unable to give them anything, and they will be a great burden upon him. And they are like all men, for they cannot survive without food, and so, since they will receive nothing from the King, they will cause great devastation out of necessity; and, in the end, they will destroy all the land, and all of them will perish one by one. So, since this lord who has bestowed such honours upon you is so well served, it is necessary that you seek to relieve him of these troops, for the sake of his honour and for their own advantage.'"[1]

The scene Muntaner reports here took place in August 1302 and the festivities mentioned were the celebrations on the occasion of the Peace of Caltabellotta. The Peace of Caltabellotta was the ending point of the

---

1 HUGHES, 2006, p. 36.

War of the Sicilian Vespers, which had been fought since 1282.[2] The man deep in thought, although there was a great party all around him, was Roger de Flor, leader of the Great Catalan Company.[3] In this function, the conclusion of a peace agreement could only be bad news for him. The Great Catalan Company was a mercenary company and for mercenaries, peace is synonymous with unemployment and unemployment is, at least in those times, synonymous with starvation. The mercenaries of the Great Catalan Company were, as Muntaner writes, of course "like all men, for they cannot survive without food".[4] Without payment or free access to food supply, they would take what they need by force and thereby "cause great devastation without necessity".[5]

I decided to begin my article with the given scene, because these considerations of Roger de Flor were the starting point for a military operation known today as *The Catalan Expedition to the East*, "perhaps the most fantastic military adventure of the later Middle Ages".[6] As we see, the question of feeding troops and food supply is not only strongly interconnected with the military aims of the expedition. According to Muntaner, it was this question, which was in fact the reason for planning such an expedition.[7] Moreover, this topic will play a major role during the entire expedition. Of course, all military expeditions in the Middle Ages, as well as in other periods of history, were subject to considerations such as: How can we feed our troops? How and which way can we transport the victuals and the equipment? What about fodder for the horses? For how many days should every soldier carry

---

2 For a short history of events and of the Company see BURNS, 1954, pp. 751f. and SABLONIER, 1971, pp. 11-17. For more historical background about the War of Sicilian Vespers see ABULAFIA, 1997, pp. 57-81, 107-112. About the Catalan Company in Greece see ABULAFIA, 1997, pp. 118-123.
3 VONES, 1999, cols. 550-551.
4 HUGHES, 2006, p. 36.
5 IBID., p. 36.
6 BURNS, 1954, p. 751.
7 The Byzantine author Gregoras also gives a close connection between the Peace of Caltabellotta, the need of the Great Catalan Company for make a living and the Expedition to the East. See KYRIAKIDIS, 2011, pp. 126f.. Abulafia calls the Catalan Company a "by-product of the War of the Vespers". ABULAFIA, 1997, p. 120.

rations in the case of emergency? However, very often the sources remain silent about the solutions, about the not so glorious day-to-day business of war. Mostly, we only receive information if things went horribly wrong, that is, for example, when a campaign had to be cancelled or that an army was defeated by famine rather than by the enemy.[8] Yet, we should not be surprised, because the logistics of a campaign usually do not produce exciting stories, at least at first glance. The "knight in the shining armour" is a more useful protagonist than the baker in the flour-powdered coat and battle cries are more easily performed in front of the audience than the maledictions of the muleteers. The chroniclers also knew about the topics, which interested their audience, usually persons of higher rank and that were narrations about other persons in power. Not only are logistics of military expeditions not very glorious, the topic is somewhat rustically and inappropriate for nobles. "While the class that would have been interested to read about logistics was not a reading class at all until the modern era, the class that did the writing thus regarded logistics as undignified, the province of its social inferiors."[9], as Edward N. Luttwak has correctly observed. In addition, chroniclers very often had no experience in warfare themselves and one could therefore suggest that some simply did not know about the problems and solutions of logistics. Nevertheless, they were experts in literary and social conventions and, as a result, the material conditions of war were drawn to the background while the literary style and the expectations of the audience came to the fore.[10]

The chronicler I would like to introduce here is an exceptional case. Ramon Muntaner was born at Peralada in 1265, where his father owned a lodging. It is very likely that he was as a young man in the service of admiral Roger of Lauria. Around 1300, he met Roger de Flor in Sicily, where Muntaner was constable in the service of Frederick III of Sicily. Shortly afterwards, he joined the Great Catalan Company where he soon took up his office as treasurer and chancellor of the company. Due

---

8   Not a disaster, but an example for several problems concerning logistics caused by a variety of reasons is the English campaign in Scotland in 1327. See NICHOLSON, 1965, pp. 26-41; HARARI, 2000, p. 319.
9   LUTTWALK, 1993, p. 6.
10 IBID., pp. 4-7. About Muntaner's literary style see AURELL, 2012, pp. 84-89 and SABLONIER, 1971, pp. 42-48.

to his office, he had significant participation in the organisation of the *Catalan Expedition to the East*. In Greece, he became captain of Gallipoli in addition to his former office.[11] Muntaner describes Gallipoli as the base camp of the company; in his own words, it was "the most important of them all, and anyone who had need of any item, whether it be clothing or amour or anything else, went there."[12] Therefore, Muntaner was, firstly, well experienced in warfare. He was a professional soldier and familiar with fighting at sea as well as on land. Secondly, he was also quite familiar with the problems and solutions of logistics at war, simply because it was his job within the Great Catalan Company. Last but not least, he was not only a professional soldier, he was a chronicler as well. He started to write his *Crònica* in 1325 and finished it in 1328. The official intention of his work is the praising of the crown of Aragon.[13] However, there is another intention, which is quite pragmatic and private. Because he had lost all of his possessions several times, he hoped that he would secure a well-paid office at court, for example. This is why his *Crònica*, at least in parts, also highlights his own abilities and skills. It is a little similar to an application letter.[14] More often, he wrote about how things were done, because he wanted his reader to recognise how well the things were done by him, Ramon Muntaner. In my opinion, these three points are good arguments for choosing the *Crònica* to obtain an insight into the organisation of food supply and logistics.

---

11 For further biographical detail on Muntaner see AURELL, 2012, pp. 72-76; SABLONIER, 1971, pp. 18-20.
12 HUGHES, 2006, p. 93.
13 SABLONIER, 1971, pp. 20-22.
14 In 1309 Frederick appointed him as commander of the island Djerba. According to the Crònica, Muntaner was chosen because of his unsurpassed experience in war and the management of soldiers. His positive qualities are given in a direct speech and put into the mouth of Frederik. Here the second intention becomes quite clear. After 1328 he moved to Majorca in order to serve King James III and was knighted shortly before his death in 1336. AURELL, 2012, pp. 73-76. See also SABLONIER, 1971, pp. 20-22.

Logistics and Food Supply

Quantities and the problem of concrete figures

Now we shall go *in medias res* and ask the very basic question: From where did the Great Catalan Company get their victuals?

In very general terms, there were three possibilities for a medieval soldier to get his food.

The first possibility: The army brought along the victuals the soldiers needed during the campaign.

The second possibility: The soldiers bought their food from merchants who accompanied the army.

The third possibility: The soldiers took their food from the area where the campaign took place, that is, the army was *living off the land*.

The kind method employed depended on the number of troops, the duration of the campaign and, of course, the situation. Usually, all three methods were used in combination and the company did so as well. All three methods had advantages and disadvantages and careful considerations were needed to find the combination, which was appropriate in the current situation.

The first possibility has a very clear advantage: The army is entirely independent from merchants as well as the area surrounding it. If the enemy employed the tactic of scorched earth, the baggage train was the life insurance of the army. If travelling by ship, the first possibility is the most ideal. At sea, there are no merchants, at least not until the ship reaches the next harbour, and to live off the land is, without land, obviously not an option.

In the spring of 1303, the Great Catalan Company started their expedition. Roger de Flor had negotiated a contract with the emperor of Constantinople, who wanted the company in his service in order to fight the Turks. The company embarked in Messina with direction to Monemvasia at the very southern tip of Greece. According to the chronicle, "God granted them such fine weather, that, in a few days, they put ashore".[15] Here, the supply method and, at least approximately, the duration are clear. What about the number of troops? Muntaner provides the following information in his enumeration: 4000 Almo-

---

15 HUGHES, 2006, p. 43.

gavers (Almogavers are a Catalan type of light infantry.), 1500 knights and horsemen and 1000 seamen. That is a total of 6500 men. In addition to that, many of the men took their wives and children with them.[16] Muntaner mentions this several times without providing a number. He also mentions that there were galley slaves and sailors who belonged to the hired ships, but again without a concrete number. Furthermore, the horsemen and knights had to take their horses, which also required fodder. About the rations the men of the company took with them, Muntaner wrote: "…to every person – man, woman or child – who was leaving with the Grand Duke [Roger de Flor], he gave a quintal of biscuit and ten pieces of cheese, and a bacon of salted pork fat between every four persons, together with garlic and onions."[17] And "knights and horsemen had double rations of everything."[18]

Now, at the first glance, it is time to pull out the calculator. However, as you can imagine, it is not as easy as that. There are several issues in the *Crònica* as well as other medieval chronicles, which prevent the historian from seeing medieval logistics as a question of basic arithmetic operations. The first problem is that there are, obviously, numbers missing. Muntaner does not tell us, how many wives, children and slaves were with the company. These persons also needed food. The second problem is that, where we do have absolute numbers, we do not know how reliable they are. It is not unusual for medieval chroniclers to exaggerate numbers, especially the numbers of troops. According to the *Crònica*, we have to calculate with 6500 men. However, we simply do not know if this is, in our sense, correct information and, ultimately, the historian just has to admit his unknowingness. It is almost the same with the statements about food in the *Crònica*. Because the intention of the *Crònica* is the praising of the house of Aragon, it is possible that Frederick of Sicily should be illustrated as particular generous. Therefore, the quantity of food provided by him could be exaggerated as well. The third problem is rather technical: How much is a quintal of biscuit? The medieval units of measurement are not familiar to us. Very often, their naming

---

16 IBID., p. 42.
17 IBID., p. 41.
18 IBID., p. 42.

remained, but their meaning changed throughout the centuries or depended on the regional traditions.

Nevertheless, in spite of all the mentioned problems, I shall attempt a calculation, using the figures we know or can estimate. The aim of the calculation is to show the dimensions with which the medieval logistic specialist had to cope. I shall try to calculate the amount of biscuit, because biscuit is the only kind of food were we get with the *quintal* an indication of the quantity. The *quintal,* originated from the *centenarius,* is a unit of measurement which meant 100 Roman pounds. It passed into the Arabic as *cantar* and returned to Europe through Arab merchants. It is similar to other traditional units of measurement as the German *Zentner* or the English *hundredweight,* the first, depending on the region, is around 50 kilograms, the second around 45 kilograms. The Spanish *quintal,* which is used for the calculation, is around 46 kilograms.[19]

According to the *Crònica,* there were 5000 men, the Almogavers and seamen, with single rations and 1500 men, the knights and horsemen, with double rations. We therefore need 5000 quintals for the Almogavers and seamen, being 230 tons, and 3000 quintals for the knights and horsemen, being 138 tons of biscuit. Therefore, based on the figures the chronicle tells us, 368 tons of biscuit were on the ships. And what about the horses? According to the work of Yuval Noah Harari, a horse needs 10 kilograms of dry fodder each day.[20] If we assume that every knight and horseman had at least one horse with him, although we know that knights usually had more than one horse when campaigning,[21] we have to add 15 tons of fodder for each day at sea. According to Muntaner, they were at sea "a few days". For only three days at sea, 45 tons of fodder are needed. This would be, calculated with the figures of the chronicle, 413 tons. To provide an impression of

---

19 HUGHES, 2006, p. 41 note 54;
 https://www.unc.edu/~rowlett/units/dictQ.html, 25.11.2015.
20 HARARI, 2000, p. 305.
21 The shipping of horses creates its own very special challenge. Conscious of the rather small flotilla and the fact that the Almogavers were infantry and that they didn't sail to enemy territory, which meant they were able to buy horses after reaching the destination, I would suggest that the number of shipped horses was rather small compared to other campaigns in the 14th century. See LAMBERT, 2011, pp. 95-100.

the dimension: Today, more than six very large freight wagons would be needed to transport 413 tons of cargo by train.[22] I would like to note that these numbers are only for fodder and biscuit. There were, as we have already seen, other kinds of food on the ships, such as cheese and bacon. Naturally, the company had to bring along their armours, weapons, several kinds of tools, cooking utensils and other things.[23] Consequently, I believe it is quite clear now that being a medieval logistic specialist was not an easy job.[24] Now, I shall now refrain from further calculations and return to the advantages and disadvantages of the possible methods of food supply.

Methods of Transport

The clear disadvantage of the "bring along your own stuff" method is the laborious transport of the things. Again, the numbers of the following considerations are taken from the work of Harari. According to him, the biggest medieval carts had a maximum load of 4 tons.[25] To transport the just calculated amounts of biscuit, 92 carts were required. To supply an army not only for a few days, but for weeks, it would be necessary to employ hundreds of carts. Even if there were hundreds of carts and animals to pull them, more difficulties would occur. The mobility of the carts, and therefore the mobility of the entire army, would depend on the existence of streets and their condition, on the landscape and on the weather. Another possibility, especially in the mountainous areas of Greece and Asia Minor, would be packhorses and mules. A pack animal could carry 150 kilograms on average.[26]

---

22 Calculated with the load limit of covered bulk goods wagons used by Deutsche Bahn. http://www.gueterwagenkatalog.rail.dbschenker.de/gwk-de/start/gattung_t_gedeckte_schuettgutwagen/3157124/Talns_969.html?start=0, 25.11.2015.
23 HARARI, 2000, p. 314.
24 Of course one could claim that the expedition of the Catalan Company was a single event and a rather small enterprise. Much more impressive, but not object of this article, are the quantities of victuals shipped to France by the English in the 14th century. See LAMBERT, 2011, p. 90 table 2.9.
25 HARARI, 2000, p. 312.
26 IBID., p. 312. Haldon gives lower loading capacities. Even small differences in the estimated average load could cause completely other

Obviously, without any calculation, one would need legions of them. Another problem of the transport by pack animals was well known by The Great Catalan Company and Muntaner, because they experienced it at the siege of Messina in the Wars of the Sicilian Vespers.

"So the siege lasted so long, that Messina was at risk of being evacuated on account of starvation. Nevertheless, the Lord King entered Messina twice, each time bringing in more than ten thousand mules laden with wheat and with flour and much livestock; but all this was as nothing, for wheat brought by land does not amount so much, since all the horsemen and the accompanying soldiers have already eaten a great amount by the time they leave. So the city was in great distress."[27]

From this we can conclude, that food transports by pack animals were useful to provide a marching army for a short time. However, they were not useful to send provisions over long distances, because much of the food was consumed during the transport. Worthless, at least in the long run, was the transport of fodder by pack animals. If we assume the already mentioned 10 kilograms of fodder each day and an average load of 150 kilograms, you will end up with a well-nourished pack animal after 15 days and a hungry accompanying soldier thinking about eating his packhorse.[28] Except from the quotation, there is no evidence for the transport of food by pack animals during the Catalan expedition to the east. Maybe, Muntaner and the company had learnt their lesson.

Another option of delivering food and equipment was to transport it by ships. In 1303, the emperor of Byzantium sent the Great Catalan Company to Asia Minor, more precise, to Cape Artaki on the peninsula of Cyzikus. They planned to march further inland in order to fight against the Turks. Muntaner tells us that it was arranged: "…that when he [Roger de Flor] moved inland with his army, his galleys should await him with food and all other provisions in appointed places."[29] The major benefit of this method of transport was the large loading capacity. A seafaring vessel could carry on average 150 tons; some even had a

---

    results to a calculation regarding the numbers of pack-animals. HALDON, 2006, pp. 5-8.
27 HUGHES, 2006, p. 30.
28 HARARI, 2000, p. 320.
29 HUGHES, 2006, p. 47.

maximum load of up to 300 tons.[30] Therefore, it was possible to supply an entire army with a small number of ships and, in proportion, the crew of a ship consumed less of the cargo.[31] The clear disadvantage was that ships were less flexible. The supply by ship could naturally only work in coastal regions or along big rivers. In 1303, the decision was seemingly correct, because we do not hear of any problems with the supply lines concerning that year.

Merchants and food trade

In October 1303, the company decided to spend the winter in Artaki. To ensure constant supply during winter, the company employed a system, which is a mixture of two methods. They lived, in a wider sense, off the land, but paid for the things they consumed. In a first step, a committee of twelve persons was founded. Six persons belonged to the Catalan Company and six were notables of the locality. In a second step, the committee assigned lodgings and thereby distributed the members of the company to several hosts.

> "And they made the followings arrangements: namely, that each person's host was obliged to give him bread, wine, oats, salted pork fat, cheese, vegetables, a bed, and everything that he might need: for, with the exception of fresh meat and seasonings, each host had to provide his guest with everything else. And those twelve men assigned a suitable price to each thing, and they instructed the host to keep a tally of each thing used by the person who was lodging in his house, and to carry this out from the first day of November until the end of March."[32]

The plan was that, in March, the money for the consumed items would be deducted from the pay of the hosted person. It is not difficult to guess that this plan worked only in theory. When, in February 1304, all members of the company were requested to bring their bills to the treasurer, it quickly became clear that "there was no one who had not

---

30   HARARI, 2000, pp. 312f.
31   IBID., p. 313.
32   HUGHES, 2006, p. 51.

consumed more by far than was warranted by the time they had stayed there."³³ In the end, de Flor generously decided to pay the bills without deducting any sums from the payments of his soldiers. At least this is the end of the story as Muntaner tells it. It is reasonable to think that not all things were paid and that the inhabitants of Artaki had to shoulder the most of the costs.³⁴ Nevertheless, the described system was, in the Catalan point of view, very useful. It was repeatedly employed during the Catalan expedition to the east.

The company bought their food through this system not only from the peasants, but also from merchants. We do not know from where the merchants obtained their goods nor do we have much information about their numbers, their origins or their trading habits. In his description of Gallipoli, Muntaner informs us that "all merchants, whatever their status, came to visit and to settle there."³⁵ Thus, there were different types of merchants; some just stopped for a visit, while others settled down. The merchants in Gallipoli are later mentioned in the *Crònica* in a somewhat untypical context: The Great Company had left Gallipoli in order to fight against the Alans, Muntaner stayed behind with only a couple of men. The emperor had learnt about the absence of the soldiers from Gallipoli and, because he and the company had meanwhile become enemies, sent eighteen Genoese galleys against Muntaner and his small force. Muntaner had therefore to organise the defence of Gallipoli with rather uncommon means:

> "I ensured that all the women we had were fully armed (since we had a large amount of armour), and I deployed them along the ramparts; and on each section of the ramparts, I placed a merchant, from among the Catalan merchants who were present, to be in command of the womenfolk."³⁶

According to this, there must have been merchants who either accompanied the company from the outset or followed them on to

---

33 IBID., p. 52.
34 The Byzantine author Pachymeres blamed the Catalan Company for impose burdens on the local population as well as for committing crimes against them. See KYRIAKIDIS, 2011, p. 123.
35 HUGHES, 2006, p. 93.
36 HUGHES, 2006, p. 104.

Greece later. Besides this military context, we, as already said, are not informed about the merchants. Muntaner possibly did not mention them, because the presence of merchants at Gallipoli was taken for granted. We learn about a disadvantage of this method of food supply in an indirect way. The problem was that the imbalance of supply and demand in times of war led to exorbitant prices for food. Usually, the payments of the soldiers, at least in part, were destined for the acquisition of food and equipment. Exorbitant prices for basic foodstuff meant that the payments were not sufficient to buy other necessary items. This could result in inadequate equipment or discontent in the army, both with negative impact on the fighting power. Because of this, a wise leader of a mercenary company needed to keep a closer eye on the prices and take countermeasures against usury.[37]

Roger de Flor was such a foresighted leader. During the War of the Sicilian Vespers, he captured several provision ships of the enemy and sold the food at giveaway prices. Occasionally, he even bought food and resold it with loss. According to Muntaner, he "announced the sale of fine wheat at thirty tarins a salma, which had cost him more than forty tarins, and which he could have sold at ten ounces a salma, if he had wished."[38] A salma was a unit of measurement for grain in Sicily; in modern terms, it was about 263 litres. One ounce valued thirty tarins.[39] Thus, Roger de Flor, according to the *Crònica*, sold the wheat with a loss of 25 percent when he could have sold it at ten times the price. Muntaner's reason for telling this story is, of course, the depiction of Roger de Flor as an able and generous leader, who is interested in the well-being of the people in general and of his men in particular. Therefore, it is possible that the proportions of the given sums are not correct. However, as already outlined, de Flor had very good reasons, besides any philanthropic considerations, to act as described in the *Crònica*.

---

37 HARARI, 2000, p. 315.
38 HUGHES, 2006, p. 31.
39 IBID., p. 31 note 35.

Living off the land

Let us now have a look at the third possibility to get victuals and other things; that is to live off the land. For the Great Catalan Company, as for the most other armies in the Middle Ages, this method of food supply played a major role. Muntaner presents the peninsula of Gallipoli as a land of milk and honey:

> "And everyone was wealthy and well-supplied, so they did not sow nor plough nor dig the vines nor prune them, and yet each year they took in as much wine and as much wheat and oats as they desired. Therefore, for five years, we lived from the crops' own regrowth. And so our raids became more wondrous than you could ever imagine, so much so that, if someone were to tell you about them all, he could not write a document long enough."[40]

Later on, the situation changed remarkably:

> "Now it is true that we had been on the Gallipoli peninsula and in that region for seven years since the Caesar's death, and we had lived from the crops' own regrowth for five years. And, similarly, we had left that entire region uninhabited to a distance of ten days' march in every direction and so, having driven out all the people, nothing could be harvested; and on account of this, we were forced to leave that country."[41]

First, the duration Muntaner states here is verifably wrong. The Company did not stay at the peninsula for five years; they stayed for two years, from the summer of 1305 to that of 1307.[42] Within two years, the company had the dubious honour to achieve the entire depopulation and devastation of the Gallipoli peninsula and the neighbouring areas. Because of that, they "were forced to leave that country." The leaving of Gallipoli is, after the leaving of Sicily and the following expedition to the east, the second example for moving the

---

40 IBID., pp. 93f.
41 IBID., p. 119.
42 IBID., p. 93 note 118.

entire Great Catalan Company to another location due to supply conditions. They did not leave Gallipoli for military aims, strategic considerations or changing politics. They left because there was nothing left in Gallipoli.

Regarding the advantages and disadvantages of the methods of food supply, we here see one of the clearest disadvantages of the "living off the land" method: it is strictly limited in time. But what is meant by living off the land? Very generally, there is a direct and a rather indirect way in doing so and it could be employed as an offensive and as a defensive weapon.[43] The direct way is, quite simply, to take the food from where the army is campaigning. Smaller groups of soldiers explored the area and raided small villages or farms. They took away the stock of the peasants and drove away the livestock in order to collect food for the army. Because of its simplicity, this seems to be a foolproof method. Yet, as most issues concerning logistics, things became increasingly complicated due to the quantity of food needed and the large numbers of people involved. I would just like to mention some problems, which could occur: firstly, the larger the army, the more raiding groups are needed. Consequently, they were difficult to coordinate. It could well have been that one group went to a village because they had heard of the large amounts of stock and just found smoking ruins, because their comrades had heard the same. Secondly, all problems I have already mentioned concerning transport and consume during the transport of food are of course also true in this occasion. Therefore, the groups could only act in a specific area; otherwise, the way back would have been too long. Thirdly, to raid a region also meant to divide the troops. Sending out groups of soldiers weakened the main force and the small groups had to be careful to circumvent the enemy. This method would only have been without risk without hostile troops around.[44]

Muntaner also had to learn this lesson, as a story about an attack on a timber transport shows.[45] He tells us in the *Crònica* that he used to send out two carts and two mules for wood every day. At this given day, the carts were accompanied by a mounted crossbowman and four

---

43 SABLONIER, 1971, p. 75; LYNN, 1993, p. 37.
44 HARARI, 2000, pp. 306-309.
45 HUGHES, 2006, p. 95f.

foot soldiers. This small escort illustrates that nobody expected an attack. Indeed, the main forces of the notorious enemies were far enough away. However, what nobody in the company knew was that a certain Sir Christopher George, a noble from the kingdom of Thessalonica, was in the vicinity with 80 mounted men. According to the description, it seems reasonable to suggest that these men were looking for an adventure as well as spoils. Nothing indicates that their actions signified a greater military offensive against Gallipoli or the Catalans. Therefore, it was quite a negative surprise for the five soldiers. They were attacked, but the mounted crossbowmen managed to escape and rode back to Gallipoli from where Muntaner sent reinforcements. In the meantime, the four foot soldiers had climbed a nearby tower and did their best to defend themselves desperately. The forces from Gallipoli appeared just in time to defeat Sir George and his group and to rescue their comrades. The fact that it was possible for the mounted soldier to ride back, fetch other soldiers, and return in time to rescue the four, illustrates that the distances travelled by the wood transports were usually rather short.

With this example, I would like to conclude my list of possible difficulties in the hope that it left at least a small impression. The indirect way of living off the land is taking everything away besides food. The acquired things could be reused, exchanged for desired goods, or simply turned into cash. In the Eastern Mediterranean, not only things, but also people were abducted and sold. The slave trade was omnipresent in this region and we know from the *Crònica* that the company held auctions at which their captives were sold.[46] It was not allowed for Christians to sell Christian slaves, but this ban was very often circumvented by arguing that the rule must only be applied for the "right", roman-catholic Christians. The Greek were orthodox Christians, i.e. heretics, and many of them thus also end up at the slave market. Sometimes, the ban was circumvented without any convincing argument. On the following day after the just outlined attack on the wood transport, such an auction was held "for the horses and the captives and for the spoils that we had acquired."[47], as Muntaner writes.

---

46 Of course, ransoms were demanded for the release of wealthy and noble captives. SABLONIER, 1971, pp. 84-86.
47 HUGHES, 2006, p. 96.

As mentioned above, the captives were men from Thessalonica and therefore most likely Christians. However, this did not seem to provoke any feelings of guilt by the Catalans. Overall, the company raised large sums of money by selling their booty, be it objects, livestock or human beings. This money could be spent on food, which leads us back to possibility number two. Because the selling of booty and the buying of food are intermediate steps, one could call this an indirect way of living off the land.

Both, the direct and the indirect way, were employed by the Great Catalan Company and both had a devastating impact on the areas in question. Not surprisingly, this method was not only used due to the need of food or money, but also as a tactical weapon, it "not only filled the cook pot of the medieval warrior but served as his sword and shield."[48] It could be used as an offensive weapon, employed with the aim to cause as much destruction as possible to the territory of the enemy, to spread fear among the population and to destroy the economic and agrarian basis of the country. As we have seen, the Catalan Company succeeded in doing so and called it the *Catalan Vengeance*[49], but noted too late that, on this occasion, they had destroyed their own basis. Usually, marching and not immobile armies used "living off the land" method as an offensive weapon precisely because of that. As *tactic of scorched earth*, it could also be used as a defence. Thereby, the own territory was devastated in the hope that the enemy would find nothing of use for him and would consequently be compelled to turn around or just perish by starvation. If there were any fortifications in the concerned area then it would be wise to collect everything useful and bring it to safety behind the walls. Thus, the

---

48 LYNN, 1993, p. 37.
49 KYRIAKIDIS, 2011, p. 124. Up to the 19th century the name Catalan was a term of reproach in some parts of Greece, e.g. in Thrace persisted the oath "May the vengeance of the Catalans overtake you!" whereas in Euboea bad conduct was commented with "Not even the Catalans would do that!". Besides the Catalan Vengeance other Catalan activities like piracy might have influenced these terms. SETTON, 1975, pp. 247f.. It has also been suggested that the prosperity gap of villages that appears in early 14th century Byzantine tax records might be related to the march of the Catalans. ABULAFIA, 1997, p. 121.

besieged would have better chances of resisting a long time and the besieging party would have the trouble.[50]

There is no explicit mention of this method during the expedition to the east, but the description of the siege of Madytos could be a hint. One of the commanders of the company, Ferdinand Eiximenis, besieged Madytos with a force of 80 horsemen and 200 foot soldiers. According to the *Crònica*, the castle was defended by more than 700 Greeks. Muntaner reports, evidently quite enervated: "In effect, the nobleman [Ferdinand Eiximenis] was besieged in reality more than those within, for it was I who sent all the bread they ate by boat from Gallipoli, and it was twenty four miles from Gallipoli to there. So the task of sending them provisions was mine entirely."[51] One explanation for the situation could be that Eiximenis was not able to send out some groups to collect food, because of his rather small force. Another explanation could be that the Greeks had employed the described method and therefore the searching for food would be useless anyway. The problems were possibly a result of both. However, in the end, thanks to the provisions sent by Muntaner, Eiximenis was victorious and took Madytos after eight months. One would not need extraordinary interpretive skills to notice that, in Muntaner's opinion, this victory was at least partly his own.

"...for they could not live in the absence of war."

But, maybe because he felt that his skills were not really valued any longer in the company, maybe because of the conflicts in the leadership circle or maybe, as he himself wrote, because Ferdinand of Majorca was in need of his service, Muntaner left the company one year after their leaving from Gallipoli and went back to the west. In 1308, he became governor of the islands Djerba and Kerkennah near the Tunisian coast.[52] The Great Catalan Company continued to make a noise in the world. In 1311, they conquered the duchy of Athens, in

---

50 LYNN, 1993, pp. 34-37.
51 HUGHES, 2006, p. 92.
52 SABLONIER, 1971, p. 19; see also note 14.

1318 the duchy of Neopatria.[53] A short description of the conquest of Athens is the last story in the *Crònica* concerning the company.[54] The Catalan rule over Athens lasted until 1388, and we know from other sources that the company as well as the inhabitants had quite turbulent times.[55] However, because none of these events are part of the *Crònica*, they fall outside the scope of this investigation.

The starting point was the Peace of Caltabellotta and the need of the Great Catalan Company to search for new fields of activity. During the Expedition to the East, the leaving of Gallipoli constituted a turning point due to supply conditions. One of the last sentences Muntaner wrote about his company concerning their life style in Athens shows that the problems concerning the relation of war and food supply remained unsolved after the conquest. The new leader of the company, Bernard Estanyol, developed a remarkable strategy to deal with the expected difficulties.

> "And Bernard Estanyol's strategy was this: namely, that they would wage one war at a time and make truces with the other parties, and that then, when they had ravaged the country against which they were fighting, they would forge a truce with that county and begin to wage war against one of the others. And they lead this same life even now, for they could not live in the absence of war." [56]

Here, Muntaner captured the essence of the problem of the Great Catalan Company as well as other mercenary companies. Their options to acquire food or other kinds of spoils depended on their possibility to wage war. The principle *bellum se ipsum alet* can be traced through the history of the Great Catalan Company as well as, of course, through the history of warfare.

---

53 SETTON, 1975, pp. 21-36.
54 HUGHES, 2006, pp. 147-149.
55 For the history of the Catalan rule in Greece see SETTON, 1975.
56 HUGHES, 2006, p. 153.

Bibliography

Sources

HUGHES, ROBERT D. (ed.), The Catalan Expedition to the East: from the *Chronicle* of Ramon Muntaner, Barcelona et al. 2006.

Literature

ABULAFIA, DAVID, The Western Mediterranean Kingdoms 1200-1500. The Struggle for Dominion (The Medieval World), London et al. 1997.

AURELL, JAUME, Authoring the Past. History, Autobiography, and Politics in Medieval Catalonia, Chicago 2012.

BURNS, R. IGNATIUS, The Catalan Company and the European Powers, 1305-1311, in: Speculum 29,4 (1954), pp. 751-771.

HALDON, JOHN F. (ed.), General Issues in the Study of Medieval Logistics. Sources, Problems and Methodologies (History of Warfare 36), Leiden et al. 2006.

HARARI, YUVAL NOAH, Strategy and Supply in Fourteenth-Century Western European Invasion Campaigns, in: The Journal of Military History 64,2 (2000), pp. 297-333.

KYRIAKIDIS, SAVVAS, Warfare in Late Byzantium, 1204-1453 (History of Warfare 67), Leiden et al. 2011.

LAMBERT, CRAIG L., Shipping the Medieval Military. English Maritime Logistics in the Fourteenth Century (Warfare in History), Woodbridge 2011.

LUTTWAK, EDWARD N., Logistics and the Aristocratic Idea of War, in: Feeding Mars. Logistics in Western Warfare from the Middle Ages to the Present (History and Warfare), ed. by JOHN A. LYNN, Boulder et al. 1993, pp. 3-7.

LYNN, JOHN A., Medieval Introduction, in: Feeding Mars. Logistics in Western Warfare from the Middle Ages to the Present (History and Warfare), ed. by JOHN A. LYNN, Boulder et al. 1993, pp. 31-37.

NICHOLSON, RANALD, Edward III and the Scots. The Formative Years of a Military Career 1327-1355 (Oxford Historical Series. Second Series), London 1965.

SABLONIER, ROGER, Krieg und Kriegertum in der *Crònica* des Ramon Muntaner. Eine Studie zum spätmittelalterlichen Kriegswesen aufgrund katalanischer Quellen (Geist und Werk der Zeiten 31), Bern et al. 1971.

SETTON, KENNETH M., Catalan Domination of Athens 1311-1388, 2nd rev. ed., London 1975.

Online Documents

Freight Car Catalog of DB Schenker, URL: http://www.gueterwagenkatalog.rail.dbschenker.de/gwk-de/start/gattung_t_gedeckte_schuettgutwagen/3157124/Talns_969.html?start=0, 25.11.2015.

ROWLETT, RUSS, How Many? A Dictionary of Units of Measurement, URL: https://www.unc.edu/~rowlett/units/dictQ.html, 25.11.2015.

VONES, L., Roger de Flor, in: Lexikon des Mittelalters Online Vol. 4, cols. 550-551, Stuttgart 1977-1999, URL: http://apps.brepolis.net/-lexiema/test/Default2.aspx, 25.11.2015.

Summary and Conclusions: Silent Men and the Art of Fighting

DOMINIK SCHUH

> "And in relation to this we learn from the above-mentioned men of worth that honor is not achieved through spending much time in keeping the body delightfully comfortable."
> (GEOFFROI DE CHARNY, p. 125, translation E. KENNEDY)

Geoffroi de Charny makes an essential point of the relation between fighters and their bodies short and clear: The body is seen as a means to an end, as an instrument to acquire honour, recognition as a (good) fighter. The papers collected in the volume at hand as the result of the conference "killing and being killed" look for this use of the body as they examine practices contrary to the preservation and care of bodies, practices aiming at the destruction or at least the disabling of fighting bodies. In this context, the call for papers asked for articles contributing to the following areas and questions, listed according to their occurrence in the life of a fighter:

a) Shaping bodies for battle:
Which practices were used to make bodies fit for battle?
What bodily techniques were taught and trained?
What was seen as a fighter's ideal physical appearance?
How did fighters physically experience the shaping of their bodies?

b) Using bodies in battle:
Which ways of using one's body in battle were existing and common? What were the conditions and objectives under which the own body was risked?
How did fighters experience physical dangers and how did they speak about them?

c) Bodily injuries through battle:
What kind of injuries and violations appeared and how frequently did they appear?
How did fighters experience physical injuries and how did they communicate about them?
How did people treat injured bodies – individually and within the social context?
How did fighters prepare themselves for physical injuries and how did they treat their injured companions?

d) Dead fighters. Dead bodies:
How did fighters experience the killing (hostile) and the dying of (befriended, allied, kindred) combatants?
How did they speak and write about it?
How did a fighter's approach to and dealing with the own mortality differ from the concepts of non-fighters?
How did they deal with their fear of death?
How were dead fighters treated? Could a fighter survive his dead body?

In the following paper, I shall attempt to sum up the answers given in the different contributions to this volume. Having in mind that those summarised articles treat events, persons and material that differ greatly with respect to their temporal and cultural context, the goal of developing a bigger picture seems disputable. Such a bigger picture cannot cover all historical specifics of its parts nor can it be seen as an overall theory of bodies in battle in the middle ages or a (virtually) complete description of the practices involved. Nevertheless, such a summary can provide some insights into the patterns that occur at several points of time and in different places in the era and henceforth lead to a first cautious draft for a synthesis of our knowledge with respect to the ways

Summary and Conclusions

bodies were used in the field of killing and being killed. Therefore, the articles shall not be summarised separately with the goal of describing their respective argumentation and contexts, but are as resources to answer the main questions of the conference.[1]

I. Shaping bodies for battle

The first set of questions asks about the practices of corporal preparation. The answers given can be assigned to three areas: The shaping by learning respectively training, shaping by equipment and – contrarily – the disabling of bodies.

The most fundamental requirement getting a body in shape for battle is discussed by JUDITH MENGLER, who informs us about the difficulties in logistics and food supply shown through the example of Ramon Muntaner's "Crònica". No body can be fully functional in battle – as in all other instances – unless it is well fed. Although this fact cannot be denied and should be considered in every research on a particular battle or military activity, little can be said about special nutritional practices for the fighter. DANIEL JAQUET provides hints to common beliefs on the right nutrition for fighters with regard to the preparation for judicial combats. According to the Königsegg treatise, "greasy food" should be avoided, "St-John bread" and "rye bread soaked in water" are beneficial.[2] The advice for fighters that they have to be able to endure without the right nutrition appears more often. As GIULIA MOROSINI demonstrates in several examples, one practice of shaping the body considered highly relevant by contemporaries was suffering as an exercise in endurance. This seems to shape not only the individual body of the fighter but also the community, the body as a corporation of fighters.[3]

Furthermore, the fight books inform us about several practices used directly to shape a body for battle. Beside some notes on possibly useful

---

1 The special character of a summary and synthesis leads to a spare use of research literature beyond the volume at hand, this paper therefore cannot claim to be a contribution to the research on bodies in battle on its own.
2 See JAQUET, p. 139.
3 See MOROSINI, p. 171, see also on suffering as a fighter's virtue and as community building characteristic of the "order of knighthood" can be found in GEOFFROI DE CHARNY'S "book of chivalry", pp. 174-177.

distractions, "'throwing stones and javelins, dancing and jumping, fencing and wrestling, mock jousting and tourneying and courting beautiful ladies'" can be found here.[4] It seems plausible to suggest that those practices – or most of them – were widespread as training methods, as they also appear in didactic literature for the knightly youth and refer to classical disciplines of bodily exercises.[5] Surely, the fight masters taught their students a broad set of body techniques directly aiming to harm or kill their opponents.

ERIC BURKART examines the ways of mediation used to make the fight students fit for combat: "At a basic level, fighters of the past were socialised into certain ways of using their bodies in combat." This process happened through "learning by imitation".[6] In addition to this widespread method of implicit learning, there were also ways of explicit mediation, which can be found in fight books. The art of fighting taught with – not just through – these books, was developed by fight masters, who had an interest in keeping their valuable knowledge secret. Therefore, they used several mediation techniques (encryption through mnemonic verses and depictions) that could only be used by those already introduced in the basics of their art of fighting and communication.[7]

In other cases, there is usually little information of the particular training fighters received – as the example of Theoderich shows, of whom we have to assume that he learned how to fight as a hostage in Constantinople, without having certain evidence of it.[8]

The state of source material for the shaping of bodies through equipment should be much better – already because of the need for inventory lists and account books. IAIN MCINNES shows several examples for the relevance of good equipment. Especially the quality of armour can be seen as a vital preparation for battle, as it could protect

---

4 Out of the Königsegg treatise, according to JAQUET, p. 139.
5 For instance in the "Ritterspiegel" of JOHANNES ROTHE from the early 15th century, line 2693f., p. 184, which refers to VEGETIUS' "epitoma rei militaris".
6 BURKART, p. 117.
7 See BURKART, p. 117-121, see also JAQUET on the topic of secrecy, p. 136-138.
8 See BERNDT, p. 27.

fighters from both missile and close combat weapons.[9] In fact, the type of protective gear worn and consequentially its ability to protect its owner much depended on the status of the fighter.[10] Another kind of shaping through equipment seems less sophisticated for the era, as ALASTAIR J. MCDONALD brought up, "Uniforms were not routinely worn", leading to the problem that "determining regular and irregular troops [...] is thus an impossible task."[11]

Disabling bodies is broached especially in the papers of BOGDAN-PETRU MALEON and ALASTAIR J. MCDONALD as ways of practising symbolic violence. Aiming to the social marginalisation by cancellation of personal identity,[12] the factual destruction of fighting capability,[13] practices of mutilation and especially amputation are to be named here.

Shaping one's body for battle took place at all times. Training techniques were used, but they were not often documented in the era discussed here. Shaping of a body does not just refer to the body as a pure anatomical thing but also to the body as a combination of equipment, flesh, and bones. In the later middle ages, several circles of experts (fight masters) in fighting and fight training become evident. One can assume that they existed long before in a lower and less formal grade of organisation. The art of fighting seems to be one of several types using the same techniques of mediation as other arts of the time and the same modes of organisation. Body shaping was a mandatory condition for taking a leading position in warrior communities and hence for taking a leading position in a society, which very much equalled *bellatores* and *nobiles*.

II. Using bodies for battle

How was the fighter's body used in battle? The findings can be assigned to four areas: Using one's body to get into battle, to avoid battle, to obtain or maintain a leading position and to act in battle. As well as

---

9   See MACINNES, p. 61, 64.
10 IBID. p. 62.
11 MACDONALD, p. 213.
12 See MALEON, p. 54.
13 See MCDONALD, p. 212.

these areas, it could be discussed how the use of bodies differs in particular fighting contexts, but as DANIEL JAQUET stated, our understanding of the distinction between "playful" and "serious" combat situations is still to be clarified.[14]

The first step in using one's body for battle is having one's body chosen by being considered fit for battle. Giulia Morosini shows a significant example of selection criteria put to account by the condottiero Braccio da Montone, who preferred recruits, "'who were respectable for the signs of the wounds in the face and who had the other limbs torn by blows'".[15] As was discussed during the conference, a fighter's body – especially the bodies of those fighter's, who made their living by means of war – was his hallmark, the medium for showing ones value on the market of violence. Beside the display of expensive cloth and weapons, scars could have played an important role for this display. In a wider sense, the fighter's body was used to get into battle – or into a battle group, one might say a community of violence –[16] by showing the willingness to expose it to violent action and ultimately to death.[17]

Certainly, a fighter's physical appearance could be used to win a conflict without actual combat – as was discussed during the conference. The presence of well-armed and trained forces, the display of their potential for violent actions and the willingness to fight was often quite a threat to enemies, and therefore led to surrender or the payment of a ransom or Danegeld.[18]

Naturally, groups of fighter's could not abstain from factual violence all the time; this is particular true for leading personalities. Besides his tactical skills and other specific qualities for leadership, the head of such a group was regularly expected to take part in combat himself, and his actions were often narrated as being outstanding and exemplary. Using one's body to prove the qualification for leadership and therefore legitimise ones position as a leader was even more necessary, as a group was held together primarily for the purpose of violent

---

14 See JAQUET, p. 146.
15 Pompeo Pellini's History and Life of Braccio de Montone (1572) quoted following MOROSINI, p. 175.
16 See BERNDT with regard to the research group „Gewaltgemeinschaften"(communities of violence), p. 18.
17 IBID. On obligation practices, pp. 20f..
18 For instance, see IBID. p. 29.

Summary and Conclusions

activities – as is shown in the examples of Gothic war bands as well as in those of the companies' of late medieval Italy.[19] A downright expressive way of displaying a leader's abilities can be seen in the narrations of a leader killing the head of the enemy forces. Those narrations can be interpreted as a symbolic expression of the victory pictured in a one-on-one combat. In addition to the opportunity to prove active skills on the battlefield, leaders had to show their ability of bearing the hardships of warfare together with their men to strengthen their position.[20] The respect of their followers could be improved by exposing themselves to the risk of being harmed or even killed.

The mentioned qualities, i.e. the ability and willingness to apply violence as well as to suffer it, were in fact not only demanded from leaders but from all fighters – although we usually only read of the deeds of higher status fighters. Related to these abilities, the question as to when to make use of them has to be raised. Before a fighter could apply violence, he had to decide on whom and when it should be applied. GIULIA MOROSINI shows several reflections on the last-mentioned question in the writings of condottieri, linked to some cultural stereotypes about foreign fighters and their mentality.[21] One element of the query whom to hit was the problem to determine who part of a violent conflict is – or, in a wider sense, who was a legitimate aim for violent actions in general. TREVOR RUSSELL SMITH shows how contemporary fighters in their records discussed this question of the distinction between combatants and non-combatants.[22] ALASTAIR J. MACDONALD discusses the issue of different war practices in the binary opposition guerrilla vs. conventional warfare, which is often applied by scholars to English-Scottish conflicts of the late Middle Ages. He therefore compares different theoretical approaches (e.g. ethnic, cultural and subcultural motives) in terms of their explanatory force. He arrives at the result that the opposition has to be rejected in the first place, because the recognition of regular or irregular troops was nearly impossible (lack of uniforms, as aforementioned). For the example of Anglo-Scottish wars, the cultural differences were not as eminent as former

---

19 See IBID, pp. 20-22, MOROSINI, p. 168, summing up p. 189.
20 See the before-mentioned remarks on suffering as a group.
21 See IBID, pp. 165f..
22 For the contemporary distinction see SMITH, p. 80.

researchers saw them and there is a lack of evidence for a particular Gaelic cruelty. Consequently, MACDONALD suggests, "there seems more promise in seeking to locate intensification of Anglo-Scottish hostilities in social make-up rather than ethnicity."[23] With regard to the question of violent practice, it can be stated that "specific circumstances, rather than typological models" have the potential to explain the grade of atrocity and brutality in warfare.[24]

III. Bodily injuries by means of battle

What were the consequences of the participation in battle for the bodies? To what risks did fighters expose their physical well-being? In his opening speech, JÖRG ROGGE stated that ignoring injuries and fighting until exhaustion was occasionally seen as proof of boldness and resistibility, examples for such narratives can be found in the self-assessments of fighters or in the battle accounts of chroniclers.[25] As discussed above, suffering visually was a suitable way for leading personalities to secure their position in a community of violence. Beside the opportunity of displaying joint pain to constitute and stabilise such a community, a leader could gain prestige by performing exemplary and outstanding acts of endurance. With regard to this, GIULIA MOROSINI shows how military mentality and its virtues could be connected with bodily practices, as the latter were used as signs or proof for the possession of the first. The most significant virtue represented through such practices seems to be fortitude. Its representation could range from withstanding attacks by enemies up to suffering the pains of medical treatment without showing any signs of hurting. The brave and therefore silent patient can hence be seen as one manifestation of the valiant fighter.[26]

Despite the sources' focus on suffering leaders, one has to assume that fighters of lower status suffered more regularly than members of the nobility. This instance can be explained as being due to their inferi-

---

23 MACDONALD, p. 217.
24 IBID., p. 219, with reference to the sack of Berwick in 1296.
25 See ROGGE, pp. 10f..
26 An expressive example can be seen in the case of Giovanni de Medici fixing and illuminating himself during the amputation of his leg, see MOROSINI, p. 182.

Summary and Conclusions

or equipment and a lesser chance of receiving mercy due to their lower value as hostages. Although as ALASTAIR J. MACDONALD puts it "the completeness of the exclusion of the lower orders from martial codes has surely been overstated".[27] Which particular injuries caused the suffering of fighters? IAIN MACINNES examines the "types of injuries involved, the areas of the body most affected and the ability – where possible to discern – of these men to survive the injuries they suffered."[28] For the Anglo-Scottish conflicts, he identifies missile weapons, especially longbows, as a prominent cause of physical harm. Although it can be suggested "that these attacks were more of an 'impediment' than they were fatal", especially injuries to the face were common occurrences.[29] The head – and particularly the eyes – of an opponent seems to be a prominent aim of violent actions in several descriptions, which can be explained as a result of less sophisticated protective gear for this area and its crucial importance for the function of a human body. A successful hit on the head could hence secure a 'quick win' and was often used – the examples given by IAIN MACINNES, and the widely spread eye gouging in trials by combat shown by DANIEL JAQUET serve as evidence for this insight.[30] The type of injury one probably received depended much on the spatial position one occupied on the battlefield. While fighters on foot had to fear mainly the aforementioned hits on the head, fighters on horseback were hit more often on legs and feet.[31] The weapons used can be seen as another strong determiner of the injury produced – or possibly just narrated.[32] However, inferences should be drawn cautiously. Although written sources seem to draw a realistic picture of the injuries narrated, they probably do not give us a fully realistic account of injuries on medieval battlefields. It is likely that their purpose in narrating wounds and sufferings is to emphasise the dangers of warfare and particularly the capacity of their protagonists to face and bear those dangers. The results of these dangers and the manner of dealing with them could be used to prove ones mili-

---

27 See MACDONALD, p. 211.
28 MACINNES, p. 60.
29 IBID., p. 62.
30 See JAQUET, p. 141-145, MACINNES, p. 61, 70.
31 MACINNES, pp. 63, 69-71.
32 E.g. lance thrusts were commonly related to torso injuries, IBID, pp. 68f..

tary activity, boldness and bravery – whether they were real consequences of violent actions or just presented as such.[33]

Furthermore, the investigation not only leads to insights on the types of injuries regularly suffered by fighters but also provides us with insight into practices applied to already injured bodies. Stories of medical treatments could serve the aim of representing the sturdiness of a fighter or his capacity to recover from former injuries – as above-mentioned –, which may explain their regular appearance in the sources; however, they can also provide us with some knowledge of the frequency of medical aid in medieval warfare.[34]

As a last example for the presentation of injuries in the sources, an episode out of the narrations about Theoderich shall be applied. On one hand an example for exemplary violence dealt by a leading fighter – as mentioned above – on the other the description of Theoderich killing Odoaker referred to by GUIDO BERNDT shows us a kind of 'counter-narration'. Theoderich's alleged statement that his opponent lacked bones, so that his sword easily penetrated his whole body, uses the ideal of an outstandingly tough leader to construct the image of a completely non-ideal leader. [35]

Suffering could have symbolic benefit. Signs of suffering could be used for future fights or to legitimise a leading position. Narrated injuries often occurred in the face (especially violations of the eyes). A man not able to take blows was seen as an unsuitable leader and, consequently, not a leader for long.

IV. Dead fighters, dead bodies

What if suffering injuries was no longer possible? The question of dealing with dead fighters was only treated to a small extent during the conference; nonetheless, a few remarks can be made on those practices. Where dead bodies were discussed, they appeared mainly as media of

---

33   As afore-mentioned in II, using bodies to get into battle. See again MOROSINI, pp. 179-181, 183.
34   See MACINNES, p. 72, asking for the access to medical care as one possible explanation for casualty rates.
35   See BERNDT, p. 31.

Summary and Conclusions

communication. BOGDAN-PETRU MALEON illustrates a slew of symbolic practices operated by the use of corpses in the Byzantine Empire. Two types of practices can be discerned: Those aiming to signal and prove the victory over an enemy and those aiming to (symbolical) destroy an enemy once and for all. The first relied on the main resource of individual recognition, the head or more precisely the face of an opponent. While the body (torso and limbs) were burned or thrown away, the head was regularly shown publically impaled on a spear.[36] The practice of stripping off the insignia of those sentenced to death before beheading them, can be seen as a practice of removing the social status of a body and therefore excluding it from a community. The ultimate exclusion was realised in those practices aiming to the complete annihilation of a body and therefore its 'owner' and his memory. One can assume the symbolic meaning of bodily parts from the practices applied to them – e.g. castration and the amputation of the right arm seem to point to their particular relevance.[37] ALASTAIR J. MACDONALD shows comparable examples for this kind of symbolic violence, namely the act of chopping William Hesilrig to pieces or the narration of fighters playing soccer with their opponent's heads as an especially brutal way to signal their supremacy.[38]

A rather friendly way of treating a dead fighter's body is shown by GIULIA MOROSINI, who gives the example of troops gathering around the body of their leader, which could be understood as a ritual to stabilize the community of fighters and therefore building up an independent company.[39]

Despite few examples of fighters acting in a respectful manner towards the corpse of combat victims, in most cases discussed here, dead fighters were treated brutally, eventually with deterrence in mind. Practices of the final destruction of bodies seem to be of particular interest in some respect to the meaning a fighter's body could convey. Following up the thought of shaping a fighter's body through equipment, plundering dead bodies could be seen as destruction of the unit of flesh, bones and armament, and therefore as disintegration of a fighter's body.

---

36 See MALEON, pp. 45-48.
37 IBID., p. 49.
38 MACDONALD, pp. 201, 211.
39 MOROSINI, p. 182f..

V. Conclusions: Fighting as a culture of body usage

What can be concluded from these findings? How do they fit together, and do they fit together at all? Do they have more in common than 'something with bodies and fighting'? First, the discussions during the conference showed that many sources were not systematically considered with regard to bodily practices and experiences; future research can react to this instance. The genre of fight books seems to be especially promising to contain valuable insights to the topic.[40] The same can be stated for the area of medical treatments. The examination of medieval fighters, their bodies and practices therefore needs a broad foundation in different types of sources, because most of the common historical material is silent on the matter. As GIULIA MOROSINI formulates, to a great extent, we have to deal with silent men if we ask fighters about their bodies.

This silence seems to be prominent in two ways: As the silence of injured and suffering fighters on their pain, which can be seen as the result of body control and the display of this control at the same time. In addition, silence as the consequence of the particular character of corporal bound knowledge, which can be understood as a form of 'tacit knowledge', as ERIC BURKART suggested. This double silence is indeed an eminent obstacle for the research on medieval fighters and their bodies, but it can partially be bypassed if other sources – especially illustrations and actual corporal remains – are involved. However, the effective combination of historical – text-based – knowledge with the findings of neighbouring disciplines still seems to be in its infancy, although the awareness for its relevance and the number of exemplary studies is growing.

These preliminary notes may provide a first impression of the main issues of the conferences discussion; nonetheless, they produced several connectible insights to our topic:

The manifest connection between the aforementioned findings seems to be their way of talking about the body, respectively the ways of handling the body talked about: The body appears as an instrument, a

---

40 See the papers of JAQUET and BURKART.

Summary and Conclusions

tool or weapon to fight. It appears as a resource and a stake to risk; and last but not least as a sign, an evidence for previous action.

The body was used as an instrument for war or more precise an instrument for enacting violence, which could be prepared for particular practices such as distinct body techniques of fighting (i.e. fighting in different terrains, situations, in single-combat or groups, with different weapons, etc.). Having this instrumental view in mind, bodies could also be prepared to be unable to enact violence or particular practices of violence.[41]

The body was therefore a resource in war, as the practice of war needs bodies able to deal with violence (in both possible directions), but it was a symbolic resource as well. Showing a well-prepared and eventually experienced body marked by scars and comparable signs of former action, could be used by fighters as a symbolic capital, which offered them a better chance to enter into (well) paid service. The body was therefore a kind of certificate or CV for fighters to proof their abilities and experiences. It could also be a symbolic capital used by warlords or other military leaders to win a battle before it even begun by means of scaring their enemies – and it could be used in the opposite way by showing the results of violent actions on the body of an enemy to prevent others from taking up arms.[42]

Following this, the body was (perhaps) the most valuable resource in violent actions; however, it was a resource that could not be saved because it was only useful if its integrity was constantly exposed to risks. Consequently, a fighter's body was the instrument of violence and the most prominent object at stake in violent contest. This multidimensional position renders it plausible to consider the body as the core element of a fighter culture, which creates meaning by using bodies in different symbolic and very practical ways. Examining this use of bodies offers – this seems to be the main result of the volume at hand – insights in a culture that recruited its political elite out of the order of fighters and therefore represented power not least through the depiction of armed and violently able bodies.

---

41 As seen in the example of amputated English archers shown by MACDONALD, p. 212.
42 See the considerations by MACDONALD – especially under the paragraph "symbolic violence", pp. 209-213 – and by MALEON.

In a second step, there is especially one practice (or group of practices) which comes to mind. ERIC BURKART spoke of a culture of fighting consisting of three items ("actual fighting practice", "body techniques of combat" and "fighting systems as [...] sets of favoured body techniques"). Such a culture could – referring to the conference title – involve two techniques: the technique of killing and the technique of being killed respectively dying. One could refer to these as cultural techniques because they are socially embedded and traditional practices, consisting of much less complex practices themselves. Therefore, formulated in basic terms, fighting could be separated into giving and receiving blows – or violence in general. While dealing out violence consists of the practice of deciding whom to hit, when to hit and how to hit, hitting itself, defeating and killing an enemy (which does not have to be part of fighting), receiving violence consists of the practice of suffering (without showing), regenerating after a fight or the art of dying honourably as a fighter.

Those two main practices of fighting can be connected to virtues associated with fighters: Giving violence in the right manner requires morality and prudence to make the right decisions, and agility and strength to follow up with the right actions. Receiving violence needs fortitude and bravery to be ready and willing to receive, and stamina and resistibility to be able to bear it. The connection between practices and virtues, the link to cultural ideals and their narrative or iconic mediation makes fighting understandable as a cultural phenomenon itself, as it combines contemplating the body and its usage with questions regarding the mental (i.e. a specific mind-set)[43] and social conditions of corporal practices.

Bibliography

KAEUPER, RICHARD W./KENNEDY, ELSPETH (eds.), The book of chivalry of Geoffroi de Charny. Text, context, and translation, Philadelphia 1996.

---

43   BURKART, pp. 116f..

Summary and Conclusions

ROTHE, JOHANNES, Der Ritterspiegel, edited and translated by CHRISTOPH HUBER and PAMELA KALNING, Berlin 2009.

The used contributions to the volume at hand are not listed separately here.

Contributors

GUIDO M. BERNDT is Researcher at the Friedrich-Meinecke-Institute, Department of History and Cultural Studies, Arbeitsbereich Geschichte der Spätantike und des frühen Mittelalters, FU Berlin, for the project "The Militarisation of Early Medieval Societies. Nature, Control and Perception in a West-European Comparison" funded by the Fritz Thyssen Foundation. He has published Konflikt und Anpassung. Studien zu Migration und Ethnogenese der Vandalen (Husum, 2007), has edited and translated the Vita Meinwerci Episcopi Patherbrunnensis (Munich, 2009) and is co-editor of Das Reich der Vandalen und seine (Vor-)Geschichten (Vienna, 2008) as well as Arianism. Roman Hereys and Barbarian Creed (Farnham, 2014). Additionally, he has published a series of scholarly articles concerning Gothic history. Dr Berndt is currently working on Lombard military history, Late Antique and Early Medieval warlords and their 'communities of violence'.

ERIC BURKART (M.A.) is a postdoctoral researcher and lecturer in medieval history at the University of Trier. From 2013 to 2015 he was research assistant in a DFG-financed project on ritualized combat in the Middle Ages ("Der mittelalterliche Zweikampf als agonale Praktik zwischen Recht, Ritual und Leibesübung") at Technische Universität Dresden. In July 2015 he defended his PhD thesis on crusading discourses in late medieval Burgundy ("Kreuzzugsbereitschaft als Selbstbeschreibung. Die Verteidigung des Glaubens als Element burgundischer Statuspolitik in den Traktaten des Jean Germain († 1461)") at Goethe-University Frankfurt. He specialises in cultural history, symbolic communication and propaganda in 15th century Burgundy and European martial arts traditions.

DANIEL JAQUET is a medievalist, currently visiting scholar at the Max Planck Institute for History of Science, Berlin. He has background in literary studies and interest in history of science and material culture in the early modern period. He received his PhD. in history at the University of Geneva in 2013. He taught at the University of Geneva and Lausanne (2008-2015) and was a visiting scholar at the Centre pour l'Histoire des sciences et des techniques (University of Paris, Pantheon Sorbonne 1, 2011). He is the co-editor of Acta Periodica Duellatorum (open access, peer-reviewed Journal dedicated to Historical European Martial Arts). His dissertation investigates the praxes of armoured combat at the end of the Middle Ages and the beginning of the Renaissance, in the light of the Fight Books. His teaching and research specialisations are history of warfare, duelling, ludic practices and knowledge transmission in pragmatical literature at the end of the Middle Age and the beginning of the Renaissance. His current research focus on Historical European Martial Arts studies, with specific interest in bodily knowledge transmission and experimentation. He edited the following collective volumes: L'art chevaleresque du combat (Neuchâtel 2013) and with Nicolas Baptiste, Experimente zur Waffenhandhabung im Spätmittelalter (Basel 2016).

ALASTAIR J. MACDONALD is Mackie Lecturer in History at the University of Aberdeen. His research deals primarily with later medieval Scottish history and he is joint-author of the chapter on that period in The New Penguin History of Scotland (ed. Houston and Knox, 2001). He is particularly concerned with two broad fields: Anglo-Scottish relations; and warfare in Scotland. He is the author of Border Bloodshed: Scotland and England at War, 1369–1403 (2000), and is working on a monograph covering Anglo-Scottish relations over a broader timespan, between 1286 and 1603. His interests in warfare are especially focused on understanding the social and cultural contexts of military activity and the impacts of war. He is a contributor to A Military History of Scotland (ed. Spiers et al., 2012). Articles are forthcoming on Anglo-Scottish relations during the reign of Henry V,

Contributors

and on the same topic during James II's reign, and on the concept of guerrilla warfare in later medieval Scotland.

IAIN A. MACINNES (PhD, History, University of Aberdeen) is a lecturer and programme leader in Scottish History at the UHI Centre for History, University of the Highlands and Islands. His research focuses on medieval Scotland, and medieval Scottish warfare in particular. He has published several articles and essays on military aspects of the period, focusing on the Second Scottish Wars of Independence (1332-1357), including pieces on: the use of terror as a weapon of war; the English occupation of southern Scotland; the campaigns of 1336; Scots in English service; the depiction of arms and armour in chronicle sources; and battlefield injury in an Anglo-Scottish context. His first monograph, entitled Scotland's Second War of Independence, 1332-1357, was published in 2016 by Boydell and Brewer, and brings much of his wider interests together in a concerted analysis of conduct and chivalry during this understudied period of Anglo-Scottish warfare. While continuing with a focus on this period and these themes, he is also currently venturing out from a strict consideration of medieval history and is focusing some time on studies of medievalism and the depiction of medieval warfare and chivalry in modern film, television and graphic novels.

BOGDAN-PETRU MALEON is Professor at the Faculty of History, "Alexandru Ioan Cuza" University of Iași, Romania. Since April 2015, he is General Director of "Mihai Eminescu" Central University Library of Iași, and during December 2010 – December 2015 he was Director of the Museum of "Alexandru Ioan Cuza" University of Iași.
The first field of research is ecclesiastical history, with focus on the status of the secular clergy. He has published several studies on the topic, as well as the PhD thesis, entitled Clerul de mir din Moldova secolelor XIV-XVI (Orthodox Secular Clergymen in Moldavia during the 14th-16th centuries). A second field of interest is the ideology, symbols and rituals of power in Byzantine and post-Byzantine space, with focus on the rituals of war and violence practiced at the level of political power. Awards: The most valuable Ph. D. dissertation in 2006 on History, awarded by the "Alexandru Ioan Cuza" University of Iași;

Alexandru D. Xenopol, awarded by the Romanian Academy for the year 2007, on December 17th, 2009 and Iustin Frățiman for essential contributions to the field of ecclesiastic history, given by Paul Gore Society of Genealogy, Heraldry and Archive in Chișinău, on December 5th, 2008.

JUDITH MENGLER is PhD student and research associate at the Research Unit Historical Cultural Sciences, Mainz. She works at the project "Fighting Bodies – Bodies of Fighting. Studies on the representation of bellicose bodies in references of the 14th to the early 16th century". Her research interests are the history of the body, medieval military history, the interdependence of warfare and medical knowledge, and the history of logistics and nutrition.
Contact: jmengler@uni-mainz.de

GIULIA MOROSINI is a Masters graduate in the Historical Sciences at the University of Padua, Italy. Her main research interests are History of Emotions, Military History of The Italian Renaissance and Early Modern Cultural History.
Contact: morosinigiu@gmail.com

JÖRG ROGGE is Professor of History, Middle Ages, at the University of Mainz, Germany. He is also Spokesperson of the Research Unit Historical Cultural Sciences, Mainz. His main research interests are methods and theory of historical cultural sciences, politics, and culture in Late Medieval Europe.
Contact: rogge@uni-mainz.de

DOMINIK SCHUH finished his studies in history and German literature at Johannes Gutenberg-University Mainz in 2011. From October 2011 to December 2012 he worked at the Research Unit Historical Cultural Sciences in Mainz and began working on his doctoral project on lay masculinities in the later middle ages. Since January 2013 he works at the university library Mainz in an academic integrity project.

TREVOR RUSSELL SMITH is a PhD candidate at the Institute for Medieval Studies, University of Leeds. He investigates the rhetoric of

English historical and political writing during the reign of Edward III, king of England (1327-77). In particular he explores these texts' implicit (yet sometimes explicit) engagement with issues of identity and the ethics of war. He shows how such texts were highly rhetorical in their representations of conflict, even if they were not all intended to serve directly as propaganda. In contrast to the orthodox view that people in the Middle Ages accepted all the acts of war as pragmatic, he argues that historical and political writers had varied moral positions and cared more about how war was fought (*ius in bello*) rather than as a whole (*ius ad bellam*). Trevor considers these issues through a case study of an often neglected northern chronicle in his forthcoming article entitled 'Ethics and the Representation of War in the *Lanercost Chronicle*, 1327-46' in the *Bulletin of International Medieval Research*, 20 (2016 for 2014).